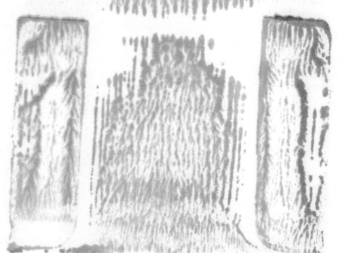

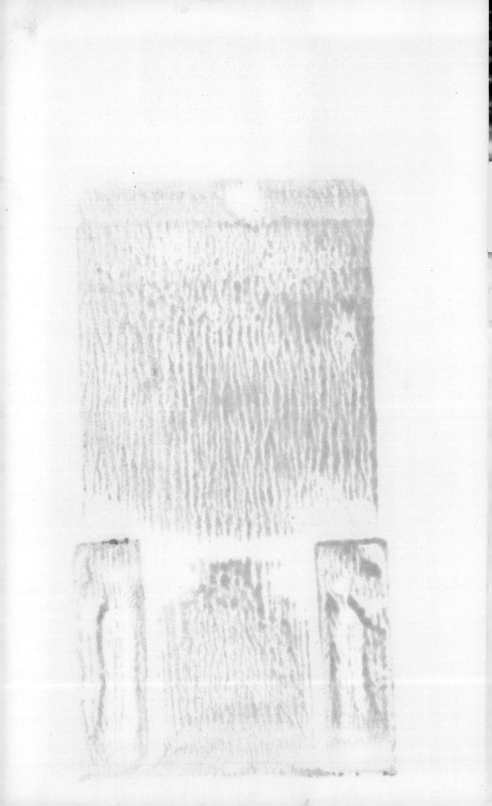

The Fortunate Slave

AN ILLUSTRATION OF AFRICAN SLAVERY IN THE
EARLY EIGHTEENTH CENTURY

Job, Son of Solliman Dgiallo, High Priest of Bonda in the Country of Foota, Africa.

JOB BEN SOLOMON

From *Some Memoirs of the Life of Job*, by Thomas Bluett, 1734. The portrait was made during Job's stay in England by 'Mr. Hoare', probably William Hoare (1707?–1792).

The Fortunate Slave

AN ILLUSTRATION OF AFRICAN SLAVERY
IN THE EARLY EIGHTEENTH CENTURY

DOUGLAS GRANT

London

OXFORD UNIVERSITY PRESS

New York Toronto

1968

Oxford University Press, Ely House, London W.1

GLASGOW NEW YORK TORONTO MELBOURNE WELLINGTON
CAPE TOWN SALISBURY IBADAN NAIROBI LUSAKA ADDIS ABABA
BOMBAY CALCUTTA MADRAS KARACHI LAHORE DACCA
KUALA LUMPUR HONG KONG TOKYO

Printed in Great Britain by
Richard Clay (The Chaucer Press) Ltd, Bungay, Suffolk

INTRODUCTION

THE theme, structure, and method of this book will, I believe, be made clearer to the reader if I explain how I came to write it.

I once bought a set of *The World Displayed; or, A Curious Collection of Voyages and Travels*, published in 1759, with a well-known Introduction by Dr. Johnson; a pretty set, in full tree calf, gilt, as the bookseller put it. I have never read through the twenty volumes from beginning to end, small though they are, as befitting abridgements, but I sometimes read in them here and there when I have nothing else at hand, or when I feel a longing for the remote and strange.

A year or two ago I happened to pick up the seventeenth volume and began to glance through Francis Moore's *Travels into the Inland Parts of Africa*, first published in 1738. I had never looked into it before, at least, not as far as I could remember, but perhaps because it concerned Africa, and Africa, in its splendours and miseries, seems to tyrannize over our imaginations today, I began to read it with attention. Francis Moore was a keen observer and a lucid journalist—in the older sense of keeping a journal—and something of his quality came across, even in the abridgement.

I had not read far before I came to a chapter with the heading, 'The History of Job ben Solomon'. Job, 'who was of the Pholey race, and son to the High Priest of Bundo, in Foota,'—I give the names as I first learnt them, in all their strangeness—was captured by his hereditary enemies, the 'Mundingoes', on the banks of the Gambia in 1731, and sold by them to Captain Pyke, a separate trader—another of the terms I was later to come to understand. Pyke shipped this 'elegant figure', as *The World Displayed* describes him, to Maryland and sold him to a planter. As Job was a Mohammedan and literate in Arabic, he managed to write a letter to his father, appealing to him to try and ransom him, and dispatched it home by one of the vessels sailing back to the Gambia by way of London. The letter fell into the hands of James Oglethorpe, the colonist and philanthropist, and when he had had it translated at Oxford, Oglethorpe was so touched by its sentiments that he arranged for Job to be redeemed from slavery and brought to London.

Job arrived in London in 1733, and was treated as though he had become an entirely different person. He made the acquaintance of Sir Hans Sloane, and being found to be 'a perfect master of the *Arabic* tongue', he translated several of the Arabic manuscripts and inscriptions in Sir Hans's collections. 'That learned Antiquary', I went on to read, 'recommended him to the Duke of Montague, who being pleased with his genius and capacity, the agreeableness of his behaviour, and the sweetness of his temper, introduced him to court, where he was graciously received by the Royal Family, and most of the nobility, who honoured him with many marks of favour. The *African* Company and the chief Merchants of the city strove who should oftenest invite him to their tables. His good sense engaged their esteem, he freely discoursed on every subject, and attended the churches of the most celebrated divines.' He was shipped back to the Gambia, with a cargo of presents, a year later, and helped from there to make his way home to Bundo, in Foota —meaningless but euphonious names. He astonished his people by his reappearance, for as he himself simply put it: 'I was gone to a land from whence no *Pholey* ever yet returned.'

I was astonished by this remarkable story. What a fantastic contrast it presented, I thought: a savage from the wilds of Africa moving in the polite society of eighteenth-century London. What on earth did Alexander Pope's contemporaries make of their visitor, newly fetched out of slavery? The oddest thing was that they apparently liked and admired him, if *The World Displayed* could be trusted, and treated him on a footing of equality. How could this have happened? The same people who shook his hand at a reception might have come from signing the papers that put up for auction several hundreds more of his fellow countrymen. The questions came quicker and quicker as I tried to visualize the two together: one of the 'celebrated divines', perhaps, and Job, the Mohammedan Pholey—simple questions, none of which I could begin to answer.

The first question seemed to be, what did Job ben Solomon's English hosts make of their involuntary guest? I quickly realized that such a question was unanswerable until I had discovered what impressions of Africa and its peoples were current in England at the time. Job could only have been understood in the light of what was already known.

Job was seized and sold on the Gambia. He was a Pholey—that is, a Fula, or a Fulani, as I began to learn—and his captors were

Mundingoes—more usually, Mandingos. Whereabouts did these people live along the length of that great river? What was their relation? Who were their neighbours? I found that the Pholeys and the Mundingoes were only two of the several tribes on the river; there were also the Joloffs and the Floops, and a smaller group, the Portuguese: the older form, Portingale, better suits their elusive character. I tried to collect what could have been known about their customs and society from accounts that had already been published by the time of Job's visit, supplementing them with information which could be plausibly conjectured to have been known by report. I have given what I found in my first chapter.

I was struck in my reading by the obvious importance of the Gambia in the early impressions of West Africa. The tribes along its banks are described with a greater intimacy and respect than any of those elsewhere in the region, the reason being that the river is the only one which the European traders could sail up for any distance, to a length of two hundred-odd miles. This brought them into close touch with the people; farther south, down the coast, they were confined to castles and conducted business through Europeanized middlemen.

The first traders on the river were the Portuguese, but the English had supplanted them by the end of the seventeenth century, trading as the Royal African Company. What were the relations of the Company's officers—men like Francis Moore, for example— with the natives, and how would their experiences contribute to the image of Africa that was slowly being built up at home, detail by detail? I have tried to show in my second chapter the manner in which these men lived, more isolated in Africa than any other Englishmen of the time, and the system under which they traded.

The Company traded in many native products, gold, beeswax, and hides, but most notoriously in slaves. Job ben Solomon had been bought as a slave and shipped to North America. He was still a slave when he was fetched to London. The fortunes of early industrial England were inseparably bound up with the slave trade. When Job confronted his hosts in some drawing-room, furnished, however indirectly, by the sale of his brothers—brothers whom he himself had, ironically, helped to sell—he was both an African and a slave. Some knowledge of the operation of the slave trade in Africa was essential to an understanding of Job, not only as an individual, but, as I later hope to show, as an idea.

I had now sketched three necessary, preliminary chapters and

could introduce Job himself and describe him against the background of the Gambia and its peoples, and relate plausibly how he
came to be captured and sold to an English slaver. If Job wrote an
account of his adventures for the instruction of his posterity, it has
not survived, and I have been forced to rely in my account of the
events that followed his capture on what he himself told his well-
wishers, supported by the information in official documents; but
as he suffered on board ship and in Maryland the common fate of
all slaves, I have been able to describe in general the experiences
he must have undergone. Once he was rescued and arrived in
London, much more information of a personal kind is available,
and it is possible to follow his movements in some detail from the
day he landed to 15 July 1734, when he sailed home in the
Dolphin, taking with him five hundred pounds' worth of presents.
All these events fall into the fourth chapter.

I had realized by this time that even if I had defined Job's
character accurately, in terms of what could have been known about
Africa and the workings of the slave trade, and had narrated clearly
the history of his year in London, I had still not accounted entirely
for the effect he had made not only upon those who actually met
him, but upon those who would have read about him, either in the
short biography of him by Thomas Bluett, which appeared immediately after his departure, or in the pages of Francis Moore,
published three years later. I knew that something else was wanted.

By a strange coincidence, Job arrived in England at a turning-
point in the relations between the black and white races. When
Thomas Clarkson, the great abolitionist, looked back to the time
when he was converted to the anti-slavery cause, he attributed his
conversion to his reading of 'the great authorities of Adanson,
Moore, Barbot, Smith, Bosman and others'. Among these others
would be William Snelgrave and especially John Atkins, whom
Clarkson credited with originating the protests against slavery.
Four of these 'authorities' published their travels at more or less
the time of Job's sojourn in England: John Barbot in 1732, William
Snelgrave in 1734, John Atkins in 1735, and Francis Moore in
1738. William Bosman had published earlier, in 1705, though his
work was reprinted in 1721, and William Smith and Michel
Adanson later, in 1745 and 1759 (English translation). Clarkson's
observation made it clear that Job stood in the centre of an impassioned argument, both philosophical and moral. Who were the
Noble Savages? Why were the Africans excluded from the charity

shed upon primitive peoples by the ideal? Could Christians en-slave their brothers? Were Africans properly to be considered men? These were great questions and I felt that I ought to discuss them before seeing Job safely home.

Francis Moore had welcomed Job on his return to the Gambia and his account has been the only information available of what occurred. I thought that I also should have to rely on Moore, sup-ported by whatever I could find among the papers of the Royal African Company. The Company had been responsible for Job during his stay in England. I had a great stroke of luck. When Job travelled up country to his home in Bundo, he was accom-panied by an Englishman, Thomas Hull. Hull was known to have kept a journal of his travels, but it had been entirely lost. I was able to trace it among the papers that had once belonged to Job's admirer, the Duke of Montagu. Hull's Journal is one of the earliest records of English exploration in West Africa and, for all its short-comings, is a most important document, in addition to helping to complete the story of Job.

Job was sent home with the intention that he should further British interests in the upper Senegal, in return for his redemption and generous treatment. The Royal African Company was extreme-ly anxious to penetrate those vast inland markets and especially to capture the trade from the French, who were already strongly placed on the Senegal and determined to defend their advantages. Job fell a victim to this national rivalry and nearly ended up as a slave again—this time, in French Martinique. The Company's efforts in the Gambia were, however, defeated by its financial instability, and with its collapse, Job disappears from sight.

I had made Job's return to his own country, and its consequences, the subject of my sixth chapter, but I felt that the book was still not quite finished, even though I had traced Job as far as I could. I was left with the mystery of Job's own character. I had come to realize that, in a sense, he had 'no character at all'. He existed only in so far as he had been interpreted according to the current notions of Africa. He himself was highly intelligent and ingratiating, but he could not really make himself known to his well disposed English hosts. The difference between their experience was too great, even though such qualities as devotion and morality might be shared and mutually respected. He faded as an individual into the enigma of his race. I have tried to suggest the mystery which enveloped him by describing in my final chapter the background out of which he came, to confront the light of an ordinary English day. The Gambia has hardly changed in two hundred and fifty years: the moral issues which centred about Job are still unresolved. He was a challenge as a guest of the Duke of Montagu; he is as much a challenge as he appears to us through the records of the time.

I have not described how the book was written in order to antici- pate criticism, but to try and explain why Job's appearance in the story is delayed for three chapters and why he is always discussed in association with such large topics as the Noble Savage, or the commercial rivalry in Africa between the English and the French. The book is not discursive; it has been planned: I hope to the best advantage of its intriguing subject.

I have a last excuse for having written at the beginning in this personal way. I was led into the subject out of interest, and my interest quickened as it opened out through extraordinary byways into the greatest issue of our age. Job ben Solomon was an African and a slave; the only one of those silent millions of whom we have any precise and extended account. Who could remain unmoved by his fate?

ACKNOWLEDGEMENTS

I HAVE not written a travel book, though travel plays so large a part in the story, but it was necessary to visit the Gambia and this I was enabled to do through the generosity of the University of Leeds. I only wish I could acknowledge fully the kindness and courtesy that were shown to me during my visit. I think that no one has written about the Gambia without remarking on these common character- istics of its different peoples.

I owe a special debt of gratitude to Sir John Paul, K.C.M.G., then on the point of retiring as Governor-General, and Lady Paul. They not only gave me hospitality, but made it possible for me to see much of the country in a very short time, including James Island and Albreda, the pleasantest and most comfortable of my excur- sions.

I received help from all sides. I could not thank everybody by name, but I must single out Mr. D. A. Percival, Economic Adviser to the Cabinet, Captain L. W. H. Dunster, Director of Marine, Mr. R. Porch, Mr. A. M. B. Clarke, Mr. J. E. Bishop, the Divisional Commissioners at Basse, Georgetown, and Mansakonko, and Mr. A. C. Andrews, Education Officer; Mr. F. H. Smyth of the Colonial Office Record Department, Mr. A. W. M. Cooke of the Medical Council Research Laboratories, and Mr. Gordon Pate, at the time engineer in charge of the erection of the G.O.M.B. mill at Kau-Ur. I am especially grateful to Mr. H. A. Oliver, M.B.E., Permanent Secretary to the Ministry of Local Government, who put his unrivalled knowledge of the country at my service. As for my fellow passengers in the stateroom of the *Lady Wright*, all native Gambians, I remember them with affection. They went out of their way to make me feel at home.

I was fortunate in tracking down the journal kept by Thomas Hull of his voyage to Bondou in 1735, and I am deeply indebted to the Duke of Buccleuch, G.C.V.O., for permission to quote extensively from it. I am also indebted to the Public Record Office, the Archives Nationales, Paris, the British Museum, the Royal Society, the Society of Antiquaries, the Spalding Gentlemen's Society, and the Society for the Promotion of Christian Knowledge, for permission to use material in their possession. I have been greatly helped by the staffs of the Public Record Office and the British Museum, and especially by the staff of the Brotherton Library in the University of Leeds, and by Mr. Frank Beckwith, the Librarian of the Leeds Library.

I have made innumerable inquiries of many librarians and archivists, and I hope I shall be excused if I thank only those who were able to answer positively: Mr. S. W. Woodward, Librarian of the Spalding Gentlemen's Society, Mr. A. E. Barker, Public Relations Officer of the S.P.C.K., Mrs. Isobel Pridmore, Archivist to the United Society for the Propagation of the Gospel, Mr. Peter Walne, County Archivist, Hertfordshire, and Mr. Geoffrey Beard, Director of Cannon Hall, Cawthorne, Barnsley. I should like to thank most warmly Mr. P. I. King, County Archivist, Northamptonshire, and Mr. D. H. Simpson, Librarian of the Royal Commonwealth Society, who have both been exceptionally kind.

I made inquiries, too, on the other side of the Atlantic and all were answered in great detail. I should like to thank Mrs. David B. Coghlan, Manuscript Librarian, Historical Society of Delaware, Mr. Leon deValinger, Jr., State Archivist, State of Delaware, Mr. John D. Kilbourne, Archivist IV, Hall of Records, Annapolis, Maryland, and Mrs. Lilla M. Hawes, Director, Georgia Historical Society.

I had already completed a draft of the book when Professor Philip D. Curtin of the University of Wisconsin, who had been editing Thomas Bluett's *Some Memoirs of the Life of Job*, 1734, called my attention to a footnote in a collection of documents published by J. Machat in 1906. The reference took me to Paris and the papers relating to Senegal in the Archives Nationales, and there I found an account of the extraordinary events that followed upon Job ben Solomon's return to Bondou. I am grateful to Professor Curtin for further help, which I have remarked on in my notes.

I have still other people to thank closer at home, in the University of Leeds. I owe more than I can briefly express to Professor William Walsh. He read the manuscript and did everything that a good friend could in the way of criticism and encouragement. Miss Claire Lamont, Research Archivist in the School of English, was tireless in pressing home inquiries, and when Miss Lamont left for Oxford, Miss Audrey Stead generously came forward to help me complete the work. Mr. D. Newlove, in the Department of Geography, drew the maps. And I am also indebted to Mr. John Bell and Miss Ena Sheen of Oxford University Press for their later advice and suggestions. I have been most fortunate in all the help I have received.

DOUGLAS GRANT

1968

CONTENTS

ILLUSTRATIONS

'He was cloath'd in a white Cotton Vest with open sleeves, and
Breeches which came to his Knees, of the same. His Legs and Arms
were bare, on his Head he had a small white Cotton Cap, and Gold
Rings in his Ears. He rode upon a beautiful Milk-white Horse, 16
Hands high, with a long Mane, and a Tail which swept the Ground.
His Bridle was of a bright Red-Leather, plated with Silver, after
the *Moorish* Manner; his Saddle was of the same, with a high Pommel, and rising behind. The Breast-Plate was of Red-Leather plaited
with Silver, but they use no Cruppers. His Stirrups were short, and
as large and as long as his Feet, so as to stand firm and easy. Upon
these he would raise himself quite upright, stand steady at full speed,
and shoot a Gun or dart a Lance as well as if upon the Ground.'

MAPS
(at end)

Moore's map has been redrawn and adapted to include the modern
version of the names of towns and districts. The modern versions
are those underlined.

The places shown are to be found either in Thomas Hull's Journal or on contemporary maps. The modern place-names are
those underlined.

'I have at length resolved to communicate to the world such particulars of the Life and Character of this *African* Gentleman, as I think will be most useful and Entertaining.' Thomas Bluett, in *Some Memoirs of the Life of Job, the Son of Solomon, the High Priest of Boonda in Africa*, 1734.

'Every thing in Africa, indeed, inclines the mind to thought, to meditation, to reflection, to comparison, to remark.' S. M. X. Golbéry.

'. . . a Country, much talk'd of, and little known.' Francis Moore.

CHAPTER ONE

The Peoples of the Gambia

ONE of the earliest and most striking images of Africa appears in the Catalan Atlas of 1375. In order to fill up the undiscovered interior of the continent, the mapmaker has introduced two outlandish figures. Below the Atlas Mountains and inland from Cape Bojador, a veiled rider advances on a camel, flourishing a whip. He is a Moor, one of the Tuareg. Facing him is a king enthroned; a Negro king, a most royal figure. He wears a crown and carries a sceptre negligently across his left shoulder, and in his right hand he holds out invitingly what lures the rider towards him, a large nugget of gold. He is, the legend informs us, 'Musse Melly, senyor dels negres de Gineua': Mansa Musa, the fabled king of Mali, who astonished Cairo with his wealth and liberality when he passed through on pilgrimage to Mecca in 1324. Offshore, on the map, floats a vessel manned by Catalans, equally attracted by the gold.

The first Europeans to explore the West Coast of Africa properly were the Portuguese, under the inspiration of Henry the Navigator. Cape Bojador was doubled by Gil Eannes in 1434 and Cadamosto reached the Gambia in 1455 and explored some way up its course. The Portuguese, as they are described in Eannes de Azurara's chronicle of their early discoveries, were motivated by a mixture of religious enthusiasm and knight-errantry, scientific curiosity and commercial greed. They intended to convert the Pagan and put down the Muslim, to win renown both for their valour in the field and as the discoverers of new worlds, and to benefit themselves and their country by trade, especially by diverting to themselves on the African coast the commerce that flowed north from Negroland to Barbary in the hands of the Moors—above all, the flow of gold.

The Portuguese dominated West Africa for two hundred years. They occupied the Atlantic islands and formed permanent settlements on the coast, and, though they exaggerated their power and range of influence, they established the pattern that other Europeans were

B

later to follow. The others were not long in coming and in challenging the Portuguese in their search for the still undiscovered mountains of gold.

The English found the Portuguese settled on the banks of the Gambia when they first attempted an exploration of the river. A sailor putting out from England and making for the African coast would be carried by the set of the winds and tides towards the Gambia, if his journey was prosperous; and as there is no bar at its mouth, unlike all the other great associated rivers that fall into the Atlantic, the Gambia was the easiest waterway to follow into the interior. When Richard Jobson anchored in the Gambia in 1623, acting as scout for an association of London merchants, he discovered among the Mandingos near the mouth a number of 'vagrant Portingall'.[1] They were Portuguese by language and sentiment rather than in appearance, for, though some were mulattoes, the majority were as black as the rest of the natives. They called themselves Christians and, whatever their hue, considered themselves to be white and took it as a deep insult to be classed with the Negroes. The river trade was mainly in their hands. Jobson had the greatest contempt for them, but as they were the instigators of the massacre of the trustful crew of an English ship lying in the river in 1618, he warned his countrymen to treat them with the caution they would show to snakes.

Jobson expected the 'Portingall' to disappear as the English established themselves on the river, but he underrated the tenacity and subtlety of these adaptable people, as well as wildly overestimating the chances of English success. A lull of many years followed his voyage and when English interest in African trade was renewed later in the century, the Portuguese were still on the Gambia, and still identifiable by their speech and behaviour, if not by their colour.

The Portuguese in the region were visited in 1686 by the Sieur de La Courbe when he inspected the French factory at Albreda on the Gambia, as an agent of the French Senegal Company. After leaving Albreda he journeyed overland to a Portuguese settlement farther south, at Cacheu on the river San Domingo.[2] He stopped on the first

[1] Richard Jobson, *The Golden Trade*, 1932, p. 37.

[2] When J. B. Labat compiled his *Nouvelle Relation de l'Afrique Occidentale* (1728) he appropriated La Courbe's journal and attributed it to the famous Director-General of the French Senegal Company, André Brüe (see *Premier Voyage du Sieur de La Courbe*, ed. P. Cultru, Paris, 1913). As a consequence, Brüe is usually referred to as the authority of the time.

stage of his journey at the village of Vintain (Bintang)[1] at the mouth of the Vintain (Bintang) Creek, that flows into the Gambia from the south a short distance upstream from Albreda. The Portuguese were more numerous at Vintain than elsewhere on the Gambia. There was a church at Vintain, and another higher up the creek at Geregia—in fact Geregia is a corruption of *igereja*, the Portuguese for a church. A priest came once a year from St. Jago, in the Cape Verde Islands, to marry and baptize. The Portuguese were also settled in some numbers at Tancrowall (Tankular) on the Gambia above Vintain, and there, too, they had a church, where Mass was celebrated every day of the priest's annual visit from St. Jago.[2] La Courbe was greeted as he came ashore at Vintain by the chief Portuguese, dressed according to custom in long black cloaks and broad black 'Quaker' hats and carrying spados, or long swords, and poniards as big as ordinary swords, and dangling copious chaplets of beads in their left hands. He was entertained at the home of the wealthy widow of a Portuguese trader, who had married as her second husband an English trader, Captain Hodges, at the time of La Courbe's visit absent on a voyage far up the Gambia.[3] Mrs. Hodges, a well-shaped mulatta of about thirty, received La Courbe on her porch, with two maids and one of her daughters in attendance. The daughter was almost white, but the maids were black, and the female slave who served La Courbe with kola nuts, a staple delicacy, was handsome and immodestly naked. Mrs. Hodges was a woman of influence, La Courbe thought, and worth the cultivating, but a month or two later he heard that when she was brought to bed of a black child shortly after her husband's return, her husband, suspecting that she had been unfaithful to him with the Alcaid of the town, took the baby, brayed it alive in a mortar, and threw it to the dogs.[4]

Vintain was a foretaste of Cacheu. Cacheu was more properly a Portuguese settlement. It had a governor and a garrison of about thirty to man its walls, a church with a resident padre, assisted by two or three indigent and ignorant priests, and even a convent of

---

[1] The different spellings of the names of towns and places in this region can lead to great confusion. I have not always found it possible to be strictly consistent, but I have tried to keep to the contemporary version, putting the modern after it within brackets when it first occurs. As the names appear in the index under both spellings, there should not be many chances for mistake.

[2] Francis Moore, *Travels into the Inland Parts of Africa*, 1738, p. 51.

[3] La Courbe called him 'Agis', but the Captain's name was actually Hodges. The story told about him was also told about another Englishman elsewhere on the coast (see J. M. Gray, *A History of the Gambia*, 1940, p. 96 n.).

[4] See *Premier Voyage du Sieur de La Courbe*, p. 204.

Capuchins, housing two Capuchins in 1686. The citizens appeared to La Courbe to dissipate all their energies on women; the streets were made unsafe at night by amorous adventurers—and by equally dangerous assassins, who affected an extraordinary costume: 'Conceive a Man, who, above his Cloaths, has gotten a Leather Apron, with a large Slabbering-Bib, which covers a Cuirass of Mail, or half-Suit of Armour. This Apron, which falls but four Fingers-Breadth below the Waist, is full of Holes, in which are stuck two or three Pair of Pocket-Pistols, and a Brace of Poniards. The left Arm is charged with a small Buckler, and the Hip with a long Sword, or Spado; whose Scabbard is split, and flies open with a Spring, to save the Time and Trouble of drawing it. When they go only on Business, or for Recreation, this Equipage is covered with a black Cloak, reaching down to the Calf of the Leg.'[1] As to their 'business', they carried it out by letting fly at their victim with a blunderbuss charged with loose shot. The Portuguese wives were strictly confined to their homes, and if they chanced to be white even the Mass was not a sufficient excuse for their going abroad by day, though only people of distinction had private chapels. The tawny and mulatto and black ones were allowed out to pray, but so heavily veiled that they showed only their toes and a single eye.

The other Europeans were all openly contemptuous of these 'Portuguese', dismissing them as debauched and degenerate, but they could not disregard them; they had to admit that they had come to terms with the strange continent. By intermarrying with the natives, they had bred into their descendants something of the necessary genius of the place. They were acknowledged to merit the arms they carried and to be intrepid middlemen, trading widely both on their own account and as agents for the interlopers and the French, who persisted at the end of the seventeenth century in trading on the Gambia, in spite of the pretensions of the Royal African Company to a monopoly. The Company's agents frequently pillaged the Portuguese traders' canoes from their armed sloops, but they could never suppress the Portuguese and found them staunch and unforgiving opponents, ready to retaliate whenever they had the chance. In the opinion of some observers, if they could have been trained to be less self-indulgent and to accept discipline, they would have made the ideal scouts to probe the mysteries of the African interior and to lead the European nation

---

[1] La Courbe's journal covering his visit to Cacheu is not extant, though it was published by Labat, attributing it to André Brüe. I am quoting from the English version given in Astley's *A New General Collection of Voyages and Travels*, 1745 (ii. 90–1).

lucky enough to enlist their services to those mountains of gold and shoals of precious stones that were supposed to lie near the headwaters of the Gambia.[1]

The Portuguese had already proved themselves to have been of far more use to Africa than they were ever likely to be as treasure seekers for Europe. They had introduced into the Gambia more comfortable and commodious houses than the ordinary native huts, and the style was copied by the African princes and nobility. They raised their houses a foot or two above the ground to escape the damp and built the walls thickly of reeds, or wattle, and mud, whitewashing them when they were dry. The windows to the several rooms were kept small on account of the heat. They ate and, in effect, lived on the verandah, open on all sides to catch the breeze, and they planted trees round about for the sake of the shade. Houses built in this style were known as Portuguese houses.[2]

Housebuilding could benefit only a few, but from the Portuguese the natives had learnt what they knew of boatbuilding and seamanship, and the use of many domestic implements. The Portuguese also introduced the orange, the lime, and the pawpaw from Brazil, and particularly the groundnut, which is today the Gambia's staple crop.[3] Jobson's 'Portingall' was less a vagrant than he appeared when seen through the jealous eyes of economic rivalry.

Creole Portuguese was a useful trading language, widespread down the coast and along the Guinea waterways, and the one most easily picked up by the English; but the chief language on the Gambia was Mandingo, and Mandingo was needed for the penetration of the mysterious hinterland into which the river led. The Mandingos were the most numerous of the peoples on the Gambia and the greatest traders among the Africans. The Portuguese might be black and outwardly distinguished from their neighbours as 'Boon Christians' only by their custom of wearing a little crucifix about their necks,[4] but through their language and their beliefs, however riddled with superstition, it was possible for the English and other European traders to feel that they shared in the same community, in spite of despising and distrusting them. The Mandingos were different, and the difference was expressed by their language. The European adventurers on the river came face to face in their persons with the alien world and bewildering culture of Africa. All they had in common with the Mandingos was their humanity.

---

[1] Labat, iv. 368–72.   [2] ibid. p. 368.   [3] See Gray, p. 15.
[4] William Smith, *A New Voyage to Guinea*, 1744, p. 25.

The Englishman who anchored for the first time in the Gambia and, idling on the quarter-deck to get the breeze, stared curiously ashore, had some notions of what he might expect to find when he landed; notions that would not be at all favourable to the character of the Negroes, whom he could now see energetically paddling their canoes towards the ship. The continent is vast, he will have been told, with stupendous differences of deserts and forests, mountains and plains, yet, he will also have been warned, instead of a corresponding diversity of character, the inhabitants are everywhere the same: 'All the people of the globe', ran the proverb, 'have some good as well as ill qualities, except the Africans.' 'Brutish, ignorant, idle, treacherous, thievish, mistrustful, and superstitious'—such they were supposed to be. 'I shall only say in one Word,' observed a doctor, extending himself to several, 'that their natural Temper is barbarously cruel, selfish, and deceitful, and their Government equally barbarous and uncivil. . . . As for their Customs, they exactly resemble their Fellow Creatures and Natives, the Monkeys. . . .'[1]

An explanation of the Negroes' extraordinary depravity was offered by the Marabouts—the priestly class of Mohammedans. When Noah died his three sons, the black, the white, and the tawny, decided after eating a good supper together to leave the division of their father's wealth until morning and went off to sleep in their separate tents. Two or three hours later the white brother cautiously got up and, loading the best horses with all the gold, silver, precious stones, and other valuables, rode swiftly away to lands where his posterity has lived prosperously ever since. The tawny brother next awoke and finding what his more alert brother had done, hurriedly followed his example, and loading the rest of the horses and the camels and the oxen with the best carpets, cloths, and everything else of value, drove them away. When the black brother rose belatedly he found that he had been left with nothing but a few coarse cloths, cotton, tobacco and pipes, millet and rice. He knew that he was unable to pursue his brothers and recover what had been stolen from him, but, after turning over the problem and puffing at his pipe, he decided to wait patiently and steal from them whatever chance threw in his way—a revenge that he strictly enjoined on his descendants.[2]

The Muslim's jaundiced view of the African could be generously

---

[1] James Houston, *Some New and Accurate Observations of the Coast of Guinea*, 1725, pp. 33-4.

[2] *Universal History*, xiv. 17–18. This moral tale was long current in Senegambia and seems to have been first recorded by La Courbe in 1685, when it was told to him by a Marabout (see P. Cultru, *Histoire du Sénégal*, 1910, pp. 94–5).

matched by the Christian who could happily recall his classics. With a few choice quotations from Lucan and Virgil, and from other authors more often consulted for profit than for pleasure, the African could be shown typically to be 'proud, lazy, treacherous, thievish, hot, and addicted to all kinds of lusts, and most ready to promote them in others, as pimps, panders, incestuous, brutish, and savage, cruel and revengeful, devourers of human flesh, and quaffers of human blood, inconstant, base, treacherous, and cowardly; fond of, and addicted to, all sorts of superstition and witchcraft; and, in a word, to every vice that came in their way, or within their reach.'[1] The opinion of pagan antiquity might be suspected as lacking in charity, but St. Augustine confirmed that one would rather take Africa, his native home, for 'a volcano of the most impure flames, than for a habitation of human creatures'. The Saint scrupled not to confess 'that it is as impossible to be an African and not lascivious, as it is to be born in Africa and not be an African'.[1] Homer had told in a strange and moving passage of how the gods liked to visit Africa each year to enjoy the festivals of the dark-skinned peoples, who lived as innocently as they would have done in the Golden Age:

> The Sire of Gods, and all th'Etherial Train,
> On the warm Limits of the farthest Main,
> Now mix with Mortals, nor disdain to grace
> The Feast of Æthiopia's blameless Race:
> Twelve Days the Pow'rs indulge the genial Rite,
> Returning with the Twelfth revolving Light.[2]

—but a poet's visions could hardly stand against the combined fulminations of St. Augustine and kindred authorities, though education saw to it that the lines were never entirely forgotten.

The gods of pagan antiquity might very well have enjoyed their annual rendezvous in the Ethiopian highlands, for nowhere else in the world was superstition inveterate enough to do justice to their fictional divinities. The Africans were addicted to idolatry, magic, and witchcraft, and worshipped anything, from the sun in the sky to the lowest piece of crawling vermin, and accompanied their worship with unspeakable cruelties and brutalities. The worst of them all were the Imbii, a tribe bordering on the Hottentots. They waged universal war on their neighbours, ate their captives after roasting them over a slow fire, and had so set their black faces against their Creator that

---

[1] *Universal History*, xiv. 18–19.
[2] Homer, *Iliad*, Book I, ll. 554–9 (Pope's trans.).

they would dance about in a frenzy of defiance, shooting their arrows and screaming imprecations against the sky.[1]

No wonder the African's complexion was black; the colour was a warning of what he was like within. The why and wherefore of his colour may have required no other explanation, but what was the natural rather than the moral cause of his dark skin? Dissection could hardly answer the question. Whether his blackness resided in the skin itself, or, what was more probable, in the epidermis, or—and this was the most advanced conjecture—in a certain reticulum of extremely soft and fine particles lying between the skin and the epidermis, was impossible to distinguish by observation. To add to the mystery, the colour was not invariable: a Negro child came white out of its mother's womb, except for a darkness about its privities and under its nails; a sick Negro could fade, even to wanness, 'like that of a maid who languishes under the green sickness'; a burnt Negro will show a white cicatrix.[2] And, a further related marvel, the lice on a black body, though identical in shape with the white lice on a white man, were also black. Among the Africans' other characteristics that might be associated with their colour were their woolly and 'bestial' poll, their round eyes, the shape of their ears, their 'tumid nostrils, flat noses, invariable thick lips, and general large size of the female nipples, as if adapted by nature to the peculiar conformation of their children's mouths'.[3]

The African was also notable for his 'bestial or fetid' smell, but as this was in proportion to his lack of intelligence and ferocity and as the natives of the Senegal and the Gambia were among the most acute and mild, the traveller whom we left lounging on deck should not have been expecting to be especially offended in this respect when he went ashore.

The choice of a particular moment in these instances may seem arbitrary, but let us suppose that our traveller stepped ashore in the Gambia on 11 November 1730, having sailed out from England in the Royal African Company's sloop, the *Dispatch*, under the command of Captain Robert Hall. He would not disembark on the mainland at the mouth of the river, but at the Company's fort on James Island, a day's sailing upstream. 'The Country look'd beautiful,' one arrival noted, 'being for the most Part woody, but between the Woods pleasant green Rice Grounds, which after the Rice is cut are stocked with Cattle.'[4]

---

[1] *Universal History*, xiv. 21.   [2] ibid. p. 20.
[3] Edward Long, *History of Jamaica*, 1774, ii. 352.
[4] Moore, p. 13.

James Island lay towards the middle of the river, opposite to the village of Albreda on the north bank and downstream from Vintain. Its defences were in good repair in 1730 and manned by a garrison of thirty-three English soldiers and a drummer, under the command of a captain and a sergeant. The garrison could be reinforced in an emergency by the many civilians in the fort, who drew a common soldier's pay of £26 a year—raised to £27 in 1734—for this service, in addition to their regular allowances.[1] The fort swarmed, of course, with blacks, slaves and auxiliaries, but the sight of the white men in charge and the way life moved to the customary rhythms of Europe prevented Africa from making its impact until the traveller went ashore, either by Company boat or in a native canoe, at St. Domingo, on the north shore, about a mile and a half distant. The Company had a well at St. Domingo and drew a daily supply of water in casks for the use of the garrison at the fort. James Island was little more than a low sandbank and was without water.

From St. Domingo, where a few of the castle slaves lived in Company huts to look after the well and to cut firewood for the fort, you could strike downstream for about a mile and a half to Gillyfree (Jufureh), where the Company had a factory, built in Portuguese style, and gardens for supplying the fort with fruit and vegetables. The grass grew eight or nine feet high and as you passed through it, lizards with heads as yellow as gold darted off the path into hiding. The ground was excellent for shooting and would have been pleasanter for walking had it been less sandy. Or you could turn in the other direction and walk two miles to Seaca (Sika), another Portuguese settlement. Seaca had a church, which the priest from St. Jago visited, but it was also noted for an enormous silk cotton tree, measuring ninety feet in circumference, taking in its spurs.[2]

Seaca had its church; Gillyfree a small pretty mosque. Gillyfree was the larger of the two places. The separate traders had to put into this port to pay the king of Barrah his customs and to take on one of the linguisters (translators) whom he alone could supply. Any linguister agreeing to serve a separate trader who had not discharged the customs due to the king was punished with slavery. Below Gillyfree lay Albreda, where the French had a factory. At the east end of Albreda was a fig tree so vast and ancient that it appeared to be several trees, and round its girth, for the sake of the shade, was the *bentang*, the open platform where the villagers lazed and gossiped or formally consulted. In a well at Albreda, Michel Adanson, the

[1] P.R.O., T.70/1451, p. 51.   [2] Moore, pp. 54–5, 67.

French botanist, found the only frogs he ever saw from the Senegal to the Gambia; in such prodigious numbers that they actually hid the surface of the water.[1]

Seaca, Gillyfree, and Albreda were all in the kingdom of Barrah. The king of Barrah himself lived below Gillyfree, at Barrinding (Berrending). The Royal African Company leased James Island from the king, paying a ground rent of £12. 10s. 0d. a year,[2] but, quite apart from questions of tenure, as the fort was completely dependent upon the mainland for its supply of water and fresh provisions, it was imperative that the governor should remain on the best of terms with the king. Courtesy visits were often exchanged, and in 1726 William Smith, who had been sent out to West Africa by the Company to survey its forts, attended Governor Rogers on a visit to the king. When the English party went ashore they were welcomed by the king, who had come a quarter of a mile out of town to meet them. He was accompanied by three or four hundred of his subjects, dancing and frisking and firing off guns, beating on large drums and sounding strident trumpets, hollowed from whole elephant tusks. The raucous and jubilant crowd brought them in triumph to the town and the king's palace.[3]

Smith called it a palace because the king lived there, but he remarked that it was nothing but a cottage—mud walls thatched with palmetto leaves. Michel Adanson, who knew the coast better than Smith, observed that the style of building in Barrah was superior to the building elsewhere in Senegambia because of the Portuguese. He lived for a time in one of the native huts at Albreda—one of the better sort, no doubt—and described it as large and commodious, though dark 'as a subterraneous cavern, even at noon-day', having as its only openings a door at each end. Adanson also described how the mud walls, if the roofs were accidentally fired, which often happened, would vitrify with the heat and appear to be beautifully coated with a brilliant red enamel.[4]

When the king had seated his visitors in state before his palace, one of the court musicians—a griot, as they were called—gave a concert on the ballafeu. Of all the strange instruments that the Europeans heard resounding across the Gambia the ballafeu, or xylophone, was the one which most impressed them, both its tones and its ingenious construction. Smith was so struck by it that he sketched the musician, squatting cross-legged before his instrument and striking the

---

[1] Michel Adanson, *A Voyage to Senegal*, 1759, pp. 171–3.
[2] P.R.O., T.70/1451, p. 87. [3] Smith, pp. 20–1. [4] Adanson, p. 163.

wooden keyboard with his padded sticks. Calabashes of differing sizes were suspended beneath the keys to amplify the sound. The musician wore in his cap a magnificent tuft of feathers, but when Smith went to take off his cap to see exactly what the feathers were, he leapt to his feet in surprise and ran away. Smith was equally taken aback, but the old hands at the fort smiled and explained to him that as the tuft was the musician's fetish, he dared not allow it to be touched by anyone other than himself. Smith had put out his hand and found that the ordinary incorporated a mystery. Nothing in Africa was what it seemed.[1]

The kingdom of Barrah was one of several Mandingo principalities lying on both sides of the Gambia. The Mandingos had descended on the river in the fourteenth century when the dominant African power was the Mandingo empire of Mali, lying to the south. In their advance they dislodged the Floops[2] from most of the south bank of the river. Cantore, Tomany, Jemarrow, Eropina, Yamina, Jagra, and Caen, all kingdoms however various in power, were governed by Mandingos, but, continuing in order to the sea, Fonia and Cumbo were Floop territories. Fonia was ruled by both a king and an emperor belonging to the Banyoons, a kind of Floops.[3] The Mandingos also spread north across the river into the territory of the Joloffs, who ruled the littoral and the countries lying inland between the Senegal and the Gambia. Barrah and Badibu and, following the river inland, the tiny principality of Sanjally were governed by Mandingos, tributaries of the powerful Joloff ruler of the neighbouring domain of Barsally. Lower Yani was governed by a Joloff; Upper Yani by a Mandingo. The greater kingdom of Woolly, whose extent, merging into the interior vastness of the continent, could be guessed only from rumours, was the last of the Mandingo realms that were known.

The Mandingos 'are Lords, and Commaunders of this country', declared Richard Jobson, 'and professe themselves the naturall Inhabitants'.[4] They were a tall and very black people. The men of the better sort wore cotton shirts reaching to below their knees, with voluminous sleeves which they looped back when they wanted to work freely, and baggy drawers of the same locally grown and home-woven material. Simple leather sandals and cotton caps, sometimes

---

[1] Smith, pp. 21, 27-8.
[2] Sometimes spelt 'Feloop' in the eighteenth century. These people are the Jolas of today.
[3] Moore, p. 24. [4] Jobson, p. 51.

decorated with feathers or a goat's tail, completed their costume. They usually carried arms. Their weapons were the assegai, or lance, six feet in length with a barbed iron head, and a short sword with an open handle, which was worn slung from a bandolier of red or yellow cloth. The chief men might also carry a bow, and two dozen or so arrows in an elaborately decorated quiver. The arrows were remarkably small, about two feet long, without either nock or feather, but the barbed iron heads were steeped in deadly poison. They handled all their weapons very dexterously.[1]

The Mandingo women's dress was even simpler. A length of blue and white striped cotton—a *pagne*—tucked in about the waist and reaching to below the knee made a skirt. They were naked from the waist up, but a second *pagne* was often draped loosely across the shoulders. They scarified their backs and breasts for decoration, especially those living along the upper reaches of the river. There Jobson saw women so elaborately worked that the patterns reminded him of 'the printed lids and covers which wee see layd and set uppon our baked meates'.[2] The women delightedly turned about to let him admire and even finger these weird fleshly embossments. They also wore round their heads a narrow roll of cotton cloth, called a *jalla*, that was caught up in several different ways and decorated with a variety of beads and coral and gold trinkets, depending upon the district.[3] They took endless trouble with their hair. They cut it in patterns, or wore it long in numerous braids; plaiting into them beads and coral, or, more fantastically, small horse-bells. Francis Moore saw and heard this tinkling headgear, and, trying as hard as Jobson had tried, in his comparison of the women's scarifications to designs on pie covers, to let his readers visualize such strange practices in terms of the familiar, remarked that the use of bells by the women in dressing up 'makes 'em look not unlike the Fore-Horse of a Country Farmer's Team'.[4]

The women were betrothed young and when a girl became marriageable she was carried away from home by the bridegroom and his supporters with an appearance of force; the moonlight rang with shrieks and yells and the clatter of arms as her own friends put up a mock show of resistance to the rape. She was not seen again in public for a time, and when she did come forth she was heavily veiled for several months, 'observing herein a shamefast modestie, not to be

[1] Jobson, pp. 60–2; Moore, p. 121.   [2] Jobson, p. 75.
[3] Mungo Park, *Travels in the Interior Districts of Africa*, 1799, p. 21; Moore, p. 75.
[4] Moore, p. 75.

looked for, among such a kinde of blacke or barbarous people'. At once, or in the course of time, she would make only one of several wives, three or four or even up to seven, each living in a separate hut and sharing the husband's favours in order. A number of concubines in addition to wives was a 'necessity', in Jobson's phrase, because intercourse was forbidden until a child was weaned, which was usually not for three years. Englishmen were always astonished to discover that, contrary to their own country's proverbial wisdom, the women of a household got on extremely well together and enjoyed the companionship. They were just as surprised by the restraint and decency shown in public between the sexes, given the provocations and the opportunities; none of them could ever say that he had even seen 'a black man kiss a woman'. They apparently required the dark to uphold their reputation for unlimited concupiscence.[1]

The women did most of the work, even the heaviest, such as pre-paring the rice and other grains, which were worked with a heavy wooden puddle in a wooden mortar. The men were occupied for only about two months of the year, at seed time and harvest. They pre-pared the ground laboriously, with a hoe; the iron for these primitive implements was one of the main items in the trade with Europe. They sowed millet chiefly, except along the river, where rice was grown in the paddy fields lying behind the dense wall of mangroves. The men worked without respite at the customary times, when their whole existence might turn on their success, but for the rest of the year they hardly seemed even to bother to hunt or fish, though game abounded and the river swarmed. They lay on the *bentang* in the shade, smoking, gossiping, and playing a kind of chess. They ate once a day, usually *couscous*, which their wives prepared by steaming granulated flour over meat or broth. A favourite ingredient of the *couscous* was fish dried in the sun and rendered to a paste. Its smell was so offensive to Europeans that it was always known as 'stinking fish'. As for meat, they ate 'large snakes, guanas, monkeys, pelicans, bald-eagles, alligators, and sea-horses', and if the idea seemed monstrous, the European who actually supped on them had to acknowledge that they made excellent food.[2] Their only liquors were palm wine, ciboa wine, honey wine, and beer, but they preferred to these European brandy and rum, when they could get them; an acquired taste that too often proved disastrous.

Eating only once a day, they were able to smoke without interruption. They hardly ever had a pipe out of their mouths. They grew their

[1] Jobson, pp. 70-2, 76.   [2] Moore, p. 109.

own tobacco. The pipe bowls were very neatly made of a reddish clay; the stems of a reed or a piece of wood, bored through with a red-hot wire, sometimes as long as six feet and ornamented with a leather tassel. The merchants carried travelling pipes, with bowls of huge—half-pint—capacity.[1] Their pipes were almost their only personal possessions, apart from their arms and their clothes, and, in the case of the women, their jewellery. A mat to sleep on, a box for clothes, a water jar, calabashes to drink and eat out of, mortars, and baskets for storage: give them these and their wants were supplied.

Their social diversions were dancing and wrestling. The wrestlers were young men stripped to a pair of short drawers and rubbed down with oil. They competed in front of the *bentang* tree in a circle of spectators, and though skill and dexterity counted, strength really told, and the champions would have proved too strong for most Europeans. They fought to the accompaniment of a drum, which to an extent dictated their movements. The drum spoke a language based on Mandingo sentences, and, with a little knowledge, it was possible to understand, for example, that at the beginning the drummer beat out *'ali bœ see'*, which would be 'all sit down', and as the contestants came to grips, *'amuta, amuta'*— 'take hold, take hold'.[2]

They danced to the drums and also to the balafeu, all through the night and sometimes for as long as twenty-four hours. The women and the men danced separately, and it was difficult for a European, accustomed to the regular figures of the dances carried out on the floor of an assembly room, to appreciate the endless and apparently haphazard gyrations and motions of dancers moving either together or at random, except as displays of agility and, in the case of the women revellers, of suggestiveness.

The dances and the drumming—endless drumming, continued all through the night, throbbing unexpectedly from any point in the distance, fraught with baffling intentions—reminded a European that those black faces represented a moral and psychological night that he did not dare to penetrate. 'A Colour, Language, and Manners as wide from ours', was how one observer put it, 'as we may imagine we should find in the planetary subjects above, could we get there.'[3] And the European was the more uneasy because he was forced to confess that in all the usual business of life, the social coming and going that befell a trader who could not count on a show of force to

---

[1] ibid. p. 76.   [2] Park, p. 42.
[3] John Atkins, *A Voyage to Guinea*, 1735, p. 34.

back up his arguments, the 'Natives, really, are not so disagreeable in their Behaviour as we are apt to imagine'—our imaginings, of course, having been done for us.[1]

The drums were specially busy at the time of religious ceremonies and it was then that they sounded most menacing, loaded with the undertones of blind and cruel superstition. Richard Jobson attended a great February feast to mark the circumcision of the young men; his own servant, Samgulley, being one of those who had to be cut. When he came to the boy's town in the evening he found it crowded with visitors from far and wide. The huts were all full and people were camping under the trees and cooking their meals over huge fires, and there was music and drumming and dancing everywhere. In the bustle and excited coming and going and trading and merriment, Jobson was constantly being reminded of some great English country fair. A few of even the most outlandish figures might have found their counterparts at a fairground. The 'juddies', as Jobson calls the griots, or chief's musicians, reminded him of the 'Irish Rimer', in the way in which they sat apart from the company and recited traditional ballads celebrating the heroism and bravery of the chief's family, or extemporized on present happenings, to the accompaniment of a 'fiddle'—a stringed instrument made from a gourd. The 'juddies' were popular and rewarded when they were alive, but when they died they were buried upright in a hollow tree and left to rot. They could not be interred in the normal manner, having had 'familiar conversation with their divell *Ho-re*'.[2]

Jobson was very fond of Samgulley and reluctant to let him be circumcised, and in the morning when the operation took place, in the open air and watched largely by women, he angrily accused the operator of cutting too deep and spoiling him. 'His answere was, it is so much the better for him, and without any curiosity taking up his cloath shewed his owne members, that it might appeare he was cut as farre; howbeit my distaste was such upon him, that I could not yeeld to give him any thing in the way of gratuitie to wash his hands withall, and as the manner of the countrey is to do by such as are friends, to the party circumcised.'[3] Afterwards, the youths were left by themselves to heal according to nature and during this period they were allowed a great deal of licence and escaped punishment. All the time of 'the cutting of the prickes' the devil Ho-re could be heard roaring, in tones like the deepest bass of a man's voice. Ho-re had to be fed and was a great eater, and if the supplies were inadequate he would abduct and

---

[1] Moore, p. 120.   [2] Jobson, p. 147.   [3] ibid. pp. 155–6.

swallow some uncircumcised youth and keep him in his belly for nine or ten days until he had been redeemed with provisions. Once released from this strange confinement, the boy had to keep entirely silent for the same number of days he had spent in Ho-re's belly. Jobson tried to get one victim to talk, even going so far as threatening to shoot him, but he could not wring a sound out of him. Ho-re's roaring at night seemed to come like a ventriloquist's voice from every direction, here and there, at hand and in the distance, and the Englishmen who dared to walk out were seized with a 'ghastly dread' and escaped home.[1]

The devil Ho-re was also Mumbo-Jumbo, the name under which all the dark vindictive spirits of Africa have come together. A century after Jobson, Francis Moore described how Mumbo-Jumbo could be seen in many villages: a long coat of bark, topped by a tuft of fine straw, making it nine or ten feet high, fixed to a tall stick, and standing in full view near the village during the day. It prowled at night, roaring and terrorizing the women, whom it was intended to keep in awe. Only men could be initiated into the society, and the better to keep its secrets they talked a cant language, also known as Mumbo-Jumbo. Even if the women understood this cant they hid their knowledge, for they would otherwise certainly have been murdered. About 1727 the king of Jagra betrayed the secrets of the society to a favourite and inquisitive wife and when Mumbo-Jumbo learnt of it he had both the king and his wife killed upon the spot.[2]

The difficulty the European experienced was in translating such apparitions as Mumbo-Jumbo into terms of his own knowledge of the occult and of his own religious beliefs and traditions. When a native died suddenly and mysteriously after having broken a taboo it was possible to accept that his death could have been caused by witchcraft; at least, witches in Europe could bring down harm on their enemies— or on those who had even unwittingly offended them—by spells and incantations, intoned secretly over some filthy brew. The legends of home coincided with and helped to familiarize what appeared to have happened. But Mumbo-Jumbo could not be so readily assimilated, and when André Brüe met him on his travels on the Gambia in 1705, he assumed from everything that he had heard about his powers and authority that he could only be, in the Biblical sense, a false prophet. One day he passed Mumbo-Jumbo's coat of bark hanging in a tree, and being told that the prophet was invisibly present he deliberately beat the garment with a stick to prove that it was empty,

[1] ibid. pp. 158–62.   [2] Moore, pp. 40, 116–18.

in spite of being warned that it was death to do so.[1] Mumbo-Jumbo excused his restraint in not striking Brüe dead by explaining that he loved him and knew he was to be converted. He later paid the Director-General a visit, nearly hidden in his trailing coat, but he refused to answer any questions and only danced a little to the beating of his drum.

The man was clearly an impostor, a false prophet, the Europeans could conclude, and dismiss his pretensions; but it was not so easy to disregard claims that were backed by evidence. The man who called himself the King of the Bees was not only followed by thousands and thousands of bees wherever he went, as if he were the shepherd and they the sheep; they swarmed all over him and especially his head, without doing him any harm, or stinging his attendants.[2]

Ho-re, or Mumbo-Jumbo, was most powerful in the dark, but idolatry and superstition thrived just as well by day. The Africans appeared ready to worship anything—a queer stone, a scrap of fur, a twist of rag. These they called their fetishes. But a fetish was not only the object reverenced; it could also disconcertingly be a spell, charm, or enchantment.

To take the *Fittish*, is, to make an oath; which ceremony is variously performed in several parts of Guinea. In some places, they drink a large draught of water, and wish their *Fittish* may kill them, if what they attest be not true; and, generally speaking, a Negro's taking the *Fittish* in Guinea may as sincerely be relied on as the oath of a Christian in Europe. To make *Fittish*, is to perform divine worship; *Fittishmen* are the pagan priests. In short, they all commonly wear their *Fittish* about them, which is so sacred, that they care not to let anybody touch it, but themselves.[3]

The witness is William Smith, who proved how sacred the fetish was when he tried to examine the feathers worn in his cap by the king of Barrah's griot.

When they read such descriptions as Smith's and turned over the reports of extraordinary happenings that were put into circulation each time a ship returned from the Guinea coast, the European

---

[1] Thomas Green, the intensely Protestant editor of Astley's *Voyages*, who could never resist an opportunity at tilting at the Roman Catholic Church, remarked at this point: 'These, doubtless, were irrefragable Arguments, to prove that the Impostor was not bodily in his Coat: But then they would be equally good against the bodily Presence of Christ in the sacramental Wafer; which, to all Appearance is as empty or destitute of a human Body, as the Impostor's Coat was. How miserably blind and contemptible must those be, who believe the very Thing which they ridicule and despise others for:' Astley, ii. 83, n. *b*.

[2] Astley, ii. 83–4, 68.   [3] Smith, p. 27.

scholars tried to account for what they had learnt by the light of reason, under the guidance of theology, and in accordance with the historical verities of the Bible. They were not long in recognizing the bestial and abominable superstitions of the ancient Egyptians that, extirpated in the Nile valley, had lingered on into the modern era among these fastnesses of savagery, in a form even more debased.

The Christian theorist was hard on the African pagan, but he was just as hard on the Mohammedan, fearing a rival. Mohammedanism is 'a religion so nicely suited to the depravity of the natives, that it did not need the help of the sword to make it spread itself far and near'.[1] Could he have put it more succinctly? He had, however, to allow that the superstitions and bestialities of Africa were such that even Mohammedanism was mutilated and depraved. At the time when Jobson was on the Gambia, at the beginning of the seventeenth century, the Mandingos were mostly idolaters, but Jobson noticed that living among these were small numbers of a group which he called 'Marybuckes or Bissareas'. The 'Marybuckes'—or Marabouts, to use the common spelling—were strict Mohammedans. They dressed the same as the pagan Mandingos—the kaffirs, as the 'Bissareas' or, more properly, the bushreens, called them—and their manner of living was very similar, but in conduct and belief they were completely different; and the difference could be bewildering to a European.

The Marabouts were ascetics. They worshipped the true and only God as devoutly and unswervingly as any Christian, and abhorred idols and religious images more violently than even the Puritan. They may have married several wives with unchristian licence, but they chose them only from among their own people and educated their children strictly in the faith. Up and down the Gambia, wherever they were settled, they conducted schools, for they alone were literate among the Mandingos. They taught the children first to read and memorize the Koran and later to write the classical Arabic in which it was written. Mandingo was a spoken language without a script, but they gave instruction in writing it with the use of Arabic characters. Classes were held in the early hours before dawn, but you could always find your way to a school, led there by the sound of children repeating at the top of their voices the verses they had learnt by heart. The pupils learnt to write using small boards of bleached wood, instead of slates or paper. Only boys attended school, of course, but the girls were not entirely despaired of: to give them a chance of entering Paradise, they, too, were circumcised.[2]

[1] *Universal History*, xiv. 24.　　[2] Jobson, pp. 92–3; Labat, iv. 353–5.

The Marabouts governed their lives strictly by the law. They prayed daily, after thoroughly washing themselves according to practice; they kept Ramadan without a single deviation; and, what was much more surprising to the ordinary European, who could only put such self-discipline down to 'enthusiasm'—the canting hypocrisy and arrogance of your straitlaced Puritan—they utterly refused to touch any strong liquors, for which the African had usually an insatiable and convenient thirst. Their detestation of alcohol was so ingrained that a Marabout who fell overboard in the Gambia from a European boat and was dragged back on board unconscious, instinctively pursed his lips to prevent spirits from being administered; upon coming round and recognizing the tell-tale smell, he affirmed that he would have rather died than tasted. However indistinguishable from the rest of the natives in other outward respects, the Marabouts could always be told by their refusal to touch Europe's tempting liquors. A further distinguishing mark was their fixed habit of telling the truth.[1] By being Mohammedans the Marabouts were eternally in the wrong, morally and dogmatically, but their rigorous practice of a system that in some respects resembled the one adopted by austere Christianity, fitted in awkwardly with the generalizations that were current about men with black skins.

The Marabouts were the great traders among the Africans, travelling with their families far afield. They took their books and manuscripts with them and instructed their children wherever they happened to stop. They brought back stories from the upper Gambia of a country with an untold wealth in gold, but at the same time they repeatedly warned the Europeans, whose cupidity they had aroused, of the incredible dangers and hardships that awaited anyone rash enough to try and mount the river above the falls at Barracunda (Barra Kunda), three hundred miles upstream, the first natural barrier to anyone trying to advance into the interior along the waterway.

The Marabouts traded among their own people in salt, which they obtained from the saltpits near the coast on the north shore of the Gambia, and they carried this coarse product far inland, bartering it for gold, or for kola nuts, a delicacy everywhere much in demand. Far in the interior the salt was exchanged for gold with a people who refused to be seen; each party in the absence of the other putting salt or gold in turn until the quantities were sufficiently matched to allow a bargain. The reason for this tribe's strange reluctance to be

[1] Jobson, pp. 102-4.

seen was their being born with a lower lip so large that it hung down
and hid their bosom. The pendulous lip putrified in the sun's heat and
salt was required to preserve it.[1]

But the Marabouts' oddest item of trade, in the view of Europeans,
was their *grisgris*—or 'gregories', as Jobson rather quaintly termed
them. *Grisgris* were verses from the Koran written out by the Marabouts on pieces of paper and sold as talismans to the deeply superstitious natives, to protect them from one or another of a thousand
possible ills and misfortunes, or to restore them if they were already
affected. Once a *grisgris* had been bought as a specific, the purchaser
took it to a craftsman and had it enclosed in a leather case, of one of
several shapes, for wearing about his person; across the head, around
the neck, about the middle, or dangling from the arm, next to the part
that was to be cured or defended. Those that could afford them carried
as much as thirty pounds' worth in weight, and bought them to hang
also on their weapons and their horses.[2] The spell could also be written
in ink on a wooden board and washed off and the dirty water drunk
as a remedy. The trade in *grisgris* was lucrative and made paper one
of the most desirable of European goods. A Marabout could travel
a long way on the proceeds of a sheet or two of paper.

Mohammedanism was more widely established in the Gambia in
the eighteenth century than in Jobson's time, but the majority of the
Mandingos were still pagans, though their beliefs and customs were
tempered by the Marabouts' example. The Floops, and the related
Banyoons, whom the Mandingos had dislodged from the river, were
more inveterately pagan. The Banyoons, living on the south shore in
the kingdoms of Fonia, Cumbo, and Geregia, had the reputation of
being civilized, industrious, and brave; in fact, the women were so
taken up by their chores that they were supposed to fill their mouths
with water in order to avoid wasting time in chat. The Floops in those
areas were also comparatively civilized, but the farther away from the
river their settlements were—and their territory stretched along
the coast as far south as Cacheu, on the San Domingo—the more
savage they appeared to become, until they were referred to as 'the
wild Floops', who, like so many African tribes, had the reputation of
being cannibals.[3]

The Floops were a stockier and more round-headed people than

---

[1] Jobson, p. 141. Stories of a 'silent trade' in gold were common from the time of
Herodotus. They are well discussed by E. W. Bovill, *Caravans of the Old Sahara*,
1933, pp. 59–60.

[2] Jobson, pp. 68–9; Moore, p. 144.   [3] Astley, ii. 86.

their bitter enemies, the Mandingos; and, unlike the Mandingos, they were not combined under a number of despots but were a federation of fortified villages, though they effectively acted in unison as far as policy was concerned. They had the reputation of being sullen and revengeful, and one of their practices would seem to confirm it. If a man was killed at one of their drunken feasts, his son wore his father's sandals once a year on the anniversary of the murder until he had succeeded in revenging him by slaying the assassin.[1]

Their principal article of trade with the Europeans on the Gambia was beeswax; from honey they made the mead on which they got drunk. Their vast and unfrequented forests were full of bees. The intermediaries in this trade were the Marabouts, no European ever trying to master the difficult Floop tongue.[2] And Europeans were well advised to have nothing directly to do with the wild Floops. They were ready to plunder anyone who attempted to pass through their domain by land, and in 1731 a shallop of the Royal African Company that ran aground on a trading voyage to Cacheu was savagely attacked in force. The shallop was manned by five white men and seven castle slaves, trained as soldiers, but though their guns were more than a match for the Floops' bows and arrows, they came away with difficulty and then only because they were floated off by the rising tide.[3] Farther south below Cacheu, at Biafara, whenever the natives came upon a vessel grounded on the coast they attacked it across the morasses by fastening pieces of bark, about two feet long and seven or eight inches wide, to their feet in the manner of snowshoes, to stop them from sinking into the ooze.[4] After such reports on the Floops, their enemies' admission that they were as prompt to repay kindness as they were in revenge suggests that the Europeans understood them imperfectly.

The other people on the Gambia who had resisted the Mandingo advance were the Joloffs. Barrah and Badibu, the Mandingo king-doms on the north shore, were tributaries of the greater Joloff king-dom of Barsally, and Barsally was only the last of the several Joloff principalities lying between the Senegal and the Gambia, an enor-mous extent, known to Europeans only through the coastal trade. The Joloffs of Barsally were a martial people and like the Spartans lived under regulations designed to keep up their fierceness and hardiness; regulations adapted to the strange circumstances of African life. No Joloff, except the royal family, dared sleep under mosquito netting upon pain of being sold into slavery; and the same penalty

[1] Park, pp. 15–16.   [2] ibid. p. 5.   [3] Moore, p. 36.   [4] Astley, ii. 100.

awaited anyone who dared to sit on the royal mat without an invitation. The king ruled absolutely, but lived on terms of equality with his soldiers, and as he paid them in plunder he was always at war, looting one town or another.[1]

The Joloffs were black, blacker than any other African people, but beautiful; tall and slender and strong in body, with black hair, 'curled, downy, and extremely fine', large well-shaped eyes, and features that pleased a European's taste with their regularity. The women were especially attractive. 'Their skin is surprisingly delicate and soft', wrote a Frenchman, and the French on the Senegal had far more to do with the Joloffs than the English had on the Gambia; 'their mouth and lips are small; and their features very regular. There are some of them perfect beauties. They have a great share of vivacity, and a vast deal of freedom and ease, which renders them extremely agreeable.' When the English translator came upon this passage he used the excuse of England and France being yet again at war to remark with repressed envy: 'The vast numbers of children, and children's children, the French begat by them, and left there, prove our author is not singular in his opinion.'[2]

The Joloff way of life was outwardly much the same as the Mandingo, but the Joloffs excelled their neighbours in at least one trade, the manufacture of fine cotton cloth. They spun the thread by hand with spindle and distaff and wove it into pieces nine inches wide and as much as twenty-seven yards long. They made from these pieces, by cutting and sewing, the lengths they needed for their *pagnes*, one for their shoulders, the other for a skirt, the invariable dress of both men and women. They dyed the cloth either blue or yellow, and the colours were so brilliant and fast that a pair of these cloths could fetch as much as thirty shillings sterling—a very steep price indeed, converted into the values of today.[3] The Joloffs' ingenuity in weaving ought to have been as difficult to square with the African's well-known inability to master any craft as their women's beauty and vivacity with the African's repulsive features and sullen bestiality, but in a continent so vast and notoriously uniform, and standing in such a curious relation to Europe, generalizations were always allowed to apply.

If the Joloffs appeared in some insignificant respects to contradict the current impressions of the African, the fourth and last of the main racial groups on the Gambia was even more of a puzzle; a people so mysterious in their looks and manner that it was impossible to tell where they had come from, or where exactly they were to be placed

---

[1] Moore, pp. 213–14.   [2] Adanson, p. 39.   [3] Moore, pp. 72–3.

among the grades of mankind. Richard Jobson found them living among the Mandingos, occasionally in settlements, but more often as nomads, herding their cattle down from the distant highlands to the savannahs along the river in the dry season. 'The wandering Fulbie', he called them, referring to their pastoral way of life, and 'the paineful Fulbie', when he considered the hardships they underwent, living in subjection to two harsh task masters, nature and their overlords, the Mandingos.

Jobson's idyllic account of the Fulbie[1] is infused with the affection that Europeans often felt for this strange people. Among the black and alien Africans they stood out as a recognizable, a non-negroid type of man; they resembled the Egyptians, Jobson wrote. They were tawny in colouring, upright and slender in stature, with fine features and long black hair, quite unlike the Negro's crisped wool.[2] And if a European could admit at least part kinship with the Fula, they, in talking about the tribes of Africa, ranked themselves as white men.[3] Many extravagant conjectures were made as to their origins: that they were descendants of the Hyskos, the Shepherd Kings, was one, but the correct view, that they were a Negro people infiltrated with Berber blood, was also established. As one observer remarked: 'Their Alliances with the *Moors* have both imbued their Mind with *Mohammedanism*, and their Skins with a Clay-Colour.'[4]

The Fula had to be always on the watch. When they drove their cattle down to water at the river, they had to beware of the ambush of the crocodile—or 'bumbo', as the beast was called on the Gambia; and at night they had to build a ring of smudge fires around their herds and mount guard to ward off the prowling ounces and lions.

The roar of a marauding lion could strike the night into terrified silence, every living creature straining to catch the noise of the kill. When a caravan of more than sixty people, with asses and oxen and protected by horsemen as outriders, was once moving by moonlight through the deserted forests lying between the Senegal and the Gambia, on the roar of a lion 'the silence which instantly reigned throughout our troop, permitted us to hear very distinctly the movements of this terrific animal through the high grass which concealed him from our view'. And then, suddenly, the momentary hypnosis induced by that chilling cry was snapped and 'women, children, all ran

---

[1] They were usually called Pholeys in the eighteenth century—by Francis Moore, for instance—but they were also known as Fulas or Foulans. Fulani is the accepted name in Nigeria. Unless quoting, I have preferred for convenience to keep to Fula, which is the name they go under on the Gambia.

[2] Jobson, p. 45.   [3] Park, p. 59.   [4] Astley, ii. 63.

pell-mell for protection to the horsemen, with such precipitation, that they overthrew one another'.[1]

Lions and crocodiles were the Fula's large enemies; smaller ones were the flies. A herdsman might be so thick with flies about his face and hands and bare legs that anyone not inured to their plague would have to carry a leafy branch to beat them off while he was bargaining over the price of a beast.[2] But in spite of the flies the Fula's sense—if not their attainable standard—of cleanliness was high. The women had the right to the milk of the herd[3] and sold it and the butter in well scoured gourds. Had a hair or a bit of dirt been found in them, 'she would have seemed to blush, in defence of her cleanly meaning'. The women of the Irish kerns were not to be compared in respect of cleanliness to these tawny milkmaids.[4]

The nomadic pastoralists were the purest of the Fula breed; they were the 'red' Fula, speaking with reference to their colour. Wherever they had settled they had intermarried with the surrounding people, but though this had darkened their hue, their ideal of beauty and appearance was still taken from their original stock, and they despised Negro characteristics.[5] Many more Fula had settled on the Gambia since they were first described by Richard Jobson, and by the beginning of the eighteenth century a *Pholeycunda*, or Fula village, was commonly found beside a Mandingo village, standing to it rather in the relation of a useful parasite. Each Pholeycunda was under the government of its own chief and was tolerated by the king of the realm in which it happened to be; should its inhabitants be ill-used or oppressed, they simply broke up the town and moved it elsewhere.[6]

The Fula were tolerated because they were useful. They were as productive farmers as they were skilful herdsmen. They cultivated cotton and tobacco, and planted maize and rice and millet, the staples of African diet. They were extremely industrious and frugal and as they were always willing to help their less provident Mandingo neighbours in such a common emergency as a famine, 'to have a *Pholey* Town in the Neighbourhood, is by the Natives reckon'd a Blessing'.[7] They also herded the Mandingo cattle with their own. The herds grazed

---

[1] Gaspard Mollien, *Travels in the Interior of Africa*, 1820, pp. 93–4.
[2] Jobson, p. 47.
[3] Derrick J. Stenning, *Savannah Nomads: A Study of the Wodaabe Pastoral Fulani of Western Bornu Province, Northern Region, Nigeria*, 1959, p. 5. Stenning is discussing the Fula of today, but it is clear from Jobson's remarks that this custom has not changed over the years.
[4] Jobson, pp. 49–50.   [5] Mollien, pp. 164–5; Stenning, p. 2.
[6] Moore, p. 30.   [7] ibid. p. 32.

all day on the savannahs, or on the lougans (the paddy fields) when the rice crop was off. At night they were driven in and tethered separately to one of the many posts that were fixed round a guard house— a platform built about eight feet above ground, open on all sides, and roofed with thatch. Five or six armed men slept there all night to give protection from the wild beasts.[1]

The village itself lay in the centre of the land under tillage, or used as a cattlefold. The Fula houses were differently built from the Mandingo and in their resemblance to tents suggested the people's nomadic origins. The walls were circular and made of a mixture of earth and dung, and the roof was constructed of long poles, tied in a cone and covered with straw. When the single door was shut the people inside were dry and warm, but completely in the dark, a small inconvenience.[2] The huts were sited to form regular streets and passages, unlike the higgledy-piggledy of the Mandingo villages, but far enough apart from each other to lessen the risk of fire. They were as clean and as well tended in appearance as the inhabitants, who dressed in white cotton of their own weaving.[3]

The nomadic and primitive Fula—those who, uncouth and dangerous, wandered most of the year through the inland forest, sheltering in huts made of branches of trees covered with a handful of straw— were pagans. Their more civilized brothers living in villages were almost entirely Mohammedans. They were a devout people, easily governed by their own chiefs, self-disciplined, and peaceable; but they were known to be courageous and to handle their arms well.

Mandingos, Joloffs, Floops, and Pholeys—these were the peoples of the Gambia, but the European traders hardly knew more about them than they could gather from coasting along the shore. Inland, they were told, the Mandingos and the Joloffs had other and far greater kingdoms than those which bordered the river. The Floops held vast territories lying to the south; even the 'poor Fulbie' had his own dominions: Futa Toro, Bondou, and Futa Jallon were lands where the Fula ruled.

[1] ibid. pp. 33–4.   [2] Mollien, p. 166.   [3] Moore, p. 35.

CHAPTER TWO

Trade and Diversions
on the River

'I MADE answer, We were a people, who did not deale in any such commodities, neither did wee buy or sell one another, or any that had our owne shapes.'

Richard Jobson's refusal of Buckor Sano's offer to sell him some black girls is among the proudest of famous replies. Jobson was eleven days' journey up river beyond Barracunda when he had his meeting with the great merchant, Buckor Sano, who had hurried down specially from Tenda to see him. The merchant had put on his best clothes for the meeting and arrived with his music playing solemnly before him in adulatory strain, and some forty attendants armed with bows and arrows. They met under a shady tree on the bank of the river, far from any sign of habitation, but within two hours of Jobson's stepping ashore from his boat, two hundred men and women had assembled. The meeting was a merry one. Buckor Sano liked Jobson's liquor so well and sucked in so much of it, that he fell asleep and was put insensible in Jobson's bed on board. He was so unwell the following day that apart from offering Jobson the girls he was incapacitated for business.

Buckor Sano was extremely surprised at Jobson's refusal. He had been used to carrying slaves, especially young women, for sale to white men. 'They were another kinde of people different from us,' Jobson replied, 'but for our part, if they had no other commodities, we would return again.' They decided to trade in elephants' teeth, cotton yarn, and native cloth, and the day after the debauch they set up a covered stall on the river bank and began dealing in these commodities against salt. Jobson and his men were desperately anxious to buy gold, but they were so frightened of betraying their purpose that they came to the point only after the most roundabout inquiries. Buckor Sano immediately offered them the gold worn in ornaments by the women present, but if it was really gold they wanted, he exclaimed, he would bring sufficient in future to buy all their goods. 'This Countrey above doth abound therewith, insomuch as these eyes of mine (poynting two of his fingers to his eyes, as the Countrey manner of speaking is,) hath been foure severall times, at a great Towne above, the houses whereof are covered onely with gold.' Jobson's own eyes nearly started out of his head at this information, the only news he had come to hear, and he asked if Buckor Sano would lead them there. They would have to travel through enemies, Buckor Sano replied. We have guns and will kill them all, Jobson boasted, in the style of the conquistador; at which Buckor Sano 'seemed to take a great deale of content'.[1]

Jobson never set eyes on the city of gold, but his purpose in publishing in 1623 *The Golden Trade*, his account of his voyage up the Gambia, was to persuade his readers that the city existed for the sake of Englishmen alone, and that it could be reached. Many attempts were made following Jobson's encouragement to reach the gold country into which the Gambia was supposed to lead; Wangara, as it had already been denominated for centuries in the European imagination.[2] Colonel Vermuyden pushed up beyond the falls at Barracunda in 1661 and claimed to have found at the farthest extent of his capacity to follow the river an 'Exceed of Gold'; a discovery most probably imagined by the Colonel to encourage others.[3]

A far more adventurous and successful search was made about thirty years later by Cornelius Hodges, the brutal captain who was married to the Portuguese widow at Vintain. He tried striking up river in 1681 and 1688 without great success, but in 1689 he crossed the wilderness lying between Barracunda and Kaynoura on the Faleme and entered Bambuk, which was really the Wangara of fable.[4] He reached the famous mine at Nettico, but found to his chagrin that it was not being worked on account of a terrible famine, which, as Hodges remarked, 'has proved ye Rewin of my Voyage'. Notwithstanding, he pushed an advance party of thirteen men north-eastwards through Bambuk and across the Senegal to the stone-built city of Tarra—probably Atar, in Mauritania—where they combined with

[1] Jobson, pp. 117-23.   [2] See Bovill, pp. 59-61.
[3] Vermuyden's journey and the journey by Hodges that followed are both usefully discussed in the context of African exploration by Robin Hallett, *The Penetration of Africa*, 1966, pp. 82-4. Vermuyden's journal was published by Moore as Appendix III.
[4] A Frenchman, the Sieur Compagnon, is the authority for 'Agis' [Hodges] having reached Kaynoura, where the French were later, in 1716, to set up a fort, St. Pierre (Astley, ii. 148). But Kaynoura would, anyway, be the natural terminus for a journey to the Faleme from Barracunda (see below, p. 168).

the inhabitants to repulse an attack by an army from Morocco—forty thousand horsemen and camels, Hodges claimed. Hodges himself failed to reach Tarra and was forced to retreat to Barracunda after enduring considerable hardships. He wrote a report on his experiences for the Royal African Company and among his information was the alarming news that the French were already sending boats up the Senegal as far as Dramanet, only ninety miles from the mines at Nettico. He anticipated that their competition might be disastrous for English trade.[1]

Captain Bartholomew Stibbs, also a servant of the Royal African Company, tried to reach the mines supposed to lie above Barracunda in 1724, optimistically taking with him a party of Cornish miners to work the ore. He, too, failed; both the man and the season were wrong.[2]

Hope never dies: Vermuyden's matter-of-fact journal was unpublished until 1738; Hodges' confused but powerful account lay hidden until almost yesterday; but tales of a successful English discovery of an enormous treasure were always in circulation. As late as 1749 a pamphleteer on an African subject was telling his readers how in Charles II's time an English gentleman had been kindly directed by some civil Negroes on the Gambia to a gold mine from which he had taken an 'immense treasure'.[3] By 1749 gold was far from being the largest item of trade on the river.

The white men who would buy the slaves that Jobson had declined were the Portuguese, which was enough to give him a contempt for the trade. He knew why they were so eager to deal in blacks. They either shipped them abroad themselves as slaves, or sold them to the Spaniards for shipping to Mexico and the West Indies to work in the mines, 'or in any other servile uses, they in those countries put them to'.[4] Jobson's reply to Buckor Sano's offer of the girls has the resonance of personal integrity and has caught, we might like to think, the national tone. We cannot remind ourselves of it too often, if we pursue the history of the English on the Gambia, inaugurated by Jobson's adventure.

Sir John Hawkins had raided the West African coast for slaves in

---

[1] Hodges' account lay among the papers of the Royal African Company until 1924, when it was published by Thora G. Stone. 'The Journey of Cornelius Hodges in Senegambia, 1689–90', *English Historical Review*, 1924, xxxix. 89–95.

[2] Stibbs's journal of his attempt was published by Moore (pp. 235–97).

[3] *The Royal African: or, Memoirs of the Young Prince of Annamaboe*, n.d. [1749], p. vii.

[4] Jobson, p. 38.

1562 and 1564, but his wild example might not have been copied by his countrymen at the expense of the national virtue, exemplified by Jobson, had it not been for the corruption of sugar. The introduction of the sugar cane into the West Indies, and the methods required to raise and harvest and process it, led to an insatiable demand for labour, to match the equally insatiable taste for sweetness at home. The demand could not possibly be met by the shipping out from England of cast criminals, political offenders, and indentured servants to work on the spreading plantations, but Africa offered an inexhaustible supply of sturdy and industrious men and women, and Spain and Portugal had already drawn on this source for hundreds of thousands of labourers to work in the fields of the New World, or down its mines. Holland and France, Denmark and England suddenly grasped the merits of the system and the simplicity of its workings and began to compete fiercely for the trade as Spanish and Portuguese power declined.

The Portuguese had settled along the length of the coast, from the Gambia to Angola, beyond the Congo, but in the gaps between their settlements, or wherever they could be supplanted, the other Europeans established trading posts. The size and establishment of these posts, or factories, as they were called, depended upon the goodwill of the native rulers and the amount of available trade, but the largest were castles—defensible and fortified compounds, commanded by a governor, manned by a European garrison, with a proper complement of merchants and clerks.

The excuse for these establishments being trade, they were not directed or administered by the national governments concerned, but by companies of merchant adventurers, acting under patent. Patents for the exclusive trade on the African coast were granted to associations of English merchants by Charles I in 1631 and by the Commonwealth in 1651, but not until after the Restoration were conditions at home favourable for serious undertakings in Africa. The leading spirit of 'the Royal Adventurers of England trading into Africa', as the Royal African Company was first called on its establishment in 1661, was Prince Rupert. He had already visited the Gambia in 1652 and piratically harassed the Commonwealth shipping in the river, and remembering the stories of mountains of gold waiting to be removed from the interior, and appreciating the possibilities of English participation in the trade for slaves, he persuaded several members of the royal family and many others to subscribe towards sending out a fleet in 1661, under the command of Major Robert Holmes.

When Holmes arrived he found, as he had expected, that the only European opposition to an English monopoly of trade on the Gambia could come immediately from the remains of a colony that had been sent out by James, Duke of Courland, the ruler of a small principality on the Baltic, who tried to make up for his lack of resources by imagination and initiative. Four men and two women, under the command of Otto Stiel, their valiant and honourable governor, were all that were left on St. Andrew's Island. They had no alternative but to surrender the fort on Holmes's demand. Holmes renamed the fort James Fort, after the Duke of York. The only other immediate consequence of Holmes's mission was Colonel Vermuyden's voyage up the river in search of gold.

The royal charter incorporating the Company in 1661 had been made out in favour of the Duke of York, but in 1663 the Duke returned it to the king, who revoked it and issued another of ampler privileges and wider scope. The Company was now put in possession of all the countries between the port of Salee in Morocco and the Cape of Good Hope, for the period of a thousand years. The only condition imposed by regal generosity was the Company's being required to present the king or his successors with two elephants each time he or they set foot in any of the countries and colonies within the grant. An elephant, supported by two Negroes, was carried on one side of the Company's seal; the king's face on the other. Such large territorial responsibilities could not be lightly discharged and the Company was to be conducted by a governor and his deputy, with the agreement of seven of a court of twenty-four assistants. They were to make regulations and inflict punishments, to transfer stock at their pleasure, to equip and send out trading vessels, and to make war in defence of their colonies. The Company's most important privilege was, however, the one that caused it its greatest difficulties: its rights to the African trade were to be exclusive and interlopers were to be punished by the confiscation of their vessels. The African coastline is long and human greed is unlimited; the exclusion was impossible to apply and brought the Company the ill will of every separate trader. But the Company stood upon the footing of this charter through all vicissitudes until 1720, when a new charter was obtained by the Duke of Chandos, in an attempt to rescue its sunken fortunes.

The unscrupulous snatching of James Island from the Courlanders and Charles's shabby refusal to give any satisfaction to the unlucky Duke, to whom Charles was, typically, indebted for aid during the time of his exile, was an appropriate inauguration of the history of the

Island under the Company. The Company's headquarters in Africa was Cape Coast Castle, on the Gold Coast—seized from the Dutch in 1664—but James Fort was of great importance and the centre of its trade in the Gambia and up and down the coast. The island's only advantage was that lying one and a half miles from the north shore and two and a half miles from the south it controlled the deep-water channels; no ship could pass up river without coming within range of its guns. All the Company had to do was to maintain the guns and provision the garrison in order to exclude all interlopers, English or foreign. What can be simply said is not always easily done, and to keep the guns in repair and a garrison in existence, in the face of natural and political hazards, often proved too much for the Company's resources.

After Major Holmes had dispossessed the Courlanders, the Dutch menaced the fort for several years, as they and the English contended for supremacy. The fort was seized by slaves in a rising of 1667, after thirty-one of the thirty-two Englishmen garrisoning it had been killed; a pirate called Anderson ransacked it in 1683, when its defenders were too weakened by sickness to resist; the French reduced it to ruins in 1695; and as a result of further action by the French, the Company withdrew from it entirely in 1709. The Company recovered the fort in 1713 and by 1718 it was again habitable, in time to be plundered in the following year by the Welsh pirate, Howel Davis, and again abandoned. The Company returned in 1721 under the inspiration of the Duke of Chandos and by 1726 the fort had been restored and remained more or less unaltered in appearance until its final destruction by the French in 1778.[1]

The Company's method of trade in the Gambia necessarily differed from the one in use elsewhere on the coast. The Portuguese had penetrated inland and settled in several places, but the other Europeans were mainly confined to trade castles on the Gold Coast; thirty-two in all at the peak of the system—English, Dutch, Danish and French, and Brandenburger. The castles, which varied in size from palisadoed mud huts to spacious and permanent fortifications, collected the trade through the caboceers—the chiefs of the villages—and transhipped it to vessels lying offshore, beyond the barrier of dangerous surf that raged along the whole length of the coast. The Europeans stationed there never penetrated inland in search of trade themselves and their only knowledge of the African character came from the black castle servants, whether slaves or freemen, who were, superficially at least,

[1] See A. W. Lawrence, *Trade Castles and Forts of West Africa*, 1963, pp. 250–61.

thoroughly Europeanized; the caboceers, linguisters, and other commercial agents; and the townspeople or villagers, whose huts clustered under protection of the castle. The natives had long been accustomed to European manners, especially as they provided the castles with women, who passed on to their folk outside their intimate knowledge of their white keepers' habits and displayed the latest European fashions on their persons. The garrisons knew nothing of the interior except what could be learnt through these local intermediaries, and could judge of what was happening only by the rise or fall in the slave supplies, unless some internal disturbance was so great that hostilities were carried even as far as the coast.

The Company's operations in the Gambia were determined by the access the river allowed into the interior. James Fort was well placed to control the river traffic, and to serve as a collecting point for goods waiting to be shipped, but trade would not flow naturally to it: 'Trade will not come without seeking', is how the matter was put by a Company agent.[1] The method of implementing this policy was to establish trading posts—factories—up river and to use small craft for communication and transport between them and the fort. The factories could not always be maintained in the face of extortionate or hostile local rulers, and often they could not be manned for want of agents, but in February 1732, for example, there were factors at Cabata (Kafuta), Vintain, Geregia, Tancrowall, and Yamyamacunda on the south bank and at Gillyfree, Colar (Koular), and Joar (Jakau-Ur) on the north. In the same month three sloops, the *Fame*, the *Sea Nymph*, and the *Adventure*, and a shallop, the *Gambia*, were in service.[2] About six months later there were factors also at Brucoe (Buruku) and Fattatenda (Fatatenda), but those at Cabata, Vintain, and Colar had apparently been withdrawn. The fleet had been increased by the *Falam*, an unidentified craft, and the *Recovery*, a schooner.[3] The penetration of the country in these ways allowed the Company's agents to see more of Africa than Europeans elsewhere on the West Coast and brought them directly into touch with the life and customs of several important tribes; it is consequently from them that the fullest and most authentic impressions of the African were to be derived.

At any of the factories there could be two, or even three, Company agents, but usually only one. During the eight months from June 1732 to February 1733, for instance, James Payzant, James Connor,

[1] See K. G. Davies, *The Royal African Company*, 1957, p. 216.
[2] P.R.O., T.70/1447, pp. 39–40.　　　　[3] ibid. p. 52.

John Harrison, and Francis Moore were serving alone as factors at Geregia, Yamyamacunda, Tancrowall, and Brucoe; the factory at Gillyfree was being run by Frederick Pritzcoe, a writer—that is, a clerk in the service of the Company and junior to a factor; and only at Joar and Fattatenda was there more than one agent. James Davis and John Brown, a factor and a writer, were stationed at Joar, and at Fattatenda, Hugh Hamilton, the factor, was assisted by two writers, Thomas Palmer and Henry Johnson.[1] These outlying and lonely Englishmen were forced to live on terms of unusual intimacy with their African neighbours, and both their success and safety depended upon their winning the natives' friendship and coming to understand their character—at least, as it showed in practice.

The establishment was not fixed at any of the factories, depending as it did upon unforeseeable circumstances. In May 1733 Francis Moore was given two writers just arrived out from England, James Roots and John Barnfather, to help him at Brucoe,[2] but in July he was ordered by Richard Hull, the governor, and John Hamilton, the chief merchant at James Fort, to replace James Connor at Yamyamacunda. Connor, as senior factor, was needed at the fort.

Moore's instructions reached him at Brucoe on the evening of 12 July, brought up from the fort by George Lawson, the master of the *Gambia*, a shallop. The shallop was a most useful vessel for such purposes. Small and light, with only a small mainmast and foremast and lugsails, that could be readily hauled up and let down as required, it was commonly a good sailer and often used as a tender upon a man-of-war. But when Moore set out three days later for Yamyamacunda, after having accounted for the Company's effects and arranged for James Roots to succeed him, the river was already running so strongly with the rains that the shallop could not make headway and he had to travel by canoe.

After taking leave of the Suma of Dubocunda (Dobang Kunda), whose protection extended to the factory at Brucoe, Moore and George Lawson crossed to Cuttejarr and hired horses to ride overland to Samy (Sami), where they stayed the night. They wanted to swim the horses across the Samy River the next day, but the owners refused to let them for fear of crocodiles. 'They are exceeding plenty in that River,' Moore observed, 'and withal very mischievous; for they often catch Men by the Legs, and carry them away as they are wading up to their Knees or Middles in the River to unload Boats or Canoas, which they are at low Water obliged sometimes to do.'[3] They

---

[1] P.R.O., T.70/1447, pp. 51–2.   [2] ibid, p. 53.   [3] Moore, p. 170.

D

crossed the Gambia by canoe, and walked to Fendalacunda, about ten miles below Yamyamacunda, where they rejoined their own canoe. Their progress against the rush of waters was so slow, however, that they disembarked again and ended the journey on foot, having taken three days. Moore was ill and found the journey very fatiguing.

The annual floods were particularly severe that year. By 16 September the waters had begun to undermine the mud walls of the factory-house and Moore had hurriedly to build a hut on higher ground, in the middle of the village of Yamyamacunda. He had no sooner transferred the Company's effects there, and entrusted his slaves to the custody of the headman of the village, than the walls of the factory fell with a thunderous crash about midnight, though the roof itself was left standing. The river brought down whole islands of earth with giant trees still attached. The only way of travelling across the drowned fields was by canoe, and provisions were so scarce there was danger of starving. Moore returned to the factory on 27 October, after hearing of a plot to steal his slaves.

The factory needed to be rebuilt and after the timbers for the *forkillas*—poles shaped like crutches—and ridgepoles had been delivered by sloop on 20 December, Moore set his servants to work on a site on rising ground about fifty yards from the river. The size of the house was to be forty square feet and beginning with the roof, which was supported on forkillas, they proceeded to the walls. The Negroes trod the mud for the walls with their feet, to temper it and prevent it from cracking, and built the walls a foot and a half thick. They raised them a foot at a time, neatly smoothing the mud with a special knife and leaving each layer to harden. The walls, which were not required, because of the forkillas, to carry any weight, came to within a foot of the roof for ventilation and were protected from the weather by overhanging eaves. The partition walls were built in the same way, those of the storeroom being of extra strength and careful design to avoid the risks of theft and fire. The roofs of both the house and the essential porch—the *alpaintre*—were thatched with mats made of straw tied in small bundles, lashed together and laid to overlap like tiles. The inside was floored with hard, rammed clay.

Moore was delighted with the native builders' skill and described their methods at length. 'I have been the longer in the Describing this,' he remarked, 'because I thought it would be amusing to the Reader, to see how easily the People, whom we call Barbarous, can procure the Conveniences of Life. Here is a House built, with a Hall 40 Foot by 13, two Lodging Rooms 20 Feet by 13, and 3 strong Storehouses, without any Iron-work, Trowells, Squares, or Carpenters Rules, and with the smallest Expence to the Company, for I did it with their Servants only, having hired no other help but the Man who laid and smooth'd the Clay. And the Inside was not only convenient and free from Vermin, but very clean, and had a cool Look, for the Clay is hard, close, smooth, and takes Whitewash very well.'[1] Four subsidiary houses, built in Mandingo style, were put up at regular distances about the main house; one served as a kitchen, two as stores for salt and for grain, and the other was used by the Company's black servants. A cirk (palisade), made of split cane woven like hurdles and standing ten feet high, was erected, enclosing about an acre of ground. Poultry were kept in the compound, of which part was used as a garden. Two stately *bishelo* trees were preserved for the sake of their welcome shade. Moore did not long enjoy his new quarters. He became so ill of the ague and fever that he begged to be relieved and returned to James Fort in January 1734.

Moore quickly recovered and was sent up river again, this time in charge of a trading voyage being made by the *James*, a sloop. The day after he arrived at Yamyamacunda, on 13 April, he discovered that the Alcaid of Sutamore had seized a horse belonging to the Company on the excuse that Moore owed him for its keep for a year. About a hundred people gathered to share in the row and Moore had at last to threaten them that unless they returned his horse and made the Alcaid apologize for the lies he had told, he would break up the factory and carry the Company's goods and servants down to James Fort. This threat was sufficient: the horse was led back and the Alcaid proceeded to beg Moore's pardon.[2]

Disputes between the Company's agents and the natives were not always so easily settled, nor could the local chiefs usually be brought to apologize for their oppressions and extortions. The outlying factors lay at the mercy of the chiefs, if they chose to exercise their power, and all that protected them was a mutual interest in the unbroken continuance of trade; an interest that was occasionally supported by friendship. Even in the happiest circumstances, both sides were out to get all they could, and if a trader could sell the bilge water out of his ship as a succedaneum, as one was sharp enough to do, a chief might retaliate on Europeans in general by squeezing out of them in 'presents' all that he dared, or, if he was powerful enough and unscrupulous, by crudely robbing them under threat of their lives. Francis Moore had a most alarming adventure of this kind when he

---

[1] ibid. p. 179.   [2] ibid. p. 187.

was sent up river for the first time in August 1731, to serve at Joar and learn the trade under the factor, William Roberts. John Harrison, a young writer, was also attached to Joar. Moore arrived on 4 September, so 'miserably mauled' on the way by mosquitoes that he could hardly drag himself up to the factory from the river, and five days later the king of Barsally and three of his brothers, Boomey Haman Seaca, Boomey Haman Benda, and Boomey Loyi Enunga, with an escort of more than a hundred horse and the same number of foot, marched into Joar. What followed is best told in Moore's own words:

Notwithstanding he has a very good House of his own in this Town, yet would he come and lie at the Factory. In the first Place he took Possession of Mr *Roberts*'s own Bed, and then having drank Brandy till he was drunk, at the Persuasion of some of his People, order'd Mr *Roberts* to be held, whilst himself took out of his Pocket the Key of his Storehouse, into which he and several of his People went, and took what they pleased; his chief Hank [longing] was Brandy, of which there happen'd to be but one Anchor, he took that out, drank a good deal of it, made himself drunk, and then was put to bed. This Anchor lasted him three Days, and then he went all over the House to seek for more; at last he came into a Room where Mr *John Harrison* lay sick, and seeing there a Case in which was six Gallons and a half of Brandy belonging to him and me, he ordered *Jack Harrison* to get out of Bed and open it; but he told him very seriously that there was nothing in it but some of the Company's authentick Papers, which must not be opened. The King was too well acquainted with Liquor-Cases to be put off so, and therefore ordered some of his Men to hold him in his Bed, whilst he took the Key out of his Breeches Pocket, he then open'd it, and took all the Liquor out of it, and was not sober so long as it lasted; but I must do the King this Justice, by saying that he very often sent for Mr *Harrison* and myself to drink with him. As soon as this Brandy was drank up, he talked of going home, upon which, his People, even his chief Ministers, who are the General, and the Keeper of his Majesty's Stores, amused themselves in taking what they thought best, which, with one Thing or another, amounted to twenty Pound Sterling; and they had the assurance to open even Chests and Boxes. What Resistance could three Men make against 300? Sometimes the King would ride abroad, and take most of his Attendance with him, but then, when he was gone abroad, we were plagued with the Company of *Boomey Haman Benda*, and his Brother, who were, if possible, worse than his Majesty.[1]

Moore had very good reason to remember Boomey Haman Benda. He once took a mouthful of water and spirted it into Moore's face. Realizing that this was an insult that it would be unwise to accept,

---

[1] ibid. pp. 83–4.

Moore emptied the remains of the mug into the prince's breeches. The Boomey furiously drew a knife on him, but on being restrained by his favourite attendant and told that he had gone too far in rudeness, he lay down on the floor in naked contrition and placed Moore's foot on his neck. Moore lifted him up and the two became warm friends.[1]

Such a scene may appear necessarily to belong to the annals of barbarism unless it is remembered that James Oglethorpe, the philanthropist and colonist of Georgia and friend of Alexander Pope, was treated in a similar way when serving as a young officer on the staff of Prince Eugene's army in Piedmont. An Austrian prince deliberately flicked some water in Oglethorpe's face at table, and he retaliated with the contents of a glass. Only the style of the apology was different. The nobility could be interchanged in these stories and discriminated only by their colour, black or white.

The king and his courtiers were all Mohammedans, but of quite another persuasion to the Marabouts, who would rather die than drink. As Francis Moore neatly remarked, the king 'will sooner die than drink Small when he can get Strong'.[2] He belonged to the lax sect of the Soninkis, who in the following century were to fight the rigid Marabouts. The king was a tall, powerful man, dressed in a white cotton cap and shirt and breeches, which admirably set off his jetty complexion, and as he enjoyed unlimited power he could freely indulge his passions. He would shoot an attendant dead for affronting him, as readily as he had thrown William Roberts out of bed. One of his amusements was to board the Company's sloop at Cahone (Kahone), the capital of Barsally, and shoot at the passing canoes, killing a man or two every day. Such were the whimsical and deliberated tyrannies of his good humour, but when he had drunk all there was in stock, for the sake of a fresh supply of liquor he would perpetrate appalling crimes.

The king filched and drank John Harrison's brandy in October, but a month after the king left Joar, Harrison himself was sent down to James Fort to recover from a flux made worse by drinking. Moore thought that Harrison's only chance of recovery was to leave off strong liquors, and, in fact, Harrison died at Tancrowall in the following February.

Drink was the curse and corruption of both black and white the length of the Coast, and the excesses it led to could be murderous or fantastic as well as sottish. On 22 May 1731 James Collins, the Company's smith at James Fort, got so drunk that he seized a musket and

---

[1] ibid. pp. 84–5.   [2] ibid. p. 85.

fired it at the ensign's head. The ball narrowly missed the ensign and two other people beside him and ended up by striking the wall close to the window of the room where the governor was sitting with some company. Collins was arrested and clapped into the slavehouse in irons. Two days later he was solemnly drummed out of the Company's service with a halter round his neck and was shipped home in the *Guinea*.[1] Collins was lucky. The demon on the African coast that took the shape of drink could sensationally arrest its victims even when they were almost out of reach. When Francis Moore was returning to England in 1735, among his fellow passengers was James Ellis, a writer, who had arrived out in the Gambia on 6 May 1733.[2] Ellis had fallen a martyr to rum and as he lay sick and fuddled in his bunk in the *Dolphin*, he could only manage to suck in his liquor through the stem of a pipe. He died 'with a Pipe and a Mug full of Bumbo close to his Pillow', and was buried at sea on 31 May 1733.[3]

Poor James Ellis; poor young Anybody. Every impartial observer blamed the exceptionally heavy death-rate among the English on their excessive drinking, and on their overeating, especially of meat.[4] Richard Jobson had noted long ago that the natives attributed their good health to their habit of eating only once a day, after dark, and then temperately. The English would not thrive in such a climate, he urged, until their governors were 'men of temperance'.[5] But men of temperance were usually not the kind who volunteered for service on the Gambia. One of the later governors, Daniel Pepper, was so drunken that in 1729 he killed a brother of the king of Barrah in an extreme bout. Luckily, the king was prepared to be compensated in money. But even had temperance been the rule of life, the climate and disease would have caused havoc. The climate is agreed to be the most tolerable on the west coast, with only four wet months, from June to September; not like Cacheu where it rains so much that it was known as 'the pisspot of Africa'; but even so, the heat and the humidity could impose an intolerable strain on men who seldom had the chance of becoming thoroughly acclimatized and continued dressing themselves in the inappropriate fashions of Europe.

When Major Holmes went ashore in March 1661 to pay a state call on the king of Cumbo he walked ten miles across bare sand, leaving the only horse to be ridden by Captain Stokes, who was 'old, fatt, and

---

[1] ibid. pp. 72–3.　　[2] P.R.O., T.70/1447, p. 53.　　[3] Moore, p. 232.
[4] William Bosman, *A New and Accurate Description of the Coast of Guinea*, 1705, p. 44.
[5] Jobson, p. 54.

burley'. One of the surgeon's mates and a greyhound in attendance fell down dead by the way from the heat and, what struck Holmes as even more surprising, a gun being carried on somebody's shoulder went off spontaneously in the heat. Holmes had to hurry back through the midday glare almost as soon as he had sat down to drink palmwine with the king, under a false alarm that his ships were in danger. Stokes and the others put up in a wood until the cool of the evening. When Holmes learnt that the guns that had recalled him had been fired accidentally on Stokes's ship he 'heartily repented' letting him have the horse and was so angry with him that he would have been 'well contented to have seen him hanged'. He suffered for several days from sunstroke and exertion.[1] The native remedy for sunstroke was to rub the forehead with a live toad, if one was to be found, but Europeans not used to handling the creatures found the remedy repugnant.[2]

Dysentery, malaria, yellow fever, sleeping sickness—endemic diseases, that could not be identified and named, except as the 'fever' or the 'flux', before the coming of tropical medicine—in combination with rudimentary hygiene, could wipe out a new contingent from England within months of their stepping ashore. 'But it is indeed convenient it should be so', one observer remarked cynically; 'another wants his place: If Men lived here as long as in *Europe*, 'twould be less worth while to come hither, and a Man would be obliged to wait too long before he got a good Post; without which nobody will easily return rich from *Guinea*.'[3] The round figures could be frightening. The Company sent out one hundred and seventy persons in 1721 to re-establish James Fort—factors, writers, soldiers, and artisans, including twenty women and children. They sailed in three ships and arrived separately in the Gambia between February and May, after undergoing various accidents. By September only seventy of the original company were left; a few had deserted to take up piracy, but the rest were dead. Three women and one child lived to escape from the river.[4] The circumstances under which these shiploads landed were exceptionally harsh, but even after James Fort had been comfortably re-established, numbers diminished faster than reinforcements could be recruited and sent out, which was one of the reasons advanced by the French for the ineffectiveness of English competition in trade, in spite of English advantages.[5] At the beginning of 1732 there were seventy-nine Company servants—factors, writers,

---

[1] Gray, pp. 57–8. [2] Adanson, p. 293. [3] Bosman, p. 107.
[4] Gray, pp. 162–4. [5] See Astley, ii. 125.

a surgeon, carpenters, masons, a wax refiner, gunners, soldiers, and so on—stationed at James Fort and the outlying factories and manning the trading vessels; by the end of 1736 there were fifty-four. Only six of the names listed in 1732 are to be found in the list of five years later.[1] Sixty-six persons of various ranks were officially recorded as having died within the period, and, as the lists were carelessly kept, the actual number may have been higher; thirty-eight were discharged and sent home; four were put down as runaways, two of them being retaken.[2]

Such startling figures can indicate the weight, but not the variety of death. The greater number died miserably and incoherently in a fever, with perhaps time in a last lucid interval to beg their friends—as William Rusling begged Francis Moore—that their bodies should be buried deep enough in the ground to keep off the jackals. But in many instances the manner of their going was extraordinary and seemed superstitiously to require comment. Joseph Railton, at Brucoe in 1733, fell down while he was thrashing his black boy, split his head open on the threshold, and died after lying speechless for twelve hours. A month or two earlier in the same year, John Phillips came down from Fattatenda to Yamyamacunda with a sore leg and a fever. A Mohammedan magician offered to cure the limb with a fomentation of herbs and was successful enough to allow Phillips to return to his factory, but he struck his leg against a tree stump when out walking and died at Brucoe on his way to James Fort in search of relief. Railton was then still alive to report on what had happened.

Philip Galand's end was even more devious. He had arrived out as a fellow writer with Francis Moore in 1730. In December 1732 Moore was urgently sent for by the Alcaid of Brucoe, with the news that the factory was burnt and that Galand, who was in charge, had run mad and tried to drown himself. Moore rode forty miles through the night from Yamyamacunda to Brucoe and arrived to find that, while the

---

[1] Frederick Pritzcoe, a factor, Henry Johnson, a writer, William Kerr, ensign, Tobias Kleusman, a gunner, and John Woodbrooke and Edward Redwood, soldiers.

[2] P.R.O., T.70/1447, pp. 40, 52, 54, 59, 61, 64, 67, 76. The deaths in order and by rank were as follows: February 1732, a factor, a sea captain, and four soldiers; February 1733, two writers, a gunner's mate, a seaman, a smith, and three soldiers; July 1733, a factor, four writers, a surgeon, a seaman, a sailmaker; April 1734, three writers, a sea captain, a bumboy, and four soldiers; December 1734, a factor, six writers, a surgeon, a sea captain, a smith, a bumboy, a butcher, and three soldiers; May 1735, a writer, a sea captain, and a soldier; October 1735, a writer and a soldier; October (?) 1736, four factors, a writer, a steward, a wax refiner, a carpenter, two coopers, a caulker, a soldier, two black Portuguese masons, and an apprentice.

fire had been exaggerated, Galand was certainly mad; though whether melancholy mad, or mad from fear of being assassinated by the natives, Moore could not decide. A few days later, against Moore's persuasion, Galand embarked in a long-boat at midnight in order to visit a private trader, moored downstream at Joar, and make purchases. The boat ran into a herd of 'riverhorses' (hippopotamus) in the dark and when a musket was foolishly fired off to scare them, one of the infuriated creatures, possible wounded, attacked the boat and sank it. Galand could not swim and was drowned.[1]

The deaths cannot always be fully accounted for, and some of the laconic entries in the official lists are as mysterious as they are pathetic. In the list submitted in 1736, which has the appearance of having been casually compiled, an additional entry reads: 'On the Fort, Mrs. Honoria Hart, a Widdow Gentlewoman of decayed Fortune sent here per one of the Owners of the Pretty Betsey, Capt. Boys.' The entry ought to be able to bear a sensible interpretation. Mrs. Hart was not given a chance to repair her fortunes and saw instead their utter eclipse. The entry is followed immediately by a note to the effect that 'Since the writing of this Died Mrs. Honoria Hart, the 17th Octr. 1736.'[2]

The women shipped out in 1721 were soldiers' wives and in spite of the disastrous losses among this party, and the belief that no white woman could live in such a climate and bear children, there is evidence of other wives being on James Fort from time to time. In fact, Francis Moore reported in April 1731 that the wife Sergeant Gilmore had given birth to a daughter and that both were doing well.[3] But there can never have been many white women on the river—and they were not needed; the opportunities for sexual indulgence with the local women were unlimited.

Hardly a traveller on the Coast did not remark on how easy it was to set up a 'wife' on something like a regular footing, or to augment the dangers of drink, fever, and the climate by engaging in a course of unremitting debauchery with several women. One or two of the observers were matter of fact in their notice of the matter. The Mandingo girls may seem modest, Francis Moore remarked, but they will give you anything in return for a piece of coral or a silk handkerchief. The Portuguese girls may offer an impression of greater reserve, but they, too, will set up with a man without any formalities, if he can keep them. Moore's tone is sensible and cool, but in

---

[1] Moore, pp. 146–51, 172–5.
[2] P.R.O., T.70/1447, p. 76.   [3] Moore, p. 70.

comments by others a hectic and strident note of moral reprobation betrays their unease in touching on such a provocative theme. The Negro women were generally blamed, of course, but the truth was occasionally acknowledged; after touching on the warm nature of the women, John Barbot remarked that they were corrupted by their association with Europeans: 'Thus we see that *Europeans* are the occasion of that lewdness they seem to find fault with.'[1] The sexual licence that prevailed seriously increased the European sense of guilt towards Africa.

In spite of every danger, physical and moral, the Royal African Company continued to trade. The Gambia, and the Senegal to the north, collected much of the trade of north-west Africa and the principal and ordinary goods were gold, ivory, beeswax, and hides, with some cotton, indigo, and dyewoods—and gum senegal must not be forgotten. The gold, that first lured the English to the Gambia, was brought down from the interior in the form of small bars shaped like bracelets—'big in the middle, and turned round into Rings, from 10 to 40s. each'[2]—called manillas. The gold came from the mines of Bambuk, but the joncoes, as the Mandingo merchants were called, were resolutely silent about the nature of the trade. The ivory was got by either hunting the elephants or collecting the broken-off tusks in the woods. Beeswax was another important article, used in the manufacture of fine quality candles. The Mandingos wove their bee-hives from straw, with a hole in the baseboard for the bees to go in and out by, and hung them in the trees. After smothering the bees, they pressed off the honey to make honey wine, and boiling up the wax with water, strained it and pressed it into cakes in holes in the ground. The price of the cakes, which varied in weight from twenty to a hundred and twenty pounds, depended upon their clearness from dirt.[3] The country abounded in bees—and they could be dangerous. A swarm could be so numerous and so vicious and persistent in its attack that men and asses and horses could die under it.[4]

The currency used in this trade was the bar. 'A Barr', Francis Moore explained, in the clearest of all explanations of a difficult subject, 'is a Denomination given to a certain Quantity of Goods of any Kind, which Quantity was of equal Value among the Natives to a Barr of Iron, when this River was first traded to. Thus, a Pound of Fringe is

---

[1] John Barbot, *A Description of the Coasts of North and South Guinea*, 1732, in Churchill, v. 239.
[2] Moore, p. 40.   [3] ibid. p. 44.
[4] See Mungo Park, *The Journal of a Mission to the Interior of Africa in the Year 1805*, 1815, p. 37. Park's expedition lost six asses and one horse in this way. See also Gray and Dochard, *Travels in West Africa*, 1825, p. 9.

a Barr, two Pounds of Gunpowder is a Barr, an Ounce of Silver is but a Barr, and 100 Gun-Flints is a Barr, and each Species of trading Goods has a Quantity in it called a Barr; therefore their Way of reckoning is by Barrs, or Crowns, one of which does not sometimes amount to above one Shilling Sterling; but that happens according to the Goods which they are in Want of, sometimes cheap, sometimes dear. These five Articles, *viz.* Spread-Eagle Dollars,[1] Crystal Beads, Iron Barrs, Brass Pans, and Arrangoes[2] are called the Heads of the Goods, because they are dearest.'[3] In all bargains for any article of value the trader would have to pay among the required number of bars so many made up of the more valuable 'heads of the goods', depending upon the state of the market.

The articles shipped from England were many and various. Beads of every shape and colour were shipped out in huge quantities: blue olivette, large oval German milk, black and white Nunge Munge, blue pipe and red pipe, striped pocado, and hundreds of others, all named—the Venetians alone had devised across the centuries at least 1,500 different kinds for use in trade.[4] Brassware, ironware, and hardware of all sorts; cloths and fabrics for service or show; cotton stuffs; hats, handkerchiefs and fine shirts; knives, scissors and needles; looking glasses; a variety of exotic fabrics from the East Indies; and, to conclude a list that illustrated exactly the range of English manufactures and the ramifications of English commerce, arrack, brandy, beer, rum, malt spirits and wines; and flint, fire steels, fuzees, muskets, carbines, blunderbusses and gunpowder. Add to these hangers, scimitars, and cutlasses, and you have pretty well the armoury of Europe.[5] Any manufactured article, used or new—for an old peruke was not to be despised by heads that had long gone without one—could find a purchaser in a country where men and women, and girls and boys, could be found to pay the price.

Francis Moore illustrated the way in which trading in bars worked. If you were buying slaves and the price of a slave was forty or fifty bars, you would agree to pay the merchant three or four 'heads of the goods', but if the price rose as high as eighty bars, as it often did, you might have to pay five or even six 'heads' upon every slave. At one time men and women used to fetch higher prices than boys and

---

[1] The so-called Spanish dollar, usually known later as the Maria Theresa dollar. The coin was minted by the Royal Mint for circulation in Africa until 1962. See *Missions to the Niger*, ed. E. W. Bovill, Cambridge, 1964, p. 159 n.
[2] A bead of rough cornelian, imported specially for the African trade from Bombay.
[3] Moore, p. 45.   [4] See *Missions to the Niger*, p. 23 n.
[5] *Universal History*, xvii. p. 15 n.

girls, but in the early 1730s the demand for young slaves was so great in Cadiz and Lisbon that there was no longer any difference.[1]

The Gambia was far from being the chief source of slaves in West Africa. The bulk was shipped from the Gold Coast and the lands lying on the Bight of Benin and reaching as far south as Angola, where slaves were the only product.[2] The Royal African Company was committed to the trade, but it did not like it. From the beginning, slaving had involved the Company in endless trouble and bitterness: with the separate traders, who grudged the Company its privileges and were determined to defy its attempts to establish a monopoly or to tax them, and with the planters in the West Indies. The planters vociferously accused it of being unable to fulfil its delegated function, which was to provide labour in a sufficient quantity and at a low enough cost to enable them to compete effectively with other nations in the production of sugar.[3]

The entire length of coast between Portendick, north of the Senegal, to Benguela—all those thousands of miles—could not provide slaves rapidly enough to fill the deserted spaces, the empty forests and savannahs of both Americas. The contract to supply Negroes—the *Assiento*—to the Spanish American colonies was one of England's prizes, in 1713, at the Peace of Utrecht; four thousand eight hundred Negroes a year, was the number agreed on. In a season of insatiable demand, the Gambia's modest tribute of about a thousand slaves a year could not be neglected.[4] The Company traded in slaves in competition with the separate traders from London, Bristol, and Liverpool, and from the ports of New England. The French traded, too, from their factory on the Gambia, at Albreda, and the Portuguese were still active, but the English had already outpaced their competitors and were to exceed them yet further in the course of the century. Had Jobson's remark been recalled in 1723 it would have seemed a hollow jest: the English had become the greatest European dealers in human flesh.

---

[1] Moore, p. 45.   [2] Davies, p. 45.
[3] See Davies, pp. 122, 180.   [4] Moore, p. 43.

CHAPTER THREE

The Miseries of Slaves

TOWARDS the end of his account of his first great journey into the interior of Africa in 1795, Mungo Park has a chapter on slavery and African society; a chapter that begins in the full, conclusive manner of the eighteenth century by asserting that 'A state of subordination, and certain inequalities of rank and condition, are inevitable in every stage of civil society.' Carried too far, he continues, subordination and social inequality become slavery.[1] The precept has the piercing rationality of the time, but reason fails before mystery and, though Park's argument might explain to an Englishman, brought up to respect the ranks above him by law and custom established but blessed with a lively sense of his own personal independence, why he was justified in his contempt of those modern slaves, the French, it hardly explained a society where, as far as Park could tell, the proportion of slaves to free men was three to one.

A slave in the kitchen, a slave driving home the cows—a few menials of this kind might seem no different from the poor English skivvy or cowherd; but slaves in such numbers that they were settled in villages indicated a degree of social and moral decadence that exceeded even the state of affairs that had brought about the greatest of political catastrophes, the fall of Rome.

Francis Moore knew of a village near Brucoe where all the two hundred inhabitants were the wives, slaves, and children of one man. As he does not describe the village, anyone searching him for evidence of the nature and effect of slavery might imagine such a situation illustrating the worst abuses of servitude.[2] But such villages were visited by later travellers and presented them with entirely different scenes from those they must have expected. Instead of dirt and idleness, apathy and brutality, when Gaspard Mollien reached the village of Pacour, in Joloff territory, midway between the Senegal and the

[1] Park, *Travels*, p. 287.   [2] Moore, p. 43.

Gambia, he found decency and industry, kindness and order. The village itself was one of the most beautiful this intrepid voyager ever came across, the cottages being set out among trees and neatly clipped hedges as if they stood in a park; and though every person there belonged to one man, having been bought by him in times of famine, they lived abundantly well under his paternal care. By the proceeds of their work, their master was enabled to double the number of slaves every year. They showed Mollien the greatest respect and in their master's absence voluntarily put themselves out to entertain him. As Mollien asked, were these 'the sentiments of barbarous slaves'? They were perfectly content with his parting present of a handful of beads.[1]

The purchasing of slaves in times of famine was a very ordinary occurrence, conducted in a most matter-of-fact manner. The chief man of a village, who would, of course, still have supplies of corn, would barter food against liberty. When Park was staying at Wonda, a town in the Mandingo kingdom of Manding, lying across the headwaters of the Niger, he watched his host, the Mansa, as the chief was called in Manding, doling out a small supply of corn each evening to five or six women. When Park asked the Mansa if this was simple charity or did he hope to be repaid, the reply was shocking and unexpected. ' "Observe that boy," said he (pointing to a fine child, about five years of age); "his mother has sold him to me, for forty days' provision for herself, and the rest of her family. I have bought another boy in the same manner." '[2] Good God, thought Park to himself, 'What must a mother suffer before she sells her own child!' and though his own position was desperately uncertain, he could not rid his mind of the horror of the idea. The next night he asked the child to point his mother out to him. 'She was much emaciated, but had nothing cruel or savage in her countenance; and when she had received her corn, she came and talked to her son, with as much cheerfulness as if he had still been under her care.'[3] Slavery was simply an escape from death by starvation.

The mother would not have thought of selling her child, even in the most desperate conditions, had she imagined that its fate might be one of degrading servitude. As the manner and behaviour of the villagers of Pacour showed, slavery had a different significance in Africa than it had elsewhere. The domestic slaves—those born to slavery—were normally protected from ill-treatment by custom. The Joloffs had the reputation of being especially kind to their slaves. They took care of their children as if they were their own; they seldom

[1] Mollien, pp. 69–70.   [2] Park, *Travels*, p. 248.   [3] ibid. p. 249.

struck them and never overworked them. In fact, the slaves of the Damel of Cayor—a kingdom at the mouth of the Senegal—could be so insolent that fetters were hung over their beds to remind them what their fate would be if they attempted to tyrannize over free men.[1] The Mandingos were even more strictly restrained by custom. The selling of a domestic slave was thought to be a very wicked thing on the Gambia; and even if a slave had committed a crime for which a free man would have been sold, he could not be sold until all his fellow slaves had consented, otherwise they would run away to the next kingdom where they could expect to be protected.[2] The custom varied and in some places the permission of the chief men might be necessary for a sale. In time of famine, a master was allowed to sell one or two slaves to buy food for his own family, and if he became insolvent his slaves might be seized and sold to pay his debts, but except in such contingencies a slave could expect to die where he had grown up and to be fed and clothed in return for reasonable labour.[3]

The number of domestic slaves for sale being strictly limited in the ordinary course of events, the supply for the local markets was maintained by war. The Africans' attitude to the choice between death in battle or slavery was practical and sensible. When they were told of the bloody campaigns in Europe they could not conceive why it was necessary to massacre men whom it would have been more profitable and humane to carry to market.[4] The warrior who lay sprawling on the ground under the threat of his adversary's spear, having displayed his courage by fighting well, was ready to barter his freedom for his life.[5] Of course, his position was far more unfortunate than that of a domestic slave—he could be sold, and as slaves were preferred who had come a great distance from home, in order to reduce the chances of escape, he would be passed on from market to market until he ended under a master speaking a language he might never have heard.[6]

The chances were, however, that the captives taken in battle, in a country where only one in four was free, were already slaves. And slaves were easier to capture. They were armed only with spears and bows and were perhaps encumbered with baggage: the free men carried better weapons and were well mounted. Should a free man be taken, he might be redeemed, at the rate of two to one, but there was nobody to be exchanged for a slave. The captives taken in an engagement were seldom recorded, but a set of figures is occasionally

[1] Mollien, pp. 58–9.   [2] Moore, p. 43.
[3] Park, *Travels*, pp. 23, 288 and n.   [4] Mollien, p. 86.
[5] Park, *Travels*, p. 290.   [6] ibid. p. 288.

available: after a day's victorious fighting, Mansong, the king of Bambarra, took in his assault on Kaarta nine hundred prisoners, of whom not more than seventy were free men.[1] The merchants actually preferred to deal in captives who were already slaves; they were inured to hardship, were easier to maintain before their sale was completed, and were more manageable.

Great and declared wars such as the conflicts between Bambarra and Kaarta were never a series of pitched battles. One battle was sufficient to end a stage in the warfare, if the campaigns were spread over several years, as they often were in a conflict between two powerful states. The vanquished army ran and the victors moved in to pillage and make captives, putting to death the useless.[2] Their method of warfare was the skirmish rather than the frontal attack. To a European brought up in the military academy, they seemed to scud irregularly over the field, stooping and gesticulating and hallooing, making the fight 'look more like Monkeys playing together than a battle'.[3] They had far more of an eye to survival and booty than to death and glory. But they were governed in their military conduct by self-interest rather than by cowardice and when they thought it necessary they could show extraordinary bravery—as in a fantastic incident of the war between the neighbouring Joloff kingdoms of Cayor and Baol. At first, the people of Baol refused to fight and hid in their woods waiting for some advantage, but when they did march out behind their king and formed up on the plain, they cried: ' "It is here that we must perish! We have been accused of cowardice, let those who thus reproach us, imitate our example: they pretend that we know only how to run away. Let each of us then make it impossible for him to save himself by flight." ' The warriors at once filled their wide breeches with sand and sinking thus immobilized to their knees, began firing the first volley. Baol lost all its warriors, but the victors from Cayor left even more dead behind on the field.[4]

Formal wars between kingdoms on particular issues were rare. The customary warfare was the result of a tacit understanding between neighbouring kings to plunder each other's territory reciprocally. At the convenient season—the dry season—the feud would be revived and, anxious to avenge some outstanding hostilities, a raiding party of as many as five hundred horsemen would push

---

[1] ibid. pp. 289–90.   [2] ibid. p. 291.   [3] Bosman (1721), p. 155.

[4] Mollien, pp. 54–5. This manner of warfare seems to have been of long standing in the Sudan. When the Songhai warriors confronted the invading Moors in 1591, they hobbled themselves in the manner of hobbling camels and fought until they fell (see Bovill, p. 160).

forward secretly and descend from the woods on some unfortunate village, plunder it, set it on fire, and withdraw with a string of slaves. A second and a third village might also be destroyed in the same raid. The insulted king would retaliate in turn and the smoke from burning villages would rise over another stretch of the frontier. Or a handful of men, or even a single desperate man, would waylay two or three of the enemy as they straggled back from the fields to their cottages in the evening, unsuspecting and unarmed. The victims of these forays and excursions were disposed of in the way of trade.[1]

Only a fanatical primitivist could believe that African life before the coming of the European was an idyll. The openly declared wars may not have ended in massacres on the field, but they were accompanied by widespread devastation, carried out according to policy, and led to depopulation and famine. Only the resilience of the Africans saved whole provinces from reverting to wilderness. The survivors would creep out from woods and caves as the raiders retreated at last before the threatening rain clouds and gaze in piteous dismay at their ruined villages—huts burnt down, wells abominably fouled, trees wantonly felled, granaries ransacked. But after a year's starvation and extraordinary effort the villages would be restored, however reduced, and the land would be at least partly under cultivation. And these extensive scenes of devastation were endlessly repeated in little whenever a raiding party crossed a frontier. But the arrival of the European slave trader in Africa helped to make warfare a brutal industry rather than a cruel diversion and destroyed the customs that had made the slave's life tolerable once he had been disposed of in the final market on his trek from home. The effects of the coastal trade spread far into the mysterious continent and resulted in atrocities that nobody could have ever imagined.

The swelling passage of the slave trade inland and its accompanying misery and disorganization could be followed chronologically. When Francis Moore arrived in the Gambia in 1730 and began his description of the kingdoms bordering the river, he remarked that while it might not seem appropriate to talk of the rulers of Cumbo and Fonia —the kingdoms lying at the mouth of the river on the south bank—as emperors, their titles stemmed from the past, before they had fatally weakened their once extensive and populous domains by selling into slavery 'infinite numbers of their subjects'.[2] And the ways in which these littoral kingdoms had been reduced could be seen at work higher up the river in the still populous regions.

---

[1] Mollien, pp. 86–7; Park, *Travels*, pp. 293–5. [2] Moore, p. 24.

The most regular method of keeping up the supply was by changing the punishment for every crime into slavery, and as judgement could be so profitable any action might be deemed criminal and condemned. Murder meant slavery—but where did murder begin and end? A man in the kingdom of Cantore, lying at the head of the known reaches of the river, found a 'tiger' devouring a deer that he had killed and hung up near his house; in firing at it he had the misfortune to miss and kill a passer-by. The king of Cantore condemned not only him to slavery, but also his mother, his three brothers and his three sisters. When this pathetic group were brought to Francis Moore at Yamya-macunda he could not bring himself to buy them; they were carried down to Joar and sold to an independent slaver instead. Petty theft was punished by the same penalty; a man lifting a tobacco pipe might find himself on sale in the market. The adulteress promptly incurred on her discovery a punishment that was both convenient and a revenge. Insolvent debtors were sold. But even the most trifling crimes could be made profitable to the judge who pronounced sentence.[1]

The law might be regular, but it was not a method that could be counted on to take care of any sudden demands for funds. A government requires not only steady returns but forced loans. When the king of Barsally had drunk up all his supplies, or wanted to reward his troops, he would simply sack one of his own villages and sell off the inhabitants. He would openly march past the village by day, but wheel back under cover of dark, set fire to the combustible dwellings, seize the villagers as they tried to escape, bind them and march them away.[2] And the conduct of the ruler of Barsally in the 1730s was being continued eighty-odd years later by another Joloff despot, the Damel of Cayor. He did not come in the night pretending that he was a foreigner but pounced brazenly by day. In 1818 Gaspard Mollien found his gloomy court in residence at Gandiolle, a village he had just pillaged for refusing to volunteer a levy of eighty-three slaves. The huts were empty or destroyed; the streets were deserted. A day or two later Mollien passed through Kelkom, another village that the Damel had visited, and saw the mutilated lying where they had been thrown, everyone else having been dispatched in fetters, sold by their monarch even before their arrest.[3]

The conduct of these great tyrants was copied by the local bullies. In many districts it was unsafe for anyone to walk alone. A herdsman might be overpowered as he slept at midday under a tree; two or three women might be assaulted as they passed through a wood on

[1] Moore, pp. 42–3.　　　[2] ibid. pp. 87, 214.　　　[3] Mollien, pp. 18, 28.

their return from the fields; and the children set among the grain to scare off the birds were an easy prey—to *panyar* somebody, it was called. The title to these properties was often so uncertain that the Royal African Company's agents would not purchase if they suspected they had been stolen, until they had consulted the Alcaid or the chief men of the place.[1]

These royal depredations and vulgar snatchings occurred under European eyes, but the wars in the interior, between kingdoms whose identity was no more than a name and a flitting position on the map, were learnt of only by rumour and seen only in their effect. In March 1733 there was a most unseasonable occurrence, thunder and lightning and rain; the natives foretold from the storm that there would be great wars—and before long, judging from the quick succession of the claps. Wars followed in under twelve months and went on for several years and vast number of slaves were taken and carried to the Company's factories to be sold.[2]

The slaves captured in the interior—Bumbrongs and Petcharies and other strange and scarcely known peoples—were led down to the river by the joncoes in coffles—slave caravans. They were sometimes tied together by leather thongs round their necks, marching thirty or forty to a string. They carried a load of corn or ivory or other trading goods on their heads, and, as their way ran through great tracts of forest, skins of water for their own preservation.[3]

Other methods of fettering were used when the slaves were being assembled for a journey and merchants had to guard carefully against their escape, a more likely contingency in the coffles that were to set out for the coast than in those departing in other directions. A couple of slaves would be secured in the same pair of irons, with the right leg of the one being secured and the left leg of the other. They could walk about slowly by holding up the fetters by a cord. Every four slaves were fastened round the neck with a strong rope and by night they were also handcuffed and linked together more securely by passing a light chain round the neck. The recalcitrant had to bear a heavy shackle, about three feet long, fitted round his ankle, made from the red wood of the *beb* tree.[4] During the day, while they were waiting to start on their journey, they were led out and encouraged to play 'at games of hazard, and sing diverting songs, to keep up their spirits; for though some of them sustained the hardships of their situation with amazing fortitude, the greater part were very much dejected, and would sit all day in a sort of sullen melancholy, with their eyes fixed upon the

[1] Moore, p. 42.   [2] ibid. p. 157.   [3] ibid. p. 41.   [4] Mollien, p. 148.

ground'.[1] They would often try to escape, occasionally with success, and others of them would be so overcome by despair as to gorge on dirt, in the hope of destroying themselves. The practice of eating dirt was not uncommon among despondent slaves and was sometimes put down to a 'vitiated appetite'.[2]

When a coffle at last started on its way the slaves might be so unsteady on their feet after months, or even years, of being loaded with chains that they could hardly bear up under their burdens and had to be allowed to march slowly at the beginning. A day or two later and they were being whipped for not keeping up and roughly dragged along. As a day's journey could be as much as thirty miles, the weak occasionally died, in spite of every means being used to save them. Rather than abandon marketable flesh, an exhausted slave might be carried forward tied like a sack across an ass. Brigands, wild beasts, thirst—many dangers had to be overcome during the months on the road before the coffle, preceded by its singing men, marched into one of the towns on the Gambia where the slaves were to be sold. Such journeys, made under terrible hardships with an appalling end in view, should have been enough to have demoralized and brutalized the most amenable slaves, and yet Mungo Park, who travelled five hundred miles with a coffle, remarked that 'these poor slaves, amidst their own infinitely greater sufferings, would commiserate mine; and frequently, of their own accord, bring water to quench my thirst, and at night collect branches and leaves to prepare me a bed in the Wilderness'.[3]

The coffles arriving at the coast were the signs of vast disturbances inland, and as the demand for slaves mounted, the wars to secure them increased in ferocity. The chances of examining the effects of this trade seldom occurred until the nineteenth century, when the mysteries of darkest Africa were at last explored by a succession of indomitable and often obsessed travellers, revealing that the blame for the excesses had largely to be laid on Europe. The natives could never resist the temptation of European goods, beads and cloth and drink and muskets—especially muskets. At first the natives wanted arms to protect themselves, but they soon coveted the weapons to hunt down slaves to sell for European luxuries. Europe was to blame, Henry Barth declared. Barth accompanied the warriors of Bornu against the pagan

---

[1] Park, *Travels*, p. 320.   [2] ibid. pp. 326–7.
[3] Park, *Travels*, pp. 356–7. Park travelled from Kamalia, near the headwaters of the Niger, to Pisania on the Gambia with a slave coffle and his account of this journey, which I have largely drawn on in describing such coffles, is one of the most extraordinary narratives of its kind in literature.

Músgu people, and saw the full horrors of such a campaign. The economy and polity of a prosperous and beautiful region were deliberately destroyed. Silence and mutilated bodies—for it was the practice to hack off a leg from the warriors whom it was too dangerous to enslave and let them bleed to death—and smoke-blackened cottages and trampled harvests were left behind as the remains of a people, mostly women and children, were tied together and marched away.[1]

The slaves making the journey to the coast for sale to Europeans were filled with a peculiar despair, for they were convinced that they were being shipped abroad to be eaten. Stories were current among the European traders that cannibalism was so usual in certain parts of Africa that human flesh was exposed for sale in the shambles as if it were beef or mutton, but the country of these abominable feeders withdrew like a mirage before any serious inquiry. As John Atkins, a sensible and humane surgeon in the Royal Navy, remarked in 1735, instances of cannibalism might occur in times of famine, or as a mark of 'intense Malice against a particular Enemy' among savages, or as a bestial rite in the cementing of some secret society, but as for cannibalism as a regular diet, that he doubted ever happened in Africa.[2] The Africans' credulity about European practices was better founded. None of the thousands of slaves that were packed annually into the ships ever returned. How else could this happen unless they were lost in the sink of millions of hungry white bellies?

The persistence of these rumours year after year is borne out remarkably by Mungo Park's experience. When he joined the coffle—that is, in 1797, a hundred and fifty years after the English started shipping slaves from the Gambia—the slaves at first looked at him in horror and repeatedly asked him if his countrymen were really cannibals. They would not believe him when he assured them that they were to be used in working the land; in fact, they could hardly credit there even being land where they were going to. 'Have you really got such ground as this, to set your feet upon?' one of them asked pathetically, putting his hand on the ground to make sure there could be no mistaking his question.[3]

At a late stage in his journey Park had the chance of catching the spontaneous terror that the idea of being sold for shipment could inspire. When the coffle reached the village of Jallacotta, on the upper Gambia, one of the male slaves being quite unable to proceed,

---

[1] Henry Barth, *Travels and Discoveries in North and Central Africa*, 2nd ed., 1857, iii. 133, 225.

[2] Atkins, pp. 123–4.   [3] Park, *Travels*, p. 319.

his master arranged to exchange him for a girl slave belonging to one of the villagers. She was ignorant of her fate until the morning of the coffle's departure when, coming with some other girls to see it leave, she was brusquely handed over to her new master. 'Never was a face of serenity more suddenly changed into one of the deepest distress: the terror she manifested on having the load put upon her head, and the rope fastened round her neck, and the sorrow with which she bade adieu to her companions, were truly affecting.'[1] The slaves told other stories among themselves about their fate: their bones would be ground up for gunpowder; the red liquor the Europeans were seen drinking was Africans' blood. But these fears were trifling compared with that of cannibalism. Had they known what was actually to happen to them, they might have preferred to have been eaten speedily.

When the slaves reached the Gambia they might be sold at any one of a dozen markets along the river, wherever the Royal African Company was maintaining a factory or the independent slavers frequented. The procedure everywhere was roughly the same. Should no purchaser appear immediately, or should the merchant judge the going price too low, he would support his slaves by hiring out their labour; otherwise they would be kept loaded with chains and in close confinement for fear they tried to snatch what they knew to be almost their last chance of escape. As the slaves were usually packed tightly together in such a trunk (gaol), with only the most rudimentary provisions for sanitation, the stink could almost overwhelm a European slaver, even to the ruination of his health.[2]

The joncoes were brokers determined to get the best price and their cattle were produced for sale looking as much as possible in the pink of condition. Their hair would be shaved close to hide the grey hair of age, their skin would be sleeked all over with palm oil, and their spirits would have been raised to gaiety by a judicious ration of liquor. The experienced slaver knew how to guard against such tricks, especially if he had a surgeon in attendance. The purchases would be made to jump and skip and rapidly stretch out their arms to test their agility and their breathing; their teeth were carefully examined for wear and decay, the signs of their true age; and their bodies were minutely gone over for any blemish or defect. Special care had to be taken to eliminate any with a venereal infection, whether the common pox or the yaws—a distemper peculiar to Guinea, whose symptoms

---

[1] ibid. pp. 353–4.
[2] Thomas Phillips, *A Journal of a Voyage along the Coast of Guiney*, 1732, in Churchill, vi. 234.

were similar to gonorrhoea—otherwise a whole cargo might be infected, in spite of all precautions that would be taken on board ship.[1]
The slaves were stripped stark naked for this close inspection, but one
observer noticed that while most of them were country people,
ignorant people, the women made the best show of modesty they
could in such humiliating circumstances and squatted all day to hide
their privities.[2]

Once the slaver was satisfied that the offerings were sound, and had
settled on a price, he proceeded to brand them. The place, either
breast or shoulder, having been smeared with a little oil, the red hot
brand was neatly applied. The mark was usually the initial letter of
the ship's name, or some other more formal seal. The pain was said
to amount to nothing and the mark entirely healed in three or four
days, appearing 'very plain and white after'.[3]

The slaves bought by an independent slaver were kept on board
his vessel until he had a sufficient consignment; those bought by the
Royal African Company's factors were sent down the river by 'parcels'
in the Company's shallops to the slavehouses at James Fort. The
slavehouses were under the soldiers' barracks, a building lying outside the walls of the main fort. The conditions in such slavehouses
were much the same everywhere, created as they were by fear and
ignorance. The slaves had to be secured and chained, and as for
hygiene, the conditions were only worse than elsewhere in the fort
because of the difficulties caused by confinement. How necessary it was
to watch these often desperate creatures was shown in the slave mutiny
of 1667, when thirty-one of the English garrison of thirty-two were
cut down. At night the gates of the fort were locked and two sentinels
constantly patrolled outside the walls to guard against a surprise
attempt by the slaves at mutiny or escape. The sentries caught the
slaves removing a bar from one of the windows in 1730, and the ringleader, who was an old offender, was ordered a hundred lashes.[4] The
additional precaution of employing spies and informers was also taken.
When Boogao, a castle slave, discovered a conspiracy among his less fortunate comrades in 1733, he was rewarded with a present valued at ten
shillings.[5]

The independent slavers, denied the facilities of James Fort,
found the loading of slaves a period of great danger. All along the
Guinea coast it was recognized that a slaver ought never to trust a

---

[1] See Churchill, vi. 234; Atkins, pp. 179–80.
[2] Atkins, p. 180.   [3] Churchill, vi. 234.   [4] Moore, pp. 15, 49.
[5] P.R.O., T.70/1451, p. 86.

cargo of slaves until he was out of sight of land. The Negroes never gave up hope until they found themselves finally at sea, in a vessel that they had not learnt to manage; and even then it was best to keep a sharp lookout in case they butchered the drunk or careless crew, and by cutting the cables risked running ashore.[1] Francis Moore thought that the dangers which threatened separate traders while they were in the river were so great that it would have paid the Company to have kept an adequate stock of slaves at James Fort to sell directly to them.[2] As it was, it might take a trader months to get a cargo and all the time he lay in the river he was hourly in danger from sickness and mutiny. And it was much easier for the slaves to escape ashore in a river than on the coast to the south, where the slaveships anchored offshore behind the tumultuous bar, in the open road.

Once the slaves were carried on board a separate trader, every precaution possible had to be taken, though the difficulties might be greatly increased by sickness among the crew. The men were shackled together in pairs, sentries were mounted on the hatchways, pistols and grenades were kept primed and ready to hand on the quarter-deck, and the quarter-deck guns stood aimed to rake the slaves with fire should they break loose.

In spite of such routine precautions a cargo of slaves would rise, seizing a moment when vigilance nodded, or making an opportunity by craft and courage; and sometimes the rising was successful. At the beginning of 1733 the parcel of slaves bought by Captain Williams, the master of a brigantine, trading in the river about Joar, suddenly rose and killed a great many of the ship's crew. Williams himself was severely wounded, his fingers being horribly mangled, but he managed to save himself by swimming ashore and, making his way safely down to James Island, took passage back to England in another ship, the *Tryal*.[3]

It was in the light of such events that some of the most experienced and hardened slavers believed that precautions had to be supported by intimidation. Some commanders recommended that while a cargo was being assembled one or two of the slaves who seemed likely to cause trouble should be singled out and deliberately mutilated, by cutting off of an arm or leg. The fear that this engendered among the others was not of pain, but of never returning home after death, which they believed they would do if they died physically intact.[4] A great

---

[1] Churchill, vi. 245. [2] Moore, p. 81. [3] ibid. p. 156.
[4] Churchill, vi. 235.

number of slavers resisted such barbarous practices, unless they were driven to inflict them as punishments.

A slave rising had to be put down without mercy: the issue was simple, the lives of the crew or of the cargo. When the naval surgeon, John Atkins, made a voyage down the Guinea coast in 1721 he visited Bence Island in Sierra Leone and called on one of the most famous and prosperous of the private traders settled there, John Leadstine, known as Old Cracker. Old Cracker showed his visitors over his slavehouses and Atkins took particular notice of one sturdy and determined slave who refused to show off his muscles when Old Cracker ordered him to. Old Cracker whipped him mercilessly with a manatee strap and only stopped short of killing him for fear of losing his profit, but the Negro bore up courageously under the punishment, and his few tears showed his humiliation rather than his pain. The man's name was Captain Tomba and as he had led the opposition of several villages on the river Nunes to the private traders, killing several of the natives who supported them and firing their cottages, Old Cracker had had him surprised and seized, though at the cost of two lives, and had now put him up for sale.

Captain Tomba was sold almost immediately, along with thirty other slaves, to Captain Harding, master of the *Robert* of Bristol. As soon as he was aboard he had begun to scheme with three or four other slaves to rise and overpower the crew and escape while they were yet within sight of land. A woman slave was in the plot and, having some freedom of movement about the ship, she brought him word one night that there were no more than five white men on deck. She handed him the only weapon she had found, a hammer. Creeping up on deck under cover of the shadows, Tomba brained two of the sailors sleeping there, and a third, who woke up and was seized by Tomba's confederates, was also dispatched with the hammer. But the rest of the watch were by now awake, and the noise of the fight giving the alarm to those asleep below, Captain Harding scrambled up on deck and, joining in the desperate scuffle, managed to fell Tomba with a handspike. He and his fellows were quickly secured in irons.

The punishments Captain Harding inflicted were ingenious, but not unnecessarily wasteful. Tomba and another ringleader were too valuable to spoil, so they were whipped and scarified, but not rendered useless. Three of the weaker and dispensable abettors were chosen as examples. After one of them had been killed, the others were made to eat his heart and liver. The feast concluded with their own cruel execution. The woman was hoisted up by her thumbs, and whipped and slashed with knives in full view of the other slaves, until she died.[1]

The separate traders were far less scrupulous in their dealings with the natives than the factors of the Royal African Company. The Company was on the Guinea coast to stay and its success over the years depended on its building up good relations. This was especially true on the Gambia, where the existence of James Island and the factories depended entirely on goodwill and the advantage to the natives of having regular centres for trade. The threat of breaking up a factory and removing it to another district was often enough to make a local king reduce his more outrageous demands. Many of the separate traders who regularly plied the coast were as careful in their dealings as the Company, but a number, in their hurry to snatch quick profits and retire, behaved as cruelly as the pirates who also haunted the coast. On some stretches the natives ran inland and hid themselves at the sight of a ship; on others they would trade from canoes, but could never be enticed on board; and on the most notorious shores, they would lie in wait to seize any Europeans who mistakenly landed, and take revenge on them for the relations lost by 'panyarring' and the villages set on fire.

The relations between the separate traders and natives were often little better than a state of undeclared war. At the beginning of 1732 a New England schooner trading at Cassan (Kass) on the Gambia under the command of Captain Major was cut off by the natives at the instigation of a Portuguese trader, Chequo Voss, who lived there, and Major was killed. About three weeks after this incident Francis Moore and Thomas Harrison, another factor in the service of the Company, stopped at Cassan on their way from Joar to Yamyamacunda and asked the *slattee*, the chief merchant, to give his account of the incident. The slattee had his account ready.

'Some Years ago,' he said, 'this Place was a Port of great Trade, which made a great many Ships resort hither; who often used us very ill, by carrying away several of our Friends and Relations by Force, without any Provocation. Even last Year Capt. *Stoneham* carried away one of my own Nephews, because Seignor *Chequo Voss*, a *Portuguese*, who lives in this Town, was not so good as his Promise, in bringing him Trade by the Time limited. Now lately, this *New England* Scooner began also to impose upon me in the following Manner. Soon after it arrived at my Port, the King of Lower *Yany*, in whose Dominion this Town is, sent a Slave to me to sell for him, which I carried aboard the Scooner, to Capt. *Major;* but he

[1] Atkins, pp. 41–2, 71–3.

having no very good Goods, at least not such as I liked, made me defer selling him, till such Time as I could acquaint the King what Sort of Goods he had; upon which the Captain desir'd I would leave the Slave aboard till the King's Answer came, which I accordingly did. At length I receiv'd Orders from the King not to sell the Slave, for he did not like the Captain's Goods. Upon that, I went on board, and told the Message to the Captain; at which he fell into a great Passion, and would not let me take the Slave out of the Scooner. I did not say much to the Captain, but came home, called all my People together, told them the Case, and then we reckon'd up the many Injuries we had received from the other separate Traders, and at last we resolved to take the Scooner, which we did the next Morning. In the Action the Captain was killed, for which I am very sorry; but as for the rest of the Men which were on board the Scooner, I gave them the Boat and some Provisions, and let them go where they pleased.'

Moore and Harrison, finding the natives prepared to defend what they had done, could do nothing but proceed on their way. The other separate traders on the river were greatly alarmed.

The schooner itself had belonged to a New England sloop, the *Bumper*, that was trading higher up the river, at Yamyamacunda, under its commander, Captain Samuel Moore. Captain Moore was already on bad terms with the natives, who had tried several times to kill him in revenge for the ill treatment they had earlier received from him, particularly the previous year when he was accused of having passed spread-eagle dollars made of pewter. Captain Moore dared not leave his ship to trade ashore, but his trade was plied very successfully for him by one of the Company's factors, James Connor—for 'very good Commissions', no doubt, as Francis Moore dryly remarked. The natives were only biding their time, and two months later, on its voyage downstream, about a hundred of them attacked the *Bumper* in the night, below Brucoe, at the narrowest passage of the river. The skirmish was extremely fierce and the sloop ran aground, but it managed to get off and made its escape with only one fatality—Mr. Lowther, the supercargo, was shot in the belly and died the next day. One native was shot and another wounded.[1]

The incident is only one in the state of undeclared war that enveloped the whole length of the Guinea coast and reached far inland. The private traders practised every cheat and chicanery and, when they dared to, violence. The natives retaliated in kind. But it would be sentimentality to imagine the manacled slaves battened down in Samuel Moore's holds as lying in a sweat of anxiety and listening

[1] Moore, pp. 102, 111-13, 148, 164-5.

desperately to their countrymen fighting to liberate them. Had the ambush been successful, the slaves might have escaped ashore, but they would then have had to evade being retaken by the captors who had already sold them. They would have been mercilessly hunted down. There were no distinct sides in this war.

CHAPTER FOUR

The Sale and Redemption
of Job

JAMES ISLAND'S only advantage as the site of a fort was its command of the channel. Ships had to pass within range of its guns, or run aground on the shoals that reach out from either shore. The river rises and falls with the tides, laying bare mud flats and shingle. At low tide, the green decayed stumps of the piling that protected the rock from further erosion can still be seen above the ooze. When the fort was busy, in the morning and late afternoon, the noise from the coopers' shop and the forge and the repair yards, the bustle and chat of the counting-house and the kitchens, the storerooms, the messes, and the surgery, asserted the regularity and seeming normality of garrison life. But at high noon and in the evening, when everything was quiet and time suddenly hung slack, the steady flood of the broad dull river, the burning vacancy above, and the far-off foreign shores, with their palisade of mangroves and sad drift of household smoke, made the place seem hideous and intolerable—a leisurely and inescapable trap. At such times of desolating introspection, the sight of an arriving sail might suddenly restore the situation and offer the wonderful possibility of news from home.

On 10 February 1731 the Royal African Company's snow, the *Success*, under the command of Captain Robert Cummins, came up to anchor at the fort. The *Success* was on her way directly to Cape Coast Castle, the Company's headquarters on the Gold Coast, but, springing a leak, it was thought better that she should put in at James Island. The next day, 11 February, at about noon, another sail was seen making up the river. The new arrival notified the fort that she was the *Arabella*, a separate trader from London, under the command of Captain Pyke. She sailed on and anchored off Gillyfree, to pay the king of Barrah his dues and take on a linguister. Pyke was in the service of Captain Henry Hunt, a brother of William Hunt, a well-known merchant in Little Tower Street, London. The *Arabella* left the following evening for Joar, a journey of one hundred and seventy miles upstream.[1]

Joar lay above the mangroves, on the north shore of a broad bend of the river. The low laterite bluffs that accompany the river, usually at a distance but sometimes rising above the water like cliffs, loop inland behind Joar and enclose an amphitheatre of flat savannah—grazing grounds and rice fields. A creek runs across this plain to the river, and at the head the Portuguese first, and then the English, maintained a factory. The creek is now overgrown with reeds, and its channel can be seen only where it widens out into broad shallow pools, the watering places of great herds of long-horned cattle, but a boat could once be taken up it. The site of the factory itself was convenient for both trade and defence. The king of Barsally had a house at Joar, but the town was greatly in decline by the time Captain Pyke anchored off it. Only about ten houses were inhabited, still by Portuguese.[2]

The situation was extremely pleasant. The savannah offered riding and good shooting, the fishing in the creek was excellent, and in the dry season there was pleasant walking among the woods on the low hills behind. In the wet season the woods were too dangerous for pleasure; they became the haunt of all the wild beasts in retreat before the floods.[3] The principal town of the region, and, indeed, on the whole river, was Cower (Kau-Ur), lying three miles to the east across the plain, on the rise of the laterite bluffs, which at that point returned to the river. Cower was a great and natural trading centre, renowned for its cotton cloths, much coveted by the women on the Gambia and very expensive. The river offered a safe and convenient anchorage at this point, and as the water there was reckoned to be extremely good, ships used to restock with it before sailing away.[4] Serin Donso, the most famous broker on the river, lived at Cower. An old man, he exercised so much authority over the merchants trading to Cower that it was useless for a separate trader to expect a cargo of slaves until he had been squared. In 1734 he became so exacting that the separate traders withdrew in protest to Yanimarew (Niani Maru) up the river and persuaded the merchants to bring their slaves to them there—a manœuvre that was almost the cause of a war between the king of Yany and the king of Barsally, who naturally resented the loss of trade.[5]

As the trade routes of the region converged at Joar, the merchants brought their slaves to that market, unless they were in a hurry to

---

[1] Thomas Bluett, *Some Memoirs of the Life of Job*, 1734, p. 16; Moore, p. 61.
[2] Moore, p. 106.   [3] ibid.   [4] ibid.   [5] ibid. pp. 102, 111.

return home or were able to make a good sale on their way down.[1] Everyone knew that this was the likeliest place for the quick disposal of slaves, especially at the right season, when the slavers were already moored in the river and anxious to load and be off, in an effort to reduce their losses from sickness or mutiny.

Among the merchants consigning slaves to Joar in the spring of 1731 was a Mohammedan priest—a high priest, an Alpha—of Bondou, a Fula principality, which lay several days' journey to the north-west of the Gambia, on the Faleme River, a tributary of the Senegal. The priest sent his son and two servants down with two Negro boys to sell, and instructed them to buy certain necessaries with the proceeds, including paper, so coveted for the making of *grisgris*, a profitable sideline of a Marabout. The son, Job, was experienced in selling slaves; he had often dealt in them and had once travelled for five weeks from home in the direction of Egypt in search of trade.[2]

When it was later of interest to know where Job had come from, Bondou was supposed to be a town rather than a country, and a misdirected effort was made to find a place for it on the contemporary maps. One description of its whereabouts reads so circumstantially that it would seem impossible to miss. Boonda, we are told—one of the spellings of Bondou—is a town in 'the County of *Galumbo* (in our maps *Catumbo*) in the Kingdom of *Futa* in *Africa*; which lies on both Sides the River *Senegal*, and on the south Side reaches as far as the River *Gambia*. The Eastern Boundary of the Kingdom of *Futa* or *Senega* is the great Lake, called in our Maps *Lacus Guarde*. The Extent of it, towards the North, is not so certain. The chief City or Town of it is *Tombut*; over against which, on the other side of the River, is *Boonda*.'[3] All these details, apparently so specific, vanish into uncertainty once an attempt is made to verify them against the map. There is no county of Galumbo, or even Catumbo, to be discovered anywhere along the banks of the Senegal, north or south;[4] nor is there a 'Lacus Guarde', though a so-called lake mysteriously appears in several maps in what would otherwise be blank spaces, mirages of desperate geographers;[5] nor is there any capital city resembling Tombut in name for Boonda to be over against.

But the description of the region in which 'Boonda' was hopefully placed is not wholly wrong. As the neighbour of the great Fula

[1] ibid. p. 22.   [2] Spalding Gentlemen's Society, First Minute Book, f. 186.
[3] Bluett, p. 13.
[4] The county of Galumbo or Catumbo is the kingdom of Galam or, more correctly, Gadiaga, which lay across the angle of the Faleme and the Senegal.
[5] The 'Lacus Guarde' is discussed by Bovill, p. 110.

dominion of Futa Toro, Bondou had fallen under Fula domination at the beginning of the eighteenth century.[1] Futa Toro reached along both banks of the Senegal, from the frontier of the Joloff kingdom of Hoval (Oualo) in the west, whose ruler, the Brak, controlled the lower reaches of the river, to that of the Seracolet kingdom of Galam, which began in the region where the Faleme flowed into the Senegal. The rulers of Futa Toro were a dynasty of pagan Fula called the Denianke: a harsh and intolerant government. The ruler himself, the supreme military commander, was known as the Siratick, whose capital in the eighteenth century was at Gumel, a village on the north shore of the Senegal.[2] The reputation of both the Siratick and his countrymen stood high among the Europeans who traded along the African coast. He is supposed to be able 'to bring fifty thousand men into the field upon occasion', John Barbot wrote; as for his subjects, they 'are accounted the most civilized people of *Nigritia*'.[3]

Futa Toro was one of the fiefs of the great disintegrating kingdom of the Bourba Joloff that once occupied all the territory between the Senegal and the Gambia, but the Fula, both as nomadic pastoralists and as settled agriculturists, had long since spread as far south as the Gambia, as Jobson tells us. Futa Toro joined Bondou to the east. Bondou itself bordered Galam in the north, and was contained to the east and south by the two great Mandingo principalities of Bambuk, where gold was mined, and of Woolly, lying on the Gambia. The third great centre of Fula power was Futa Jallon, far to the south, in the highlands of upper Guinea, the watershed of both the Gambia and the Senegal. Fula power was based on these regions and their armies in alliance were later to dominate West Africa.

The Fula of Futa Toro had long since begun to merge by marriage and concubinage with the surrounding Negro peoples, the Joloffs and the Serreres, to produce a race of mulattoes called Torodos, from whom Futa Toro ultimately derived its name.[4] These Fula were excessively proud and aggressive and, when they were Mohammedans, zealous and ready to convert by means of the sword. A Fula might be so carried away by fanaticism that, pulling out his dagger, he would exclaim: 'I will plunge thee into the heart of a Pagan.'[5] But the spread of Mohammedanism among the Fula and the other peoples living between the Senegal and the Gambia cannot be attributed primarily to fear. A simpler explanation, and one in accord with the genius of the religion, is that the schools kept by the Marabouts were attended by

---

[1] See André Rançon, *Le Bondou*, 1894. [2] Astley, ii. 57.
[3] Churchill, v. 57. [4] Mollien, p. 158. [5] ibid. p. 296.

all the children, whether or not they were already Mohammedans, and that the persons of these priests were held as sacred even by the pagans. They were superstitiously believed to hold direct communication with the Deity, and they consolidated their influence by the sale of *grisgris*, which were accepted everywhere as talismans of unlimited power. As the Marabouts had to be of irreproachable character, as well as being able to read Arabic, both the Koran and certain secular texts, their standing was usually justified. The few who added to these qualities and attainments the faculty of composing in Arabic, were entitled to wear a scarlet cap and were known among the Fula as Tomsire or Alpha, meaning Doctor.[1]

The Alpha, or High Priest, from Bondou who had sent his son down to the market at Cower was called Solomon (Suleiman), one of a family called Dgiallo (Diallo). His father, Abraham (Ibrahima), had emigrated from Futa Toro to Bondou in the reign of Siratick Bubakar, some time about 1680, and had founded a town. He was granted the proprietorship and governorship of this new foundation by Siratick Bubakar, in addition to being its high priest or Alpha.[2] The Marabouts were always called upon to administer justice—to settle inheritances, for instance[3]—but as proprietor, governor, and Alpha, Abraham had the settling of all the civic laws and regulations. Among his provisions was one that, by asserting the law of the Koran, contributed greatly to the town's growth and prosperity: he provided that no one fleeing there for protection 'that can read and know God, as they express it',[4] could be made a slave—no one, that is, who was a Muslim. Abraham's founding the town is an instance of how the Fula were constantly in movement; a movement so gradual that their occupation of new territory and growth in power could scarcely be perceived.[5]

When Abraham died, Solomon succeeded him in the priestly office

---

[1] ibid. pp. 61–3.

[2] The history of the migration of the Dgiallo family from Futa Toro to Bondou is highly confusing. Job ben Solomon told his biographer Thomas Bluett that his grandfather Abraham—I have anglicized the names—'founded the Town of Boonda, in the reign of *Bubaker*, then King of *Futa*', about fifty years ago. He certainly did *not* found Bondou, whose first rulers were the family of Sisibe. I have tried to square Bluett's account with the useful dynastic and historical information offered by P. D. Curtin in *Africa Remembered*, 1967, pp. 23–8. (Curtin prefers to call Job by the proper modern rendering of his names, Ayuba Suleiman Diallo; but since he has been known for more than two centuries as Job ben Solomon, this seems an unnecessary improvement.)

[3] Mollien, p. 62.   [4] Bluett, p. 14.

[5] See Alphonse Gouilly, *L'Islam dans l'Afrique Occidentale Française*, Paris, 1952, p. 18.

F

and, in recognition of his high character and learning, Gelazi, who had succeeded his brother Bubakar as Siratick of Futa Toro, put his son, Sambo, to school under him. Solomon's own son, Job, who had been born to his first wife, Tantamata, about 1702,[1] became the young prince's companion and fellow student. In due course, Sambo succeeded Gelazi as Siratick, and Job began to assist his father in the priesthood.[2] He was then fifteen. At about this time he married his first wife, the daughter of the Alpha of the town of Tombut. She was eleven and gave birth to her first son, Abdullah, when she was thirteen. Job had two other sons by this marriage, Abraham and Sambo. When he was about twenty-seven—that is in about 1729— he married as his second wife the daughter of the Alpha of Tomga. He called their child Fatima, after the daughter of the Prophet; another mark of the Dgiallo family's zeal. As his second marriage proves, he was becoming prosperous, although a younger son, and at the time of setting off for the Gambia he owned, besides his own plantation, three houses and eighteen servants, and seventy-three head of black cattle, as well as asses and other things.[3]

Eventually, Job reached Cower while Captain Pyke was bargaining for slaves, and offered him the two boys. But slaves were in good supply at the beginning of 1731 and either Job did not like the price, or Pyke would not pay it on account of discovering some physical defect, and they failed to strike a bargain. Job decided to try and sell the boys elsewhere, on the other side of the river.

Cower was in Barsally, a Joloff kingdom, but the kingdoms on the opposite bank, Caen and Jagra, were Mandingo. Bondou was at the time at war with the Mandingos, which, not to speak of more inland wars, would explain the glut of slaves on the market, and Solomon had particularly warned his son not to cross the Gambia and risk putting himself in their hands. But Job, thinking that there could be little real danger and that the possible returns were worth the risk, decided to cross against his father's advice and sent his two servants

---

[1] Spalding Gentlemen's Society, First Minute Book, f. 186.
[2] I have kept to Bluett's account for want of a better. As Curtin shows, Bubakar was certainly succeeded by a brother, but that brother was most probably Sire Tabakali, not Geladio Jegi, who seems to be meant by Gelazi. Geladio Jegi came to the throne much later and was deposed in 1718. The son, Sambo, who succeeded him—according to Bluett—was Samba Geladio Jegi, famous for his struggle with his brother Konko Bubu Musa for the throne of Futa Toro. He is not supposed ever to have occupied the throne, but Job's testimony that he at least held it in 1731 is supported by other evidence—see below, p. 172. (See Curtin, *Africa Remembered*, pp. 37–8.)
[3] Spalding Gentlemen's Society, First Minute Book, f. 186.

home to inform him of what he had done. As Job could not speak Mandingo, and also needed help in escorting his slaves, he engaged as an interpreter Loumein Yoai, another Fula from Bondou, and together they crossed the river.

The largest market on the other side was Tancrowall, which lay about sixty miles downstream, travelling in a direct line, in the kingdom of Caen. The Royal African Company had a factory at Tancrowall, but it was more important commercially as the residence of the great Portuguese merchant, Antonio Voss. Voss 'trades very largely with most of our *English* separate traders who use this River', Francis Moore observed,

and very often trades with the Company. He is reckon'd to be worth 10,000 *l.* Sterling, has got a vast Number of House-Slaves, (*viz.* Slaves which live with him as Servants, a Grandeur much used by the *Portuguese* and *Spaniards*) which he keeps for Service and Breed, and are esteemed by him almost as much as his own Children. And as he has got a great many Canoes, he sends his own Men-Slaves with them to all Ports of Trade up the River, and by that Means engrosses a great deal of Trade; insomuch that he has commonly a great many Slaves, and good Quantities of Elephants Teeth and Beeswax by him, with which he turns a Penny with the separate Shipping, and is well skilled in his Way of bartering, he being thoroughly Master of the prime Cost, in *England*, of all sorts of Goods, taking always care to keep his Warehouse well stocked with Goods, and has the upperhand vastly of some of his Neighbours, who are sometimes obliged to stand still half a Year together for want of Goods to trade with.[1]

Disappointed by Captain Pyke, Job and Loumein Yoai carried their two slaves in the direction of Tancrowall and Antonio Voss. They might have dropped down as far as Tancrowall by canoe, which would have been the quickest and most convenient way to travel, or having crossed the river they could have continued on foot, hoping to meet a purchaser on the way, thereby shortening their journey. Job may have sold the slaves to Voss, but either at Tancrowall or somewhere else on the road he succeeded in disposing of them at a satisfactory price and acquired instead, in the spirit of the Fula, twenty-eight head of cattle.[2] Job and Loumein Yoai started to drive the cattle home, intending to cross at Yamina, which lay on the south bank of the river opposite to Cower. At some point on the return journey,

[1] Moore, pp. 49–50.
[2] Spalding Gentlemen's Society, First Minute Book, f. 186. Bluett, p. 17, says 'some cows'; Moore, p. 69, gives the approximate number of cattle.

probably near Damasensa, where there was a Fula village, Job stopped at an old acquaintance's to shelter from the midday heat and refresh himself. He took off his weapons because of the heat and hung them up inside the hut. The Fula, especially the Fula of Bondou, were the most industrious and skilful metalsmiths in these parts of Africa, inferior only to the Moors in ingenuity,[1] and the manufacture and decoration of Job's weapons would either represent Fula skill at its best, or have been of even finer quality, brought in from abroad. They were certainly valuable, being a present to Job from his old school-fellow, Sambo, now Siratick of Futa Toro. They consisted of 'a Gold-hilted Sword, a Gold Knife, which they wear by their Side, and a rich Quiver of Arrows'.[2]

As it would be impossible to drive a herd of nearly thirty cattle for any distance through even the most deserted country without its movements becoming known, in a country where villages are frequent and report runs between them faster than any single traveller, Job could hardly have expected to return to Cower without being observed. He was probably trailed from the moment he exchanged the slaves for cattle, and the glitter of his weapons as he hung them up was an unwitting signal to his watching enemies that he was now defenceless. Suddenly, seven or eight Mandingos burst in through a back door, and before Job or his interpreter had a chance to grasp their arms, they were seized and pinioned.

The gold-handled sword and the gold knife and the rich quiver of arrows, and whatever weapons Loumein Yoai carried himself, were splendid booty, and so were the twenty-eight cattle now going in want of an owner, but Job and his interpreter were also of some value. The heads and beards of those taken prisoner in battle were customarily shaved and as prisoners could be sold as slaves, a shaven head was the sign of a marketable property. The Mandingos promptly shaved their captives' heads and, carrying the men across the river to Joar, sold them both to Captain Pyke on 27 February,[3] not stopping to bargain too closely as Job had done earlier.

The Company's factors on the river would not buy any slaves unless they were certain they were entitled to be sold; in doubtful cases they took the advice of the Alcaid of the place. We have already seen Francis Moore refusing to buy a whole family unjustly condemned for manslaughter but the private trader to whom they were next offered bought them without scruple.

Even the best-intentioned slaver could not have afforded to look

---

[1] Mollien, p. 165.   [2] Bluett, p. 17.   [3] ibid. p. 18.

too closely at the methods by which his complement was filled. If he was slaving regularly, and not trying to make a quick profit at a single venture, he would certainly not *panyar* anyone, or make a purchase that seemed likely to endanger future goodwill; otherwise, he would take what was offered and disregard the desperate entreaties of those protesting that they had been kidnapped or decoyed. The way of trade and not the demands of justice was the only practicable rule of thumb. When Job and Loumein Yoai, smarting under the indignity of having their heads shaved and the shock of finding the roles of master and slave dramatically reversed, were first carried on board the *Arabella* on 1 March,[1] Captain Pyke may not have recognized Job as the man who had earlier tried to sell him the two boys; but when Job found means of letting him know who he was and what had happened, Pyke agreed to ransom both him and Loumein Yoai, at the price of two slaves apiece. As it was already Sunday and he intended weighing anchor on Friday, Pyke could allow Job only a few days.[2]

The Fula were entirely loyal to each other. They were charitable to their people in want; they supported their blind and old and lame; they never sold each other into slavery, and made it their duty to redeem any of them taken and sold.[3] Job had every reason to believe that he would be ransomed if only his plight was known. He managed to pass his news to an acquaintance of his father living near the Gambia, and the friend at once dispatched a messenger to Bondou. But Bondou was far away; a journey beset with wild beasts and brigands and traversing a wilderness which could often only be crossed in safety by joining a caravan.

The loading of the slaves continued all the time. After they had been offered in the market at Cower and examined and bought, they were branded and led on board and shackled in pairs. The routine will have been the same on most ships, since general experience over many years would have taught the most convenient and economical practices. The slaves were brought up to be fed twice a day, in the morning at 10 o'clock and in the afternoon at 4 o'clock. They were divided up into messes of ten, which had been found to be the most manageable number; the men messing on the main deck, where they could be kept under close observation with the guns trained on them, the women on the quarter-deck with the crew, and the girls and boys

[1] ibid.
[2] One source says that Pyke allowed only four days (Spalding Gentlemen's Society, First Minute Book, f. 186), but this is most unlikely as Job's home was more than four days' journey from Joar (see below, p. 181).
[3] Moore, pp. 32-3; Mollien, p. 165.

on the poop. Once they had been sorted out in this way and had learnt their places, the arrangements went along smoothly enough. Their chief diet was a kind of pudding prepared from Indian corn ground small and boiled in a large copper furnace. About a peckful, served up in vessels called crews, was allowed to each mess, and it was eaten flavoured with salt, peppers, and palm oil. Another important article was horse beans, shipped out specially from England. The beans were served three times a week, and not only were they relished by the slaves but they had a 'binding quality' and helped to prevent the flux, or dysentery, one of the greatest health hazards on a slaveship. They had to put down all their rations under threat of a whipping. After they were fed, the slaves were each given on their way below a pint of water to drink, ladled out of a large tub. The only other times they were allowed up on deck when the vessel was moored offshore was to use the privies. These were fitted to overhang both sides of the ship. They seated about twelve apiece, and were mounted by broad ladders.[1]

The slaves had to be watched closely, not only for signs of mutiny but to prevent them from destroying themselves. They could become so deranged at the idea of leaving their native land and being committed to a hopeless future that they would seize any chance to fling themselves overboard and hold themselves submerged until they drowned. A more skilful way of suicide for the slave was to swallow his own tongue and die of suffocation.[2] Or they might deliberately set out to starve themselves to death. In that case, they had to be flogged until they were prepared to eat and if punishment failed to restore their appetite, they had to be forcibly fed. Their front teeth might be knocked out to allow the passage of food, or an instrument specially designed to prise the jaws open might be introduced. Such treatment was essential if a valuable commodity was to be saved, but the more scrupulous slavers also believed that they had a moral as well as a commercial duty to save a fellow creature from eternal damnation by suicide. Sometimes an exceptionally sensitive slave would droop resistlessly and die of a broken heart, and no instrument was cruel or ingenious enough to stir up his faltering spirit.

The Fula were, of all the Africans, the most prone to despair. Even in ordinary life their features seemed to carry a melancholy and serious expression. They had an inbred horror of slavery and were ill adapted to support its conditions, morally or physically. The African traders recognized their general unsuitability and attributed it to

[1] Churchill, vi. 245.   [2] Chambers, *Cyclopaedia*, s.v. 'slave'.

their lighter colour. As a man of rank, and literate, Job might have succumbed under the idea of his fate had he not been filled with a sense of outrage at the indignity inflicted on him, and been hopeful until the last that a messenger would return from his father with means of redemption. Anger and hope are wonderful preservatives. He had also the companionship of Loumein Yoai to keep his spirits up.

But Job's hope was hardly reasonable. The messengers in either direction, journeying as expeditiously as possible, had days of travelling in front of them, making no allowances for accidents and supposing that Solomon could find the ransom without even a moment's delay. And Pyke was most unlikely to extend the time. A slaver hoped to load as speedily as possible. The longer he stayed on the river the greater the danger and the expense. The slaves had to be kept shackled and strictly confined while the vessel lay offshore, in order to prevent mutinies and escapes, and while they were confined there was a greater chance of some general infection breaking out; and even if only their general condition deteriorated, the heavier would be the losses that would be certain to occur later at sea.

The risk to the crew was more serious. Several of them might be fresh from England and immediately vulnerable to the river fevers, but even the hardened might succumb—if not to the fever, then to the temptations of drink and women. The ship would buy fresh meat and greens and fruit if they were available locally, but the bulk of its victuals, those needed to last out a long and hazardous voyage, came from England, and any captain was uneasy to see these essential supplies reduced. Once the loading was complete and the ship watered, nothing ordinary would stop a captain from weighing anchor and falling down the river. The temperature mounts steadily in April on the Gambia and in June the rains begin, a season that a wise slaver sought at all costs to avoid.

On 11 April, in the evening, a sail was seen making up river towards James Island. A shot from the fort brought her to and she was found to be a separate trader, the *Mary* from Glasgow, under the command of Captain Gordon. She was carrying a cargo of rum and sugar from Barbados and as Francis Moore, who was there to greet the vessel, laconically observed: 'Sure never was a Vessel's Arrival more welcome than this to our common Gentry, who were afraid they would have been obliged to be without Liquor all the Rains, but now their Fears were over.'[1] Later in the evening the *Arabella* arrived from Joar, with Job and Loumein Yoai still on board.

[1] Moore, p. 69.

Captain Pyke stopped for a day or two at James Island. A messenger from Job's father had not arrived before the *Arabella* had left Joar, and none reached the fort while Captain Pyke unaccountably delayed, possibly to make a further purchase of slaves or other goods. Once he had completed his business, and still without news from Bondou, he set sail for Maryland. The low shores of the Gambia dropped quickly and steadily behind as the *Arabella* put out to sea with the tide, at the beginning of a journey from which no slave had ever been known to return. On the same day another vessel, the *Elizabeth*, under the command of Captain Carruthers, who had also been loading at Joar, came down the river with its complement of slaves.[1] Trade had been brisk; a good season.

Once out of sight of land the slaves' condition became easier, if the weather held. As the risk of their combining and mutinying almost ceased as soon as they were out of sight of land and found themselves utterly dependent on the crew for the working of the ship, the men could be unshackled and allowed up on deck, either in the evening[2] or, in more exceptional cases, for the whole day.[3] The women and children, who were never shackled, were allowed more freedom of movement, though this was not without its dangers, as the story of Captain Tomba will have shown; but strict precautions were taken to keep the men apart from the women, 'yet do what we can they will come together', as one slaver resignedly remarked.[4] They were brought up not only for the sake of fresh air, but of exercise. The exercise was needed to keep them sound and in good spirits, and, after the practice of the African merchants, they were encouraged to sing and dance. If they hung back they could be made to jump to the whip. On some ships pipes and tobacco were issued to the men once a week, and the women given a handful of beads to divert them.[5] On a well-run ship, under the impartial discipline of a conscientious master, the slaves' lot cannot have been intolerable—if the weather held. The apologists for the traffic were fond of imagining these dusky passengers drumming and dancing under a warm southern sky and squatting down to scoff the ample provisions, when gaiety at length gave way to appetite. Had their journey not been involuntary, they might even have come, it was almost suggested, for the sake of the cruise.

The weather was the greatest threat. When the slaves were being loaded the object was to pack in as many as possible. The figures are

---

[1] ibid.   [2] Churchill, vi. 246.
[3] William Snelgrave, *A New Account of Guinea*, 1734, p. 164.
[4] Churchill, vi. 234.   [5] Snelgrave, p. 164.

not certain, but it seems that the average ratio was about a Negro to every fifth of a ton; the ratio being lower for ships of smaller burden, where the worst cases of overcrowding usually occurred. But statistics tell us nothing in human terms. The fact is that if the market was good a captain would load slaves until simple prudence told him to stop. They would be compelled to lie head to foot and side by side, so close that they could hardly turn over, and if a supplementary platform was inserted between decks in order to take more rows, they might not even have room enough to sit up straight. A bucket in the corner was the only receptacle for slops. Even in fine weather, when the air-ports could be left wide open at night, the ventilation must have been poor, but in bad weather, when the slaves could not be brought up on deck and most of them were sick and the air-ports had to be battened down, the conditions below often passed belief. The stink and mess were hardly to be borne, the heat generated by so many bodies packed tight into a small space was intense, and the air was foul enough to extinguish a light.[1]

The weather might defeat a captain: foul weather by forcing him to keep his cargo below, and a calm by endangering his water supplies; but the chief danger came from disease, especially smallpox and dysentery—the flux. The slaves were carefully examined before purchase, but as the brokers were skilful in doctoring them, several infected and many unfit ones were passed. Once they were on board, a lazaretto was set up to isolate the sick as soon as they were discovered, and the healthy were made to scrape down the decks every morning and sluice them with vinegar, but nothing could be done if the ship itself was in danger, or if disease became epidemical.

Thomas Phillips, captain of the *Hannibal,* who slaved between Whidaw, on the Guinea Coast, and Barbados in 1693 and 1694, described graphically enough the hazards attending a voyage, and his complaints must have been typical of the tone that many adopted in talking of the trade:

But what the smallpox spar'd, the flux swept off, to our great regret, after all our pains and care to give them their messes in due order and season, keeping their lodgings as clear and sweet as possible, and enduring so much misery and stench so long among a parcel of creatures nastier than swine; and after all our expectations to be defeated by their mortality. No gold-finders can endure so much noisome slavery as they do who carry

---

[1] Alexander Falconbridge, *An Account of the Slave Trade,* 1788 (pp. 24–5), has a grim description of such conditions as viewed by a ship's surgeon.

negroes; for those have some respite and satisfaction, but we endure twice the misery; and yet by their mortality our voyages are ruin'd. . . .[1]

Phillips sailed from Whidaw on 27 July 1694 with a full complement of 700 slaves, 480 men and 220 women, lodged in the *Hannibal*'s 450 tons. He had already lost 12 of his earlier purchases by wilful drowning, and an unspecified number of others had starved themselves to death. He delivered 372 slaves alive at Barbados three months later, on 5 November, selling them at about £19 a head.

The Committee of the Privy Council investigating the slave trade in 1789 found that the death-rate in the slave ships had dropped from 23½ per cent towards the end of the seventeenth century to 10 per cent by 1734, when the captains had become more expert in and the ships better adapted to the traffic.[2] But these are average figures. The mortality in the *Hannibal* in 1694 was 46·9 per cent, although the ratio of slaves to tonnage—1 : ·64—was much better than average.[3] Many *Hannibals* made the crossing, and many other ships foundered with the loss of all the slaves on board. 'I have received your Favours of the 8 and 25 Feby.,' Edward Grace wrote on 23 April 1770, in reply to Messrs. Stevenson and Went, 'with the Account of the unfortunate Loss of the Sloop Expedition which foundered at Sea with 110 Slaves on board. . . . Capt. Williamson's protest has enabled me to adjust a Loss of £3200 which I had insured on the Sloop and her Cargo, which I suppose is full as much as they would have produced if they had arrived at a Market.'[4]

But taking the figures as a whole, Job ben Solomon and Loumein Yoai stood a better chance of surviving than their predecessors along the route and were the beneficiaries of experience, provided that the *Arabella* was sound and was not becalmed or storm-tossed in the frightening Middle Passage. Many of the captains were humane and decent men. Had they been accused of deliberately pursuing a bestial trade they would probably have replied in something like the words of John Newton: 'Custom, example and interest had blinded my eyes. What I did, I did ignorantly; considering it as the line of life which Divine Providence had allotted me.'[5] Thomas Phillips refused to

[1] Churchill, vi. 253.   [2] Davies, pp. 292–3.
[3] This was approximately the ratio prescribed by the Act of 1788 for regulating the number of Negroes to be carried, for ships of more than 160 tons burden (see Davies, p. 194).
[4] Edward Grace, *Letters of a West African Trader*, 1950, p. 38.
[5] Quoted in Averil Mackenzie-Grieve, *The Last Years of the English Slave Trade*, 1941, p. 89.

mutilate one or two of his slaves as a warning to the others, as he had been advised, whatever his final thoughts were on the nature of his cargo, and Captain William Snelgrave roundly declared that wherever 'I have commanded, it has been my principal Care, to have the *Negroes* on board my Ship kindly used; and I have always strictly charged my white People to treat them with Humanity and Tenderness: In which I have usually found my Account, both in keeping them from mutinying, and preserving them in health.'[1] But the trade was brutalizing in itself. Discipline had to be maintained at all costs. The whip was in constant use, often applied by the Negro overseers chosen to marshal their fellows and prevent their quarrelling, but the punishments had sometimes to be more sanguinary: for killing a seaman the punishment could be burning alive.[2]

The crews themselves were mainly recruited from among the riff-raff of the English ports. The mortality rate among those serving on a slaver was so notorious that only the desperate would volunteer; the rest had to be bribed or decoyed. The weeks, or, more likely, months, spent in collecting a shipment on a coast where malaria and yellow fever were endemic, wore down the resistance of the survivors and made them more susceptible not only to any outbreak of disease that might occur on the ship, but to the debaucheries of the voyage. The sailors could not be kept away from the women, even in ships where the discipline was tight, and some captains allowed their men to have intercourse with any who would consent. The officers, having greater freedom and range of choice, were sometimes 'guilty of such brutal excesses, as disgrace human nature'.[3] And what concupiscence did not accomplish, drink might. Thomas Phillips could not prevent his men from getting drunk on a punch made from the rawest of spirits, though he punished several of them and threw the sugar and rum overboard whenever he found any, and his trumpeter, Lord, had to be put in irons for promoting their carousals and for attacking the sleeping boatswain with a knife. Lord was kept in irons on the poop both day and night for two months, without any shelter other than 'the canopy of heaven'; yet, as Phillips sourly remarked, 'he was never troubled with any sickness, but made good the proverb, *That naught's never in danger, or that he who is born to be hang'd*, &c.'[4] The best-run slaveship was an offence against humanity, but the ships in which human nature was given a licence to do its worst still seem to cast a lurid glow on the black waters of the Middle Passage.

[1] Snelgrave, p. 162.   [2] See Davies, p. 290.
[3] Falconbridge, pp. 23–4.   [4] Churchill, vi. 252.

Attempts have been made to show that the horrors of the Middle Passage have been exaggerated and that, anyway, the slaves suffered no more than other transatlantic voyagers suffered during this period, whether they went as indentured servants, or settlers, or, involuntarily, as transported convicts.[1] And many figures can be offered to support this challenge to sentimentality. In the reign of Queen Anne, for instance, thirteen thousand Palatines fled to England within three years in the hope of emigrating to North America. They were shipped there under such appalling conditions that of the four thousand sent to New York, one thousand seven hundred died on the voyage, or shortly after disembarkation.[2] The mortality rate on emigrant ships from overcrowding and sickness and lack of sanitation and ventilation continued to be heavy until the middle of the following century, when the Mormons showed how conditions could be drastically improved.

But one set of horrible circumstances cannot be excused by quoting another and pretending they are identical, though it may be useful to compare them. The emigrants from Europe to North America went voluntarily, or, if that would seem to obscure the compulsion and persecutions they fled from, they exercised their choice in the hope of bettering their condition and believed the future worth the risk. The people transported on some trumped-up charge for the sake of recruiting indentured labour had no choice in their fate, but their judges and their masters spoke their own language and shared the same colour of skin; and the numbers were never large, except at the time of such a windfall as the Monmouth rebellion. The African slaves were purchased and disposed of in the way of trade without any regard at all for their rights as human beings. Their movement was involuntary; their treatment was heartless; their numbers were enormous. In the regularity and size of the trade, in the contingent and incalculable suffering, in the utter disregard of all the affectionate bonds that prevent men from descending into bestiality, in the extenuating and hypocritical argument that the commercial end for which the slaves were bought and shipped and sold justified the filthy means—there lies the difference between the slave trade and the European exodus. The imagination is not at fault when it perceives something special in the facts of the Middle Passage.

As the voyage came to a close, the slaves were dressed for market,

---

[1] The argument is set out most forcefully by Eric Williams, *Capitalism and Slavery*, 1944, p. 35.
[2] Leslie F. Church, *Oglethorpe*, 1932, p. 144.

supposing the weather permitted. Unless the slaver was singularly skilled or fortunate, the African dealers would certainly have managed to sell him one or two slaves who were either broken or infected, and the long voyage, trying under even the best of conditions, would have weakened others and spread such diseases as the smallpox, not to mention the pernicious and more subtle effects of despair and melancholy. The slaves had to pass the experienced scrutiny of the planters before they were sold, and had to give the impression of being in health. The buyers handled them 'as the Butchers do Beasts in Smithfield, to see if they are Proof in Cod, Flank, and Shoulders'. And the women who owned plantations were just as thorough in their appraisals, to the disgust of some observers.[1]

The slavers practised many deceptions, but the favourite method of producing a glossy skin, a sure sign of health, and dispelling any outward marks of infection, was to rub down the slaves three or four times with a compound of gunpowder, lime juice, and oil. Some experts recommended the addition of iron rust to the mixture.[2] The particular use this unguent was put to, apart from its application as a burnish, was to hide the slave's possible infection with the yaws. The method was so successful that a whole parcel of slaves might be found to be suffering from the infection two or three weeks after they had been bought. The plantation doctors commonly used mercury in its treatment, but its drastic operation either reduced the patient's resistance to other diseases or brought on fatal complications. It was reckoned that a third of the slaves landed died within three years of this disease, or of the effects of the cure.[3] Smallpox was another fearful killer.

The last horror of the trade itself was often delayed until the moment of sale. A complete family, or mother and child, might have managed to stay together through all the vicissitudes that followed their capture or original sale, but when they were finally auctioned it was as separate parcels, and no account was taken of any connections, except in instances of unusual charity. Wives and husbands, mothers and children, were ruthlessly sold apart and packed off in spite of their tears and entreaties, expressed in languages that no one needed to understand, to far-lying plantations in different quarters of the territory. When such close ties were disregarded, it is hardly surprising that after the *Arabella* had anchored safely at Annapolis in Mary-

---

[1] *London Magazine*, 1746, p. 325 n.
[2] J. Harry Bennett, *Bondsmen and Bishops*, 1958, pp. 47–8; Long, ii. 433.
[3] Long, ii. 434.

land, Job ben Solomon should have been sold away from his servant, Loumein Yoai.

Captain Pyke delivered his cargo to Vachell Denton, factor to William Hunt, the London merchant, for disposal. Denton was a substantial citizen, well connected by marriage to some of the leading figures of the time in Annapolis.[1] He promptly sold Job for £45 to Alexander Tolsey, who, after bestowing on him the convenient name of Simon, set him to work on his tobacco plantation on Kent Island, Queen Anne's County, in Chesapeake Bay.[2] Loumein Yoai was as speedily disposed of elsewhere.

The importing of slaves into Maryland was a trade of long standing. The only aspect of it that had troubled the colonists was the uncertainty of the effect of the slaves' possible conversion to Christianity upon their status. In 1671 the legislature, noting that 'several good people' had been discouraged from purchasing slaves because they thought that slaves upon their conversion must be set free, and that other people, no doubt equally good, neglected to instruct their slaves in the Christian religion for the same reason, passed an Act affirming that the situation was quite different, and that the slaves' adoption of Christianity could not literally set them free. The Act was re-enacted in 1692 and made permanent in 1715.[3] Job and his fellow travellers could not hope to find any worldly advantage in changing their religion.

Maryland, like its neighbour Virginia, derived great advantage from its slaves. A traveller though the colony in the 1740s noted that 'Prodigious Numbers of Planters are immensely rich', and, he continued, 'I think one of them, at this Time, numbers upon his Lands near 1000 Wretches, that tremble with submissive Awe at his Nod, besides white Servants: Their Pastures bless'd with increasing Flocks, whilst their Yards and Closes boast Hundreds of tame Poultry, of every Kind, and their Husbandry is rewarded with Crops equal to all their Ambition or Desires.'[4] A slave was thought at about this time to be worth £40 a year in the product he raised.[5] Much of the grain and livestock raised by slaves in Maryland was profitably

---

[1] Denton was married to Ann Brice, daughter of Captain John Brice of Annapolis. He died in 1752 (information supplied by the Hall of Records, Annapolis, Maryland).

[2] Bluett (p. 19) calls the purchaser, whom he knew, 'Mr. Tolsey'; the account in the Spalding Gentlemen's Society, First Minute Book (f. 186), adds the Christian name.

[3] Jeffrey R. Brackett, *The Negro in Maryland*, 1889, p. 29.

[4] *London Magazine*, 1746, p. 322.

[5] *The Trade to Africa Consider'd*, n.d. [1709?], p. 2.

shipped to the West Indies. The slaves lived in their own quarters at some distance from the mansion house and, though they enjoyed a 'pretty deal of Liberty' there, these collections of hovels and patches of garden were 'true Pictures of Slavery, which begets Indolence and Nastiness.'[1]

Tolsey must have been either careless or inexperienced in the managing of slaves to have set Job immediately to the heavy work of a tobacco plantation. A new Negro ought never to be severely tried before he had been seasoned; 'for it is well known that these new Negroes are always much indulged during the first two or three years after their arrival, being put to the gentlest work, that they may be gradually seasoned to the change of climate, and trained by a slow easy progress to undergo the same degree of labour as the rest'.[2] A new arrival ought always to be treated with the greatest care for two or three years, in the opinion of the experts; he should be systematically built up with good food and warmly dressed and bedded in a dry place. But even after all the obvious precautions had been taken, a planter could expect to lose a third to a half of his new Negroes from disease.[3] And the usual harsh discipline had to be avoided at all costs in case the newcomer either tried to escape or committed suicide. They must often have seemed to act out of pure cussedness: in 1714 three in a parcel of ten slaves bought by the Codrington Plantation on Barbados 'destroyed themselves after a great deal of good Usage'.[4]

But while the new Negroes might themselves temporarily escape the lash, on the usual plantation they had only to look around to see what their fate was likely to be once they were fit to receive punishment. The argument that the slave was such a valuable property that it was not in his master's best interests to mistreat him serves to correct the impression that cruelty was ordinarily resorted to, but the most diabolic punishments were kept in reserve to enforce discipline and applied without the least compunction. The great Sir Hans Sloane, a cultured and humane person, who has yet to make an appearance in Job's story, listed without the slightest hint of disapproval the punishments that were administered when necessary in Jamaica:

The Punishments for Crimes of Slaves, are usually for Rebellions burning them, by nailing them down to the ground with crooked Sticks on every Limb, and then applying the Fire by degrees from the Feet and Hands, burning them gradually up to the Head, whereby their pains are extravagant. For Crimes of a lesser nature Gelding, or chopping off half of the

---

[1] *London Magazine*, 1746, p. 324 n.   [2] Long, ii. 433.
[3] See Bennett, pp. 48–9, 58–9.   [4] ibid. p. 49.

Foot with an Ax. These Punishments are suffered by them with great Constancy.

For running away they put Iron Rings of great weight on their Ankles, or Pottocks about their Necks, which are Iron Rings with two long Necks rivetted to them, or a Spur in the Mouth.

For Negligence, they are usually whipt by the Overseers with Lance-wood Switches, till they be bloody, and several of the Switches broken, being first tied up by their Hands in the Mill-Houses. Beating with *Manati* Straps is thought too cruel, and therefore prohibited by the Customs of the Country. The Cicatrices are visible on their Skins for ever after; and a Slave, the more he have of those, is the less valu'd.

After they are whip'd till they are Raw, some put on their Skins Pepper and Salt to make them smart; at other times their Masters will drop melted Wax on their Skins, and use several very exquisite Torments. These Punishments are sometimes merited by the Blacks, who are a very perverse Generation of People, and though they appear harsh, yet are scarce equal to some of their Crimes, and inferior to what Punishments other *European* Nations inflict on their Slaves in the *East-Indies*, as may be seen by *Moquet*, and other Travellers.[1]

A comparative study of the cruelties practised on slaves in the various American islands and colonies would be difficult to make, in spite of Sir Hans's hint as to its possibility, but wherever there were slaves that needed driving to work, or slaves in sufficient numbers to offer a constant threat of a bloody and revengeful uprising, brutality was used, as a goad or for intimidation. In Maryland, as everywhere, the whip was the usual means of punishment. George Whitfield, the evangelist, in a letter addressed from Georgia in 1739 to the inhabitants of Maryland, Virginia, and both the Carolinas, exclaimed in horror over the cruelty shown by planters to their slaves; their horses, and even their dogs, were better treated, as 'the long furrows' down the Negroes' backs too sadly told.[2] And the gay traveller who perambulated the colony in 1743, rejoicing in the good breeding and heartiness and cleanliness that he found everywhere, and enjoying a hospitality that put him in mind of 'the old roast Beef Ages of our Forefathers', had also to deplore the other sights that met his eyes: 'Slavery, thou worst and greatest of evils.' He himself saw a Negro strung up by the wrists, with his toes touching the ground—the preferred arrangement—being beaten into unconsciousness by his master with a large cane, after the overseer had whipped him for an hour with a 'cowskin'—a large thong of cowhide 'twisted into the

[1] Hans Sloane, *A Voyage to . . . Jamaica*, 1707, i. p. lvii.
[2] Anthony Benezet, *A Caution to Great Britain and her Colonies*, 1784, pp. 12–14.

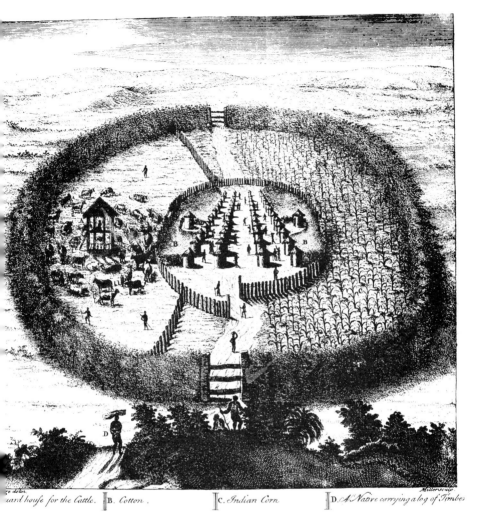

uard house for the Cattle. | B. Cotton. | C. Indian Corn | D. A Native carrying a log of Timber

'DRAUGHT OF A PHOLEY TOWN AND PLANTATIONS ABOUT'

From *Travels into the Inland Parts of Africa*, by Francis Moore, 1738.

BOOMEY HAMAN SEACA

From *Travels into the Inland Parts of Africa*, by
Francis Moore, 1738.

'He was cloath'd in a white Cotton Vest with open
Sleeves, and Breeches which came to his Knees, of
the same. His Legs and Arms were bare, on his
Head he had a small white Cotton Cap, and Gold
Rings in his Ears. He rode upon a beautiful Milk-
white Horse, 16 Hands high, with a long Mane,
and a Tail which swept the Ground. His Bridle was
of a bright Red-Leather, plated with Silver, after
the *Moorish* Manner; his Saddle was of the same,
with a high Pommel, and rising behind. The
Breast-Plate was of Red-Leather plaited with Silver,
but they use no Cruppers. His Stirrups were short,
and as large and as long as his Feet, so as to stand
firm and easy. Upon these he would raise himself
quite upright, stand steady at full speed, and shoot
a Gun or dart a Lance as well as if upon the Ground.'

Shape of a swish Horse-Whip, and as hard as a Bull's Pizzle'. And he reported that another master continued beating a girl long after she had confessed to a theft, screaming out in his frenzy, 'God damn you, when you go to Hell, I wish God would damn me, that I might follow you with the Cowskin there.'[1] The words may be apocryphal, but the sentiment must many a time have urged on the lash.

Tolsey showed that he was as unfamiliar with the African races as he was with the proper method of seasoning a new Negro. It was precisely for the benefit of such inexperienced or incautious planters that Dr. Collins later drew up his 'practical rules' for the management and medical treatment of Negro slaves. Dr. Collins showed how the handsome natives of Senegal could be discriminated from among the other tribes by their features, which resembled 'the whites', and their 'tall and well limbed' bodies. 'Many of them converse in the Arabic language,' he went on, 'and some are sufficiently instructed even to write it. They are excellent for the care of cattle and horses, and for domestic service'—and now came his warning—'though little qualified for the ruder labours of the field, to which they never ought to be applied.'[2] As an outward sign of their 'greater acuteness of understanding and mildness of disposition', this 'herd' had a less 'noxious odour' than the other different 'herds' of Negroes.[3]

Uninformed though he was in eye and nose, Tolsey recognized in its effects that the work he had set Job was too hard. Job began daily to appear more distressed and when he was clearly weakening under the effort, Tolsey, who was not one of the more fiendish planters but a humane man, took him off the plantation and set him to herd the cattle. Such work was certainly easier and, whether Tolsey knew it or not, would give Job the chance of indulging the extraordinary affection for cattle that was such a marked characteristic of the Fula; but Job was being worn down not by the weight so much as by the indignity of labour. The African slave brokers preferred to deal in slaves who had been brought up in slavery for the very good reason that, being habituated, they were more resilient, morally as well as physically. If an ordinary slave might die under despair and melancholy, or be driven to suicide, how much greater must have been the sufferings of one who had been a chief in his own country, a disposer of slaves? Job wearied and sickened, but he did not die; and he was saved from

---

[1] *London Magazine*, 1746, p. 325 and n.
[2] Collins, *Practical Rules for the Management and Medical Treatment of Negro Slaves*, 1811, p. 37.
[3] Long, ii. 353.

G

attempting suicide by his religious faith—Allah could preserve him if He would. As a devout Mohammedan, he left his cattle and went and prayed in the secrecy of the woods at the prescribed times.

We do not know how Job prayed, but we know from the report of another Mohammedan slave, a Negro from Timbuctoo, the spirit in which he must have said his prayers. 'My parents' religion is that of the Mussulman', wrote Abou Bekir Sadiki, *alias* Edward Doulan, in Jamaica, in 1834, and they pray and fast and 'fight for their religion'. They also refrain from unclean meat and wine. 'They do not associate with any that worship idols, nor profane the Lord's name, nor do dishonour to their parents, or commit murder, or bear false witness, or who are covetous, proud, or boastful for such faults are an abomination unto my religion. They are particularly careful in the education of their children and in their behaviour, but I am lost to all of these advantages since my bondage I am corrupt and I now conclude by begging the Almighty God to lead me into the faith that is proper for me for he alone knows the secrets of my heart and what I am in need of.'[1]

Unfortunately, Job had been carefully watched while he prayed, perhaps because of his unusual features and conjectures as to where he could have come from and what he might have been in his own country, and when he withdrew to pray he was regularly followed by a white boy, who, amused by his prayers and the accompanying ritual of abasement, began to mock him 'and throw Dirt in his Face'. 'This very much disturbed Job, and added considerably to his other Misfortunes; all which were increased by his Ignorance of the *English* Language, which prevented him complaining, or telling his Case to any Person about him. Grown in some measure desperate, by reason of his present Hardships, he resolved to travel at a Venture; thinking he might possibly be taken up by some Master, who would use him better, or otherwise meet with some lucky Accident, to divert or abate his Grief.'[2]

Thomas Bluett, Job's biographer, introduces Job's escape as though it was the beginning of a picaresque adventure, but it was common for slaves to run away, and in Maryland several Acts had been passed to check them. People arresting runaways were rewarded and those caught harbouring them were punished; the Indian tribes were tempted to hunt down the runaways with the promise of two blankets and a gun for each returned slave, and in 1723 it was enacted that any slave outlying in the woods and resisting recapture might be shot

[1] *Journal of Negro History*, 1936, xxi. 55.   [2] Bluett, p. 20.

dead without the hunter incurring any penalty.[1] All the colonies bordering Maryland had similar laws that provided for the arrest of any slave, or indentured white servant, travelling without a pass, and for his being gaoled until fetched by his master. If he was not found and redeemed he could be put up to auction. When Job took to the backwoods, supposing he survived starvation in the wilderness and avoided the Indians, he was certain to be gaoled wherever he came upon a white settlement and failed to explain himself—a likely contingency when he could not speak English.

After crossing the channel that separated Kent Island from the mainland, Job struck north through the woods until he came to Kent County on Delaware Bay. There he was arrested and being unable to explain himself was promptly clapped into gaol. The gaol was also the tavern.

The settlers in both Maryland and Virginia lived entirely on their plantations and the towns were small and insignificant—even the capitals, in spite of offering the social attraction of governor and legislature. The great places of general meeting were the court-houses,[2] and as a court was being held in Kent County at the time of Job's arrest, some of the gentlemen attending the sessions, hearing of the strange Negro, sent for the gaoler and had Job brought into the tavern. They tried to question him, by word and sign, but all they could make out from 'Allah' and 'Mohammed' occurring in some lines that he wrote down and read to them, and from his refusing a glass of wine, was that he was a Mohammedan. They were left guessing where he had come from and how he had got to Kent County; 'for by his affable Carriage,' one of these gentlemen, Thomas Bluett, remarked, 'and the easy Composure of his Countenance, we could perceive he was no common Slave'.[3]

Bluett had earlier been an attorney practising in Kent County, but in 1727 he went to England for ordination—surprisingly, in view of his poor reputation, particularly for intemperance—and returned in 1728 to the mission maintained by the Society for the Propagation of the Gospel, based on Dover in Kent County. At first his congregations objected to him, but they were later reconciled.[4]

---

[1] See Brackett, pp. 72–7.
[2] See *London Magazine*, 1746, p. 323.   [3] Bluett, pp. 21–2.
[4] Nelson W. Rightmeyer, *The Anglican Church in Delaware*, 1947, pp. 54–5. Mrs. I. Pridmore, Archivist of the United Society for the Propagation of the Gospel, informs me that the Society's records show only that Bluett was a missionary of the Society from 1745 until his death in 1749, based on Dover, Kent County.

The gentlemen left Job to the gaoler, but some time afterwards an old slave in the neighbourhood, who could speak Joloff, found out from him who he was, where he had come from, and why he had run away. Tolsey was sent for and, on getting him home, very decently let him have somewhere private to pray in, and tried to make his slavery as easy as possible by indulging him in other ways. The hint of Job's being a prince in his own country may very well have made the difference.

Job had learnt from his experience the impossibility of running away, except to lose himself in the wilderness, and the only hope he saw now of being released was to write to his father and beg him to try and somehow redeem him. He wrote his letter, in Arabic, and sent it to Vachell Denton for forwarding by Captain Pyke to Africa. As Pyke had already set sail for London, Denton enclosed Job's letter in a packet being sent to Captain Hunt in London by another ship, with the request that he should ask Pyke to carry it when he sailed for Africa and completed the triangular trade route.

Tolsey's and Denton's anxiety to help Job ought to be put down to kindness, but such kindnesses were so unusual among a group of men accustomed to dismissing any distress among their slaves as the ordinary problems incident to seasoning, that it is hard not to believe that the old Joloff slave not only gave a glorified impression of Job's rank and power, but let it be known that great advantages might come from helping him. And it is also clear that he had already gained the goodwill of Thomas Bluett and some of the other clergy.

Job's letter was safely delivered to Captain Hunt in London, but once again it was too late to reach Captain Pyke; he had already sailed for the Gambia. Job had now just missed being helped for the third time, but when Fate seemed to have set itself sternly against him it suddenly relented. Hunt was left with Job's letter on his hands and as he had not himself a second ship sailing immediately for the Gambia, and being unable to read Job's letter and judge its importance, he showed it as a curiosity to Joseph Ames, a ship-chandler in Wapping. But Ames was an exceptional tradesman; he was also a well-known antiquary and bibliographer. He took a copy of the letter and tried to get it translated.[1] Hunt also consulted his friends in the Royal African Company about the letter, perhaps with a view to arranging its expeditious dispatch to the Gambia.

The Deputy Governor of the Company was James Oglethorpe.

---

[1] Spalding Gentlemen's Society, First Minute Book, f. 186. As the account given there was written by Ames, it may exaggerate Ames's importance.

Oglethorpe had entered the Army as a boy of fourteen in 1710,[1] but he was more widely known as a philanthropist than as a soldier, and was thoroughly to deserve Alexander Pope's famous tribute to his character:

> One, driv'n by strong Benevolence of Soul,
> Shall fly, like *Oglethorp*, from Pole to Pole.

As M.P. for Haslemere he served in 1729 as chairman of the Parliamentary Committee on conditions in debtors' prisons; the leader of the 'generous few' who, in the words of James Thomson,

> touch'd with human woe, redressive sought
> Into the horrors of the gloomy jail.

The Committee's report had inaugurated the first in the series of reforms of the prison system.

Oglethorpe was elected to the Court of Assistants of the Royal African Company in 1730 and on 27 January 1732, after qualifying by buying £1,000 of stock, he was appointed Deputy Governor, under Sir Bibye Lake; it was probably on account of his position as well as his philanthropy that Job's letter was brought to his attention. Whether or not he knew of Ames's effort to get the letter translated, he was so struck by its curiosity and unusual history that he decided it ought to be translated and sent it for this purpose to Oxford, where the Huguenot, John Gagnier, held the Laudian Chair of Arabic. When the letter was returned in translation, Oglethorpe was so deeply moved by it and impressed by the sense of its author's character that he decided without hesitation that such a person could not be left in slavery and must be redeemed. The only way this could be done was through Henry Hunt and his factor in Maryland, Vachell Denton. In June 1732 Oglethorpe gave his bond to Hunt for the payment of £45—Job's purchase price—upon Job being delivered to him in London.[2] Instructions were sent to Annapolis and Denton in his turn quickly arranged for Job's release, Tolsey not finding much use for him.

A delay occurred before Job could be shipped to England. The winter was so unusually hard that the Maryland rivers were frozen and impassable to shipping, and Job had to board with Denton in Annapolis until the weather improved. He spent a great deal of time with one of the ministers, John Humphrys,[3] teaching him Arabic, and

---

[1] See above, p. 37.   [2] P.R.O., T.70/302, p. 68.
[3] Spalding Gentlemen's Society, First Minute Book, f. 186.

he also became very friendly with Jacob Henderson, another learned minister, and Commissary of the Bishop of London. Henderson was greatly struck with both Job's learning and his piety—but he made a good impression on everyone who met him, 'and indeed his good Nature and Affability gain'd him many Friends besides in that Place'.[1]

The harbours unfroze at last and in March 1733 Job embarked for London in the *William*, commanded by Captain George Uriell, the consignee being William Hunt.[2] Among his fellow passengers was Thomas Bluett, who had first seen him in the gaol-house in Kent County. Bluett was probably travelling to England on business for the Society for the Propagation of the Gospel. Both Bluett and Uriell were so struck by the good character that Job had earned in Annapolis that they decided they could best be of service to him by trying to teach him English properly. He had only managed to pick up a few words so far, and those he pronounced unintelligibly. They set to work immediately after hoisting sail and within a fortnight they had taught him the alphabet and how to spell 'almost any single Syllable, when distinctly pronounced to him'.[3] Unfortunately the weather was very bad all the way and since both Job and Bluett were sick, the lessons were seriously interrupted. Nevertheless, by the time they reached England about eight weeks later, at the end of April, Job was able to understand much of what was said to him and to express himself tolerably to those used to his accent.

A stranger contrast to his first crossing of the Atlantic could hardly be imagined. Instead of the stinking hold and the enforced feeding and the whip, Job now enjoyed the captain's tuition and freedom to practise his devotions; and once it became known that he could not eat flesh unless the animal had been killed by himself or another Mohammedan, he was often allowed to slaughter the fresh stock carried on board. And the sailors were so struck by his 'good Nature and Affability' that they went out of their way to help him, and, when they were sailing up the Channel, pointed out to him the headlands and other interesting places. He noted all these down so that if he met with an Englishman after his return to Africa he would be able to convince him that he had really been to England by a recital of facts.

The *William* docked in London towards the end of April. Unfor-

---

[1] Bluett, p. 24.
[2] Uriell—Bluett spelt the name Uriel—was the Captain of the *William* in 1729, with Hunt as the consignee. Hunt was still the consignee as late as 1748, though Uriell had died and the *William* was under a new master. (Information supplied by the Hall of Records, Annapolis, Maryland.)
[3] Bluett, p. 25.

tunately for Job, Oglethorpe was not there to greet him; in fact, he was no longer in the country, having sailed for Georgia at the beginning of the year. Before leaving, he had retired from the Royal African Company, selling his stock on 21 December 1732.[1] The reasons for Oglethorpe's disassociating himself from the Company are not at all clear, but in addition to the very heavy duties he had voluntarily taken upon himself when he became one of the trustees of the new colony of Georgia, he may have had scruples about being active in any business concerned with slavery. At least he had condemned it on general principles by ensuring that it was banned from Georgia. Largely through his opposition it was kept out of the colony for eighteen years, in spite of all the agitation and economic arguments put forward in its favour.[2] The foundation of Georgia was both philanthropic and military, corresponding to the dominant aspects of Oglethorpe's character. The trustees intended it to be both a refuge for deserving paupers—who were quickly to be joined by German Protestants in search of toleration—and a defence of the more northerly colonies against the hostile encroachments of the Spaniards from the south. Oglethorpe had the success of this great venture so much at heart that he had sailed himself with the first colonists in January 1732 in order to supervise their settlement.

Job was met instead by Captain Hunt, whose slave he still was—until Oglethorpe had redeemed his bond—and Hunt put him up in lodgings arranged for him in Limehouse. His trusted friend, Thomas Bluett, set off immediately to visit friends in the country. Job was now on his own and his position was far from secure.

Many Negroes were already living in London at the time of Job's arrival. They had usually been brought to England in the first place as servants to West Indian planters, returning home either to live or on a visit. As the property of their masters they were unpaid and could be freely disciplined, with the further advantage of being disposable. Unfortunately for this idyll of the labour market, the belief that a Christian could not be a slave was as current in England as it had earlier been in Maryland, and was even more strongly held. As a consequence, the new slaves arriving in the country hurried to find a clergyman to baptize them and some well-wisher to stand as their godfather and protector. Well-wishers were readily available. The Quakers, at a meeting of their whole Society held in London on 1727, passed a resolution censuring slavery as 'not a commendable nor

[1] Amos A. Ettinger, *Oglethorpe*, 1936, pp. 147–8.
[2] Church, pp. 161–7.

allowed practice'.[1] Once baptized, the slave could claim to be free and to stand on the same footing as any white servant, with all that servant's right to liberty and wages. The Negroes who had already managed to break loose were active in encouraging their fellows to make the attempt, and they had the effective support of the London mob, which was always ready to prevent the arrest of a runaway.[2]

The planters and merchants concerned were in a dilemma, and in 1729 they decided to consult the Attorney and the Solicitor General for an opinion on the position of slaves in England. The opinion ran according to their best hopes. The law officers declared that according to their lights, 'a slave by coming from the West Indies to Great Britain or Ireland, either with or without his master, doth not become free, and that his master's property or right in him is not therefore determined or varied, and that Baptism doth not bestow freedom on him nor make any alteration in his temporal condition in these Kingdoms; we are also of opinion that the Master may legally compel him to return again to the plantations.'[3] This opinion, which it took more than fifty years to overturn, was a great encouragement to the slave owners and to those interested in the trade. But the effect of this 'cruel and illegal opinion' is best given in the shocked words of the indefatigable abolitionist, Thomas Clarkson:

The planters, merchants, and others, gave it of course all the publicity in their power. And the consequences were as might easily have been apprehended. In a little time slaves absconding were advertised in the London papers as runaways, and rewards offered for the apprehension of them, in the same brutal manner as we find them advertised in the land of slavery. They were advertised also, in the same papers, to be sold by auction, sometimes by themselves, and at others with horses, chaises, and harness. They were seized also by their masters, or by persons employed by them, in the very streets, and dragged from thence to the ships; and so unprotected now were these poor slaves, that persons in nowise concerned with them began to institute a trade in their persons, making agreements with captains of ships going to the West Indies to put them on board at a certain price.[4]

Job would certainly not have been safe going out on the streets, nor was his future by any means firmly settled, but Hunt at least showed

---

[1] Quoted by Thomas Clarkson, *The History of the . . . Abolition of the Slave-Trade*, 1808, i. 112–13.
[2] See Dorothy George, *London Life in the Eighteenth Century*, 1930, pp. 134–8.
[3] Quoted in E.C.P. Lascelles, *Granville Sharp and the Freedom of Slaves in England*, 1928, p. 21.
[4] Clarkson, i. 65–6.

himself very willing to discharge his part in the original bargain. He immediately informed the Royal African Company when Job had arrived in the river and made a tender of him to the Company at £45, in the terms of Oglethorpe's bond. Charles Hayes, Oglethorpe's successor in the Deputy-Governorship, reported this to the Court of Assistants on 3 May and the Court then agreed and ordered 'that as Mr. Oglethorpe is now absent and that in regard the said Negro understands and writes Arabick and may be of service to the Company on giving him his freedom and sending him to Gambia, which is his native country, the Company do take the said Negro on their own account and that Captain Hunt be paid the said sum of £45 for the same upon his delivering up Mr. Oglethorpe's bond.'[1]

These negotiations seem perfectly straightforward, but when Thomas Bluett rode up specially from the country a few days later to call on Job at Limehouse and see how he was getting on, he found him in some distress. He had learnt, Job said, that some persons were making approaches to Hunt with offers to purchase him. Their excuse was that they intended to send him home, but he suspected that they either meant to sell him again as a slave or 'if they sent him home would expect an unreasonable Ransom for him'.[2]

Job's account may have been a garbled version of Hunt's negotiations with the Company, but Bluett acted immediately by taking Job up to London with him and asking Hunt for his permission to carry him down on a visit to Cheshunt. Hunt was quite willing to let him go. He told Bluett that 'he had been apply'd to, as Job had suggested, but did not intend to part with him without his own Consent; but as Mr. *Oglethorpe* was out of *England*, if any of Job's Friends would pay the Money, he would accept of it, provided they would undertake to send him home safely to his own Country.'[3] He promised that, in any case, he would not dispose of Job until he had heard from Bluett.

Bluett's own plan was perfectly simple. If the Company took up Oglethorpe's bond and redeemed Job, the transaction would only amount to a change of ownership; Job would still be a slave. On the other hand, if Bluett and his friends could raise the money to reimburse either Captain Hunt or the Company, they could present Job formally with his freedom. As far as slavery was concerned, judging by his silence, Bluett accepted it uncritically as an ordained and necessary institution; but he liked Job greatly as a man and admired his character, and put himself out to help him.

[1] P.R.O., T.70/93, p. 243.   [2] Bluett, p. 27.   [3] ibid.

Cheshunt lies fifteen miles from London, on the river Lea, in Hert-fordshire. The village was then deep in pleasant country. The great palace of Theobalds had stood there until its wanton demolition by the Commonwealth government in 1651, but though the Court no longer frequented Cheshunt the locality was a favoured one for the wealthy London merchants who wanted a country house conveniently placed for the City. Cheshunt offered good and comfortable society, and as soon as Thomas Bluett had carried Job down to his friends there he began to introduce him. Job made an immediate and favour-able impression; as Bluett remarked, he 'had the Honour to be sent for by most of the Gentry of that Place, who were mightily pleased with his Company, and concerned for his Misfortunes'.[1]

The courtesy and hospitality shown to Job in the country by people who were accustomed to think of Negroes as savages at home and drudging slaves abroad, except when they were snatched young from barbarity and trained up to become faithful and fashionable domestic servants, was due to a romantic interest in his rank and fate. One of the causes of this interest was Mrs. Aphra Behn's famous novel about the love and sufferings of Oroonoko, the African prince, who died a slave. Her tale and some, at least, of her views had reached an even wider audience by being used by Thomas Southerne in his tragedy of *Oroonoko*, which was first performed in 1695 and remained in the repertory throughout the eighteenth century.

Aphra Behn's novel is far from being a simple tale of sentimental woe. At the beginning, when the handsome and chivalrous Oroonoko discovers to his chagrin that the beautiful Imoinda is destined for the old king's—his grandfather's—bed, the action takes on the air of vaunting impossibility and rhodomontade that we associate with even such a rational example of the heroic play as Dryden's *Aureng-Zebe*, which exploits a similar theme. But once the action is brusquely transferred from the coast of Africa to the English settlement of Surinam in the West Indies, the happenings, however seemingly extreme, begin to put on an air of reality. Mrs. Behn knew Surinam and the conditions there from having spent her girlhood on that island.

The old king, upon discovering that Oroonoko had entered the harem and slept with Imoinda, takes his revenge by selling her into slavery—a common enough punishment for adultery in Africa, as we have already seen. He tells Oroonoko that she has been put to death. In spite of his grief, Oroonoko loyally accepts what has happened,

[1] ibid. p. 28.

according to the best conventions of the heroic play. The novel could not have borne so far in any way, except geographically, on Job ben Solomon, though he had been forcibly parted from two wives and their families, but once Oroonoko has been lured on board an English ship, panyarred, and carried off to Surinam and sold there as a slave, his tale does run somewhat parallel to Job's, except in its sentimental interest and its appalling conclusion. In Surinam, Oroonoko is reunited with Imoinda, whom he discovers in slavery there, as chaste and beautiful as ever, but in consequence of his leading a slave revolt, she dies at his hands rather than submit to the brutal lust of a white overseer, and he is tortured to death as a warning to others.

The sentiment may come to the top in a retelling, but it does not detract from the tragedy and pathos of the action. Oroonoko is everywhere shown as fully possessing all the qualities of the courageous prince and the refined lover, in spite of his skin and his condition. After he has been bought by the generous Cornishman, Trefry, who is more a friend than a master, he still shows his rank through the coarse suiting of a slave by his presence and behaviour: 'The Royal Youth appeared in spite of the slave, and people could not help treating him after a different manner, without designing it. As soon as they approached him, they venerated and esteemed him; his eyes insensibly commanded respect, and his behaviour insinuated it into every soul.'[1] He always acts as a hero, especially in leading his oppressed fellow Africans in revolt, and at the end, when he has slain Imoinda to prevent her violation, and failing in his attempt to commit suicide is nursed back to health only for the purpose of being tortured, with the extreme ingenuity described as customary by Sir Hans Sloane, a reader could not but help exclaiming against the injustice and brutality of the system and see men where he had before noticed only those bloodless and unfeeling abstractions—slaves.

Of course, when Job was introduced into the drawing-rooms of Cheshunt the guests assembled to meet him would not draw in their breath and murmur 'Oroonoko!' But Aphra Behn's novel would be one of the influences that unconsciously led them to respect Job as a ruler in his own country, and to sympathize with him in his dependency and in his narrow escape from the humiliations and brutality that had been inflicted on Oroonoko. They were probably more familiar with Southerne's play than with the novel, but in spite of its being a vulgarization of the story, it still exercised some of the

[1] *The Novels of Aphra Behn*, ed. E. A. Baker, 1905, p. 41.

original's power. When it was reprinted in 'Bell's British Theatre' in 1791, at the height of the anti-slave-trade agitation, the editor remarked that 'it may be imagined this play cannot easily be popular' in Liverpool, the centre of the trade. 'It ought to be itself the death blow to that most infernal of all commerce, the traffic of our Fellow Creatures.' And carried away by this idea, he turned from criticism and dramatic history to an impassioned denunciation of the trade:

Raised by the happy progress of cultivation to superior powers of mind, there is no reason, that is not sordid, for our violating the native liberties of Man even in a Savage State.—Barren as the Slave may be of all the trickeries upon which we value ourselves, and to our eye degraded by the unsightly opposition of his colour, he possesses feelings which it is tyranny to wound, and importance which it is treason to annihilate.—He has also resentments vivid, keen and implacable, which, if we provoke by cruelty, as well as fraud, he drags a life of torment only in the hope to exercise in vengeance.[1]

This fiercely radical denunciation was written more than a hundred years after Aphra Behn's novel appeared and was the result of decades of unremitting agitation inspired by more searching and committed pens than hers, but as the first, and one of the most imaginative, her protest was not negligible. The politeness shown to Job ben Solomon was an instance of the unease that was coming increasingly to be felt as the English began to realize more clearly the extent and enormities of the trade.

Thomas Bluett admitted that his friends found some difficulty in talking with Job because of his poor command of English, but those used to his manner of speaking, and willing to make allowances for him, found him an entertaining companion. What was life like in Africa? he was inevitably asked. Very different from life in England, he would reply; life was harsh in Africa, but as his people were inured to it from birth, they contented themselves with the bare necessities, knowing no better. They lacked proper implements to till the ground, or to reap their scanty harvests. They pulled the ripened corn up, roots and all, and ground it into flour between two stones with their hands.[2] All they had was their physical strength and their powers of resistance, which was why they made such excellent slaves. As for the conveniences of life, there were none; when darkness fell they crept into their huts and lay there until dawn, and those who were literate,

---

[1] *Oroonoko*, 1791, pp. iii–iv.
[2] Job's listeners clearly mistook him. This 'corn' must have been the groundnut, as Curtin suggests (see *Africa Remembered*, p. 47).

like Job, had to read by firelight, at the hazard of their eyes. The gap between Job and his audience at this point must have been complete, though if he had been able to exchange the lush meadows and comfortable dwellings of Hertfordshire for the barren wastes of Yorkshire, or the colliery villages of South Wales, he might have found analogies at hand to illustrate and explain his account.

The poverty and primitiveness of Job's countrymen must have strained his English to the limit, but he had other stories that could be more readily expressed. Hunting the elephant for ivory was the chief occupation of some of his countrymen, he explained, and one of the hunters had once told him that he had seen an elephant seize a lion and, splitting a tree down the middle, imprison the lion's head in the trunk. Job would not swear to the truth of this incident, not having been there, but he had seen an elephant thrust a lion's head first into a slough and hold it down until it was smothered.

He often introduced lions into his conversation, especially when he saw how much they were appreciated, and another of his anecdotes was how he had once killed two lions which had been marauding his father's cattle. He had killed both with poisoned arrows. The poison was made from the juice of a tree and stupefied the creature, allowing it to be captured and killed by slitting its throat, 'as their Law directs'.[1] The flesh was unaffected by the poison. Should any of their own people be struck by a poisoned arrow, they had a herb as an antidote; probably the root 'contrayerva', which the Moors came specially to Bondou to trade in.[2]

The other staple in such exchanges of national information was inevitably the sexes, and Job explained in some detail and, under repeated questioning, with some accuracy how the suitor arranges the bride price and the dowry with the girl's father, the marriageable age for girls, of course, being much younger than in England. 'But now comes the great Difficulty, *viz.* how the young Man shall get his Wife home; for the Women, Cousins, and Relations, take on mightily, and guard the Door of the House, to prevent her being carried away; but at last the Young Man's Presents and Generosity to them, makes them abate their Grief. He then provides a Friend, well mounted, to carry her off; but as soon as she is upon Horseback, the Women renew their Lamentations, and rush in to dismount her.... After this they

---

[1] Bluett, p. 39.

[2] Spalding Gentlemen's Society, First Minute Book, f. 186. This root was brought into England from Peru and used as an anti-epidemic; see Chambers, *s.v.* 'contra-yerva'.

make a Treat for their Friends, but the Woman never appears at it.'[1]

The last point led Job to compare the position of women in Bondou with that of English women. Once married, his countrywomen put on the veil and wore it so scrupulously that for three years even their husbands were not allowed to see their faces. In his own case, Job had been married to one of his wives for two years and had had a daughter by her, but he had never yet seen her unveiled. How did he manage with two wives? was a question that was bound to be eagerly pressed. By dividing his time equally between them, he explained, and doing it so exactly 'that if one Wife lies in, the Husband lies alone in her Apartment those Nights, that are her Turn, and not with the other Wife'.[2] And this topic led on to divorce and the ceremonies of circumcision and baptism and burial, and, as far as his halting English allowed, Job went on to explain how they dressed, the type of houses they lived in, and the general ordering of their daily lives.[3] Some of what Job told them they might have learnt from the already published accounts of West Africa, but how different to hear it from his lips and to verify in his person that the extraordinary facts he retailed had actually and successfully co-operated in producing an intelligent being, albeit a black one.

Job's own curiosity, as distinct from the astonishment that he must have felt at the unrolling spectacle of English life, was directed chiefly to implements and mechanical devices. He recognized at once that they were the cause of the gulf between the material well-being of his own people and of the English. He was extremely quick in understanding the purpose and operation of any tool or machine that was demonstrated and explained to him. Once a plough or a grist mill or a clock had been taken to pieces in front of him, he was able to reassemble them without further directions. He was helped in this by his natural quickness of mind and determination, but also by his remarkable memory, trained by having had to learn the Koran by heart before the age of fifteen. He could write out the whole book from memory; in fact, he made three copies while he was in England, without once referring to the text. When his English friends told him they had forgotten something he would laugh and remark that 'he hardly ever forgot any Thing in his Life, and wondered that any other body ever should'.[4]

---

[1] Bluett, p. 41.   [2] ibid. p. 42.

[3] Bluett just mentions these topics because, he remarks, they had already been described in several books.

[4] Bluett, p. 48.

Job made a very good impression upon society at Cheshunt, especially upon his host, Thomas Bluett, who had reason to know him best. He had the advantage of being a handsome man, standing about five feet ten inches, with a good figure, refined features, and an expression 'exceeding pleasant, yet grave and composed'.[1] 'In his natural Temper,' Bluett continued, 'there appeared a happy Mixture of the Grave and the Chearful, a gentle Mildness, guarded by a proper Warmth, and a kind and compassionate Disposition towards all that were in Distress. In Conversation he was commonly very pleasant; and would every now and then divert the Company with some witty Turn, or pretty Story, but never to the Prejudice of Religion, or good Manners.'[2]

Bluett and his friends found it easier to like and sympathize with Job because in his self-assurance and his assumption of a right to command he resembled them rather than the Negroes whom they knew as domestic servants in England, or as slaves on the plantations. He appeared to differ from the mass of his black countrymen even in his colouring and features; and his hair was long and curled, quite unlike the wool of the ordinary Negro.

One of the stories that Job liked to tell struck Bluett as showing how far his courage was belied by his usual air of mildness, but it also helps to explain how he and his listeners could share a common identity as they stood gossiping together in front of a drawing-room fire in Cheshunt. As he and four of his servants were leading home one day through Arab country a parcel of Negroes that he had just bought, they were set upon by fifteen wild Arabs. Job left one of his servants to guard the Negroes and with the other three began fighting off the banditti. One of Job's men was killed and Job himself was run through the leg with a spear, but after two Arabs had been slain and the captain of the band himself and two horses, the rest of the robbers fled, leaving Job still in possession of his Negroes. Job must have told the story well, in spite of his elementary English, and whatever difficulties his audience may have found in visualizing this skirmish—whose violent, romantic movement had to wait for Delacroix to fix its image —they could test the truth of its having happened by Job's sincerity and sympathize with him. He, too, like themselves, was one of the masters.

But more than his appearance or his good manners or his rank, it was Job's religion that commanded respect. He was a devout Mohammedan, and a priest. While a slave in Maryland, he had been pelted

[1] ibid. p. 46.   [2] ibid. pp. 48–9.

for saying his prayers; he had refused to eat meat on board the *William* unless the beast had been slaughtered according to his own rites; and while he was in England, he kept Ramadan so strictly that he began to look rather 'lean and weakly'.[1] Mohammedanism might be deplored as a corrupt deviation from Christianity, or, with the memory of centuries of conflict in mind, as its most implacable foe, but it could not be disregarded as a system, nor overlooked as a civilization; in every respect, it was comparable with Christianity. Job was so evidently a believer that his hosts had to identify him with Muslim culture and were impressed. He could not be condescended to as a pagan savage, who worshipped some idol in the secrecy of his room. He detested idolatry, of course, and, indeed, believed that Christians must be idolaters themselves, having seen religious pictures in the chapel in the French factory in his neighbourhood at home, as he told Bluett; a clue to the whereabouts of 'Boonda', had Bluett been sharp enough to have followed it up.[2]

As Thomas Bluett and probably several of his friends were devout Evangelicals, religion occupied much of their conversation with Job. They recognized that he was clearly prejudiced in favour of his own faith, but they had to admit that he seemed anxious to consider their arguments impartially. They discovered under questioning that he did not believe in 'a sensual Paradise', which they had always understood to be an article of Mohammedanism designed to draw converts, that he seemed remarkably free from all superstition, and that he believed absolutely in one God, to whom alone he addressed his prayers. He never pronounced the name of Allah, as Bluett noticed, 'without a peculiar Accent, and a remarkable Pause'. Indeed, as Bluett went on to admit, 'his Notions of God, Providence, and a future State, were in the main very just and reasonable'.[3]

Job knew, of course, the historical parts of the Old Testament, and as he was perfectly willing to examine the truth of the Christian revelation, he read through a New Testament in Arabic with the greatest care, looking especially for texts to support the doctrine of the Trinity. He could find none, as he explained to Bluett. 'I did not care to puzzle him,' Bluett observed, 'and therefore answered in general, that the *English* believed only in one God.'[4] Oddly enough,

[1] ibid. p. 46
[2] See ibid. p. 44. Thomas Green saw the importance of this remark. When reprinting Bluett, he remarked that Bluett should have told his readers where this factory was, there being none nearer than Kaygnú [Kaynoura] on the Faleme, or Mankanet [Macanet] on the Sanaga'. (Astley. ii. 240 n.*e*.)
[3] ibid. p. 52.   [4] ibid.

Plate 4.

The South-west Prospect of James Island on the River of Gambia, Drawn 1727.

Sold by I. Clark Engraver & Printseller in Gray Inn.

The River GAMBIA, on which is the Northernmost English Settlement in Guinea, is said to be Navigable about 200 Leagues. it Lyes from ye Rivers Mouth at James Island, whereon stands a strong regular well=built Fort, belonging to ye Royal African Company of England, which commands both ye North & South Channel on each Side of it: This Part of Africa, tho' full as Wealthy yet it is more Fertile then any other Part: I have Seen, & produces greater Plenty of Beef, Pork, Mutton, Goats, & Fowls. On ye North Side of Gambia, near ye River's Mouth, are the Kingdoms of Burfally, & Barra. On ye South side, are ye Emfior of Fonia, & Kingdom of Cumbo. Their Religion is partly Mahometan, some Christian, but most Pagan. on either Side the River: their Language is so different as not to understand each other; Their chief Commodities are Ivory, Wax, & the best of African Gold.

JAMES FORT

From Thirty Different Draughts of Guinea, by William Smith, 1728.

'WANDERING FOOLAH'

From *Travels in Western Africa*, by Major William Gray and the late
Staff Surgeon Dochard, 1825.

the freethinking Aphra Behn had made the Trinity Oroonoko's chief obstacle in comprehending Christianity. He 'would never be reconciled to our notions of the Trinity,' she wrote, 'of which he ever made a jest; it was a riddle he said would turn his brain to conceive, and one could not make him understand what faith was.'[1] Job, too, lacked the faith necessary to accept such a rare truth, but not the intelligence or even the learning, for his learning, in spite of there being few books whence he came—as few as thirty, Bluett thought—and those all in manuscript and on religion, was 'far from being contemptible'.[2]

The Arabic text in which Job read the New Testament was the one issued by the Society for the Promotion of Christian Knowledge in 1726. One of the correctors was the Orientalist, George Sale. Sale, who was a member of the Society, wrote to the Society in June requesting a New Testament and Psalter and a *Catechetical Instructions* in Arabic, which had all been prepared for and issued by the Society,[3] for the use of the 'Poor Mahometan Black redeemed by order of Mr. Oglethorpe', a request which, according to the Society's Minute Book, was granted on 26 June 1733.

George Sale was one of the most remarkable scholars of the age. He was born about 1697,[4] and after reading law, a profession in which he appeared to have an eminent future, he devoted himself to the study of languages, especially Arabic. He was a sociable and good-looking man; married, with several children. He had almost certainly heard of Job in connection with Job's letter to his father, which Oglethorpe had sent to Oxford to be translated. And as Sale was completing at this time his great work, a translation of the Koran, which is acknowledged to be the finest into any language, the idea of meeting a devout Mohammedan, who was also fluent in Arabic, must have made him eagerly seek out Job on his arrival.

The S.P.C.K. was most anxious to promote the knowledge of the Gospel in the Arabic world; for this reason it had raised and spent about £3,000 on the New Testament and the other two translations, published in 1726. But while it would have welcomed the chance of converting Job, it was not especially anxious to extend its mission to Africa, in spite of its founder Thomas Bray's warm sympathies for the Negro. The Society had already had a most unfortunate experience of

---

[1] *Novels of Aphra Behn*, p. 48. [2] Bluett, p. 52.
[3] For details of these publications, see W. K. Lowther Clarke, *A History of the S.P.C.K.*, 1959, pp. 116–18.
[4] His obituary, in the *London Magazine* for November 1736, says that he was under forty.

Africa and would certainly have looked askance at anyone claiming to be an African prince, or a high priest, or anything like it.

In 1721 a slave trader called Captain White, while at Delagoa in Mozambique, enticed on board two Negro youths, supposed to be princes, and carried them to Jamaica where he sold them. A Mr. Bowles, hearing their tale and taking pity on them, bought them from their master and sailed with them for England. The ship was wrecked off Cuba, but the youths, fortunate again, were rescued by a Captain Towgood and taken to London. The Royal African Company and the East India Company were both eager to patronize them, in the hope of getting a foothold in Delagoa through their supposed princely connections, and squabbled over them for a year. James Macquillan Mussoom and John Chaung Mussoom, as the youths were now called, were at length brought to the attention of Thomas Bray. Bray was appalled by the way the youths had been spoiled and pampered, and immediately set out to educate them in the tenets of Christianity, with the idea of using them to set up a mission in Africa.

When Bray was satisfied with their sincerity and progress he issued an appeal for funds to return them to their country, accompanied by two suitable missionaries. The appeal was launched 'out of a hearty desire to propagate the light of the Gospel into those dark regions of the earth, and in hopes that it may please God to bless an endeavour promising so great a harvest for his glory'. Unfortunately, only one missionary, Marmaduke Penwell, could be found willing to make the journey, and he, as the Society admitted, though the best available, was far from satisfactory. Penwell and the youths, with a fair amount of stores and full instructions as to the best ways of civilizing the natives before attempting their conversion, sailed for Delagoa in 1722. The voyage could hardly have been more unfortunate. One of the 'princes' went ashore when the ship put in at a West Country port and hanged himself in an orchard, either 'in a phrenzy' or on account of a quarrel with his brother. And when the vessel at last arrived at Delagoa, the second 'prince' retired to his mother's house and shut the door in Penwell's face. Penwell waited outside for six hours before his charge opened the door, and when he did so, he gave Penwell 'such frowns and looked so surly upon him', that he hurried immediately down to the ship and returned to England.[1]

The experience effectively discouraged the S.P.C.K. from trying to set up missions in Africa, or equally outlandish parts, and while

---

[1] This account of the 'princes' is taken from Clarke, pp. 96–8, and H. P. Thompson, *Thomas Bray*, 1954, pp. 93–4.

charity would persuade them to give Job the chance of being redeemed
by means of a Testament in Arabic, they had probably decided from
the moment they had heard of him to decline any suggestion that he
might make a useful agent in a scheme for the conversion of Africans.
As it happened, Job was proof against apostasy.

Other figures in the world of intellectual London besides George
Sale had hurried to make Job's acquaintance on his arrival, and among
them was Sir Hans Sloane, physician to Queen Caroline, and the
greatest collector of 'rarities' of his age. Sir Hans was already familiar
with the Negro, as a slave in the West Indies. He owed part of his
personal fortune to slavery. As a young man, he had practised medicine
in Jamaica, and while there had met the woman whom he was later to
marry, the widow of a wealthy planter. He had made further good use
of his spell in Jamaica by collecting materials for his splendid and
valuable, if somewhat diffuse, natural history of the island. In the
Preface to the first volume, which appeared in 1707, he gave the
gruesome and matter-of-fact account of the punishments ordinarily
meted out to disobedient or rebellious slaves, which was to become
one of the favourite texts of abolitionists. He was not without sympathy for the Negroes—at least, he denies the common charge that
they voluntarily and casually sold their own children into slavery; but
he considered them, on the whole, to be 'a very perverse Generation
of People', and describes their sale and management as if they were
livestock or another kind of article to men.[1] He was, however, far from
lacking in charity, and in his ordinary affairs was a kind and generous
man. When Oglethorpe appealed for funds to help in establishing his
colony in Georgia, Sir Hans came forward with an annual contribu-
tion of £20, and it was on his advice that steps were taken to introduce into the new territories useful drugs and plants from other
countries.[2]

Sir Hans could have learnt from Oglethorpe of Job's strange
history, but he would have looked forward to his coming out of
self-interest, as well as curiosity. The range of his collections, which
were housed at this time in Bloomsbury, was extraordinary: mineral
specimens, precious stones, birds and butterflies from both Indies and
elsewhere, mechanical contrivances, Egyptian mummies, Roman
antiquities, miscellaneous curiosities, and medals and books—42,000
books and manuscripts, all superbly bound.[3] Among the medals and

---

[1] Sloane, pp. lvi–lvii.
[2] See G. R. de Beer, *Sir Hans Sloane*, 1954, pp. 101–2.
[3] See ibid. pp. 129–33.

manuscripts were many in Arabic and these, Sir Hans had hoped, Job would be able to translate.

Sir Hans was not disappointed; at least, he was satisfied with Job's efforts and impressed by his learning. A year after Job's return to Africa he told a correspondent that he had had some of his Arabic coins 'interpreted by a native of the inward parts of Africa, a black Mahometan priest who had great knowledge of the Ancient as well as modern Arabick'.[1] But there were other matters in which Job might also be helpful, and Sir Hans foresaw that he could make a useful correspondent on his return home, and an agent for forwarding curiosities.

Job was already known to one among Sir Hans's circle of acquaintance—Joseph Ames, who had tried to get Job's letter to his father translated. Ames had begun collecting for his great work, *Typographical Antiquities*, which eventually appeared in 1749, and Sloane's museum with its extensive library was put at his use. He took a great interest in Job and tried to help him all he could, and though his kindness to a homeless Negro must be put down to his character, for even his critics admitted that he was a 'friendly and good-tempered' man,[2] he was in this typical of the radical and nonconformist class, which powerfully championed the Negroes' cause. He was 'an Independent or Anabaptist, with a great Spice of Deism mixed with it',[3] and Ames partly admitted that there was some justifiable criticism in the charge when he regretted to a correspondent having once wasted his time on Anabaptist books.[4]

Another busy and versatile scholar and man of affairs whom Job met through Sir Hans was Dr. Cromwell Mortimer, Sir Hans's assistant in his medical practice. Mortimer was also his assistant in another capacity. Sir Hans had been elected President of the Royal Society in 1727 and Mortimer, who was made a Fellow the following year, became Secretary to the Society in 1730. One aspect of the Society's policy was to initiate and encourage the recording of any strange or practical knowledge that could be discovered abroad, and such a person as Job might possibly be useful as an informant and later as a correspondent. Ames and Mortimer used frequently to meet Job in Bloomsbury. 'I am now going to meet him [Mortimer] at Sir Hans Sloans,' Ames wrote on 3 October 1733, 'with the Black that

---

[1] B.M., Sloane MS. 4068, f. 276; 16 September 1735, to an unknown correspondent.
[2] William Cole's view; B.M., Add. MS. 5831, f. 174 b.   [3] ibid.
[4] Ames to the Rev. J. Lewis, 24 March 1741; B.M. Stowe MS. 1049, f. 14.

understands the Arabick to read some of Sir Han'ses [*sic*] stones with these characters.'[1]

The strangest evidence of Job's adoption by the group of scholars and virtuosi surrounding Sir Hans Sloane was his later election to the Gentlemen's Society of Spalding. The Society was founded in 1710, in emulation of the Society of Antiquaries in London, of which it considered itself to be a cell, and many distinguished antiquaries, scholars, men of letters, scientists, and amateurs were members of this first and most distinguished of provincial societies: Richard Pococke the Orientalist for example, Michael Rysbrack the sculptor, Alexander Pope and Sir Isaac Newton, with Sir Hans Sloane among them—Maurice Johnson the founder, was a collector in more than one field. William Bogdani, the Clerk of the Ordnance at the Tower of London, who was a friend of Joseph Ames and a relation by marriage to Maurice Johnson, was the principal mover in Job's election, but Job was formally proposed by George Holmes, Deputy Keeper of the Records in the Tower, a most distinguished scholar, and by James West, who was as skilful a politician as he was a competent antiquary. Long after Job had returned home, West demonstrated his versatility by becoming Secretary to the Lords of the Treasury and President of the Royal Society. Job applied to be admitted to the Society as an honorary member on 23 May 1734, dating his letter from the Tower of London, and his request—in English, but with the address and subscription in Arabic—was placed before a meeting of the Society in Spalding on 6 June, accompanied by a brief account of Job written by Joseph Ames. The Secretary entered in the minutes that the 'learned and worthy Job Jalla was upon Ballott elected and admitted an Honorary Member of this Society'.[2]

But Job's principal business was not to argue over the Trinity with his evangelical friends, or to translate Arabic inscriptions for Sloane; he had somehow to secure his freedom and get a passage back to the Gambia. The Royal African Company clearly recognized that they were under an obligation to discharge the responsibility that Oglethorpe had undertaken—they kept Job in funds, noting that they had given him a guinea on 27 September 1733—but they seem to have been undecided how this could best be done to the Company's advantage. At length, the Company's secretary, Richard Spence— the brother of Joseph Spence, Pope's friend and memorialist—arranged with Captain Hunt that he should come to Africa House, the Company's offices in Leadenhall Street, on Thursday 15 November at

[1] ibid. f. 18.   [2] Spalding Gentlemen's Society, Second Minute Book, f. 109.

10 o'clock, requesting 'that you will bring with you the bond you have of Mr. Oglethorpe's, as also the black whom you brought from Carolina'.[1]

The financial arrangements were concluded rather more expeditiously than the personal. The Company agreed to repay Captain Hunt the full principal of £45 on Oglethorpe's bond, and the interest on the principal from 3 May, when the *William* docked in London, to 15 November, being the sum of £1. 3s. 11d; in addition, the Company reimbursed Hunt for £13. 3s. 0d., being Job's maintenance and other charges.

Job was now the Company's property, as Joseph Ames explained to an anxious Sir Hans Sloane, and, having paid off Hunt, they sent for Job on Tuesday 20 November and told him to get his things ready and move into Africa House, where they had appointed the caretaker, James Forbes, to look after him. They were not able to tell him when they would send him home, but they gave the impression of its being soon, for Job sent a message to Sir Hans: 'He desires to return you thanks for all your favours,' Ames wrote to Sloane on 21 November, 'and is ready to make you all the returns he can.'[2] The Company were fitting up a ship to sail for the Gambia about Christmas and they probably intended Job to take a passage in it.[3]

Job had no longer any need to fear being sold again as a slave by Captain Hunt, but he was still uneasy and convinced 'that he must pay an extravagant Ransom, when he got home'.[4] And some of his friends were profoundly dissatisfied with the turn his affairs had taken. In their opinion, whatever the Company's good intentions, Job had simply switched owners, and they were not prepared to rest content until he was his own master. They proposed raising the money to purchase Job his freedom by a public subscription. Among the friends that Job had made through Thomas Bluett were several influential in the City, especially Samuel Holden, a merchant connected with the African trade, and Nathaniel Brassey, a banker in Lombard Street, who later sat as M.P. for Hertford from 1734 to 1754.[5] The promoters moved rapidly and a subscription was opened for Job on Friday 30 November. Thomas Bluett wrote to Sir Hans Sloane on 3 December, explaining the situation:

Mr. Holden desir'd me to acquaint you that a ship of Mr. Hyde's going very soon to Job's country, he with Mr. Brassey and other gentle-

[1] P.R.O., T.70/47, p. 125.   [2] B.M., Sloane MS. 4053, f. 90.
[3] ibid. f. 112.   [4] Bluett, p. 29.
[5] See Cussans, *History of Hertfordshire*, 'Hundred of Hertford', 1876, pp. 103-4, 114.

men have begun a Subscription in order to redeem Job and send him in [blank] ship. He hopes you'll use your interest with the Queen and with your own friends in contributing to so charitable a design, and then we doubt not, but what we wish may be soon effected.

The money given is paid into the hands of Mr. Richard Harding at Hamlin's Coffee-house, Swithin's Alley, near the Exchequer.[1] The Subscription began on Friday night and seems to promise fair.[2]

The impetuosity of this group of Job's friends seriously alarmed the others, including Sloane. They were convinced that the Company, although Job was now their property, would behave honourably towards him, and that he was, in fact, more secure by being their responsibility. In addition, they felt that nothing ought to be done without James Oglethorpe's consent, he having himself arranged for Job's redemption. Sir Hans did not know Bluett personally, but he was so alarmed by his letter that he sent Joseph Ames with Job to meet Bluett at Hamlin's Coffee House and to argue the case for Job remaining with the company. As soon as they met, as he later reported to Sir Hans, Ames told Bluett that, in Sir Hans's opinion, Job was 'now in good hands'. Bluett disagreed and said 'with an air' that he thought not and that Job should be purchased from the Company. 'I argued with him,' continued Ames, ' 'till he was warm and left me representing to him, *How if the Company will not part with him? have you asked them the question? what will Mr. Oglethorpe say?* etc. I have enquired how they go on, and hear that they have collected together 28 pounds or Gineas. I desired they would make use of it to his benefitt.'[3]

The most surprising of the subscribers to Job's fund were the envoys of the Bey of Tunis to the Court of St. James's, who had arrived in October 1733, bringing five Arab horses as a present to the king.[4] Job waited on them on Friday 7 December. They received him 'very civilly', made him stay to dinner, and, as a token of their sympathy for the sufferings of a co-religionist, presented him with a guinea. One of the envoys, at least, would be able to sympathize fully with him: the one who appeared in mourning at the royal audience at Hampton Court on 11 October, having learnt since his arrival in England that his father, mother, wife and five children had all died of the plague.[5] Job arranged to call on the envoys again on the following

---

[1] It is not without interest that Hamlin's Coffee House seems to have been frequented by Dissenters; see Bryant Lillywhite, *London Coffee Houses*, 1963, p. 261.
[2] B.M., Sloane MS. 4053, f. 105.   [3] ibid. f. 112.
[4] *London Magazine*, 1733, p. 528.   [5] ibid.

Friday, though he was kept very busy with his friends and with getting ready to leave—in a week or so, as he anticipated. 'His time is much taken up by one or another,' Ames observed to Sloane, 'and he had many gifts, among others a watch with which he is very much pleased. He collects all his things together and packs them up, that he may be in readiness, but I must take care of your two books.'[1]

Sir Hans was far from being reassured by Ames's report, and he wrote to him within the week asking for further news and urging Ames to use his influence to deter Job from falling in with Bluett's and his friends' scheme. In his reply, after remarking that he was glad Sir Hans continued to concern himself 'for the poor man's safety', Ames had to admit that Job was refusing to see him, now that he knew that Ames disapproved of the scheme to buy him his freedom; and he had also to report that Holden and Brassey were that very day, 20 December, meeting with Sir Bibye Lake at the African Coffee House in Leadenhall Street, in order to discuss purchasing Job from the Company. Ames was beginning to fear that they might succeed. 'I may know hereafter what is done,' he remarked, 'but may be too late to do any good. They had the Day before yesterday collected for him forty one Gineas, besides what has been given to himself. Sir Charles Wager has given him two Gineas, and he continues to receive from one another many gifts.' Job's subscription was going very well indeed when it could draw in such contributors as Admiral Sir Charles Wager, the First Lord of the Admiralty, but nothing could deflect Ames from thinking that the best course would be to leave Job in the Company's hands. 'I know the Company's ship is fitting out,' he wound up, 'and believe he can do no where so well.'[2]

The promoters of the scheme for Job's freedom were successful. Holden and Brassey persuaded Sir Bibye Lake at their meeting that their proposal was just and practical, and in his turn Sir Bibye convinced his fellow officers in the Company. At a meeting of the Court of Assistants held on Thursday 27 December it was ordered:

That a certificate be prepared setting forth that Simon otherwise called Job the Gambia black lately brought from Maryland, is acquitted and discharged from all claims or demands that this Company have or can have against him on any account and further declaring him to be a free man; and that he is at liberty to take his passage to Africa in any of the Company's ships, or in any other ship or ships that he shall choose in order to return to his native country, and that the Company's seal be

---

[1] B.M., Sloane MS. 4053, f. 112.
[2] ibid. f. 118.

affixed there to and the same be thereupon delivered to the said Simon otherwise called Job.[1]

The certificate of manumission, 'handsomely engrossed' and authenticated with the Company's seal,[2] was formally conveyed to Job, and conferred his freedom on him in the most unambiguous and formal terms:

Know all Men by these Presents That we the Royal African Company of England have acquitted and do by these Presents acquit and for ever discharge Simon, otherwise called Job a black lately brought over from Maryland of and from all and all Manner of Claims and Demands of us against him on any Account whatsoever, And we do further hereby for us and our Successors declare that from and after this day the said Simon otherwise called Job is a free Man and is at Liberty to take his Passage to Africa in any of our Ships or in any other Ship or Ships which he shall chuse, in order to return to his Native Country. In Witness whereof we have caused our Common Seal to be hereunto Affixed this 27th Day of December in the Year of our Lord 1733.

By order of the Court of Assistants of the Royal African Company of England.

Rich. Spence.[3]

The business was finally completed on 10 January 1734, when Nathaniel Brassey reimbursed the Company for £59. 6s. 11d., being the sum it had paid out to Captain Hunt. The subscription was still short of this total by about £20 but Brassey, who had opened the subscription and promised 'his further Assistance at a dead Lift',[4] had generously made up the difference. The Company agreed to support Job until his return.

Job was extraordinarily reassured by his certificate and, being now convinced that he was truly his own master and could not be claimed on some pretext or another, he moved about much more freely between his friends' houses, in town and in the country. He continued to put up at Africa House in Leadenhall Street, where he was looked after by the caretaker, James Forbes, who was allowed eight shillings a week for boarding and lodging him and ninepence for his laundry.[5] Sir Hans Sloane bore him no grudge for having taken his other friends' advice rather than his own, and when Job mentioned to him one day at his house that he would dearly like to see the royal family, Sir Hans arranged an audience. The only difficulty was his

---

[1] P.R.O., T.70/93, p. 284. [2] Bluett, p. 30.
[3] P.R.O., T.70/1424, p. 18. [4] Bluett, p. 29.
[5] P.R.O., T.70/302, p. 111.

costume. He normally wore European clothes; indeed, shortly after being given his freedom, the Company ordered a suit of drugget cloth for him at a cost of £2. 10s. 0d.;[1] but it was felt appropriate that on such an occasion as being presented at Court he should wear his native garb. Nathaniel Brassey paid for the material and the making and a gown of rich silk was prepared under Job's direction. In this fashion he was taken to Court and introduced to the King and Queen and other members of the royal family. Queen Caroline graciously presented him with a gold watch.[2]

After being presented, Job dined in company with the Duke of Montagu, who among his many honours and promotions held the Court sinecure of Master of the Great Wardrobe. Montagu must have already learnt about Job's history from Sir Hans Sloane and his friends, for he closely shared their interests; he was a Fellow of the College of Physicians, and a Fellow of both the Royal Society and the Society of Antiquaries; and as the Lord of the Manor of Theobalds he also had a connection with Cheshunt. After the dinner the Duke and others of the nobility who were there made Job a 'handsome present'.[3]

Montagu was an eccentric, who delighted in practical jokes, much to the exasperation of his mother-in-law, the great Sarah, Duchess of Marlborough. 'All his talents', she wrote in 1740, 'lie in things only natural in boys of fifteen years old, and he is about two and fifty.'[4] But in spite of his painful jokes he was an extreme humanitarian, refusing to let any cattle or horse be killed on his estate at Boughton near Northampton. He was naturally generous and, in the opinion of competent judges, far from being a fool. 'His loss will be extremely felt!' Horace Walpole wrote at the time of his death in 1749; 'he paid no less than 2,700 l. a year in private pensions, which ought to be known, to balance the immense history of his places. . . . My father had great opinion of his understanding. . . . In short, with some foibles, he was a most amiable man, and one of the most feeling I ever knew.'[5]

He took an immediate liking to Job and became his patron. He brought him down with him several times into the country and showed him the tools that were used for tilling the garden and the farm and got his servants to demonstrate to Job exactly how they were used.

---

[1] ibid. p. 141.   [2] Bluett, p. 31.   [3] ibid.

[4] Quoted by Stuart Piggott, *William Stukeley*, 1950, p. 145. Piggott has an interesting discussion of Montagu in connection with the antiquarian movement.

[5] Walpole to Mann, 24 July 1749; Walpole's *Letters*, ed. Toynbee, 1903, ii. 400–1.

He presented Job with many of these tools himself; 'several other Noblemen and Gentlemen', particularly the Earl of Pembroke, made him presents of others; and all the gifts, a considerable number, were by Montagu's arrangement carefully packed up in chests ready for Job's return voyage.[1]

Job had received many sentimental as well as useful gifts and as he had no way of returning them with souvenirs of his visit, he fell in with his friends' request that he should sit to the young artist William Hoare for his picture.[2] Having all the Muslim's superstitious and scrupulous objections to the making of images, Job was reluctant to sit until he had been reassured that his portrait was wanted not for worship, but as a reminder of him when he had gone. He had not forgotten the use made by the French of the portraits in their chapel. After Hoare had finished the face itself, he asked in what dress should he depict him? Job asked to be drawn in his native dress and when Hoare replied that he could not draw it without having first seen it, he exclaimed triumphantly: '"If you can't draw a Dress you never saw, why do some of you Painters presume to draw God, whom no one ever saw?"'[3] Hoare's finished sketch showed Job wearing a turban and gown—probably the one in rich silk made specially for his audience at Court—and carrying a copy of the Koran round his neck. The handsome, regular features and the alert, confident expression, which is so admirably caught in the portrait, help to explain Job's extraordinary success.

Job's baggage was not entirely made up of tools and implements. Cromwell Mortimer wrote to the S.P.C.K. on 18 May recommending to them 'the making a present if they should think it proper of a Copy of the Polyglott Bible to Job a Mahometan Priest now in London who is very desirous of carrying a Copy of the Old Testament in Arabick to his own Countrey in the Midland parts of Africa'. The Society agreed to the request and asked George Sale to put the matter in hand.[4] Henry Newman, Secretary to the Society, was able to reply to Mortimer on 5 June, telling him that the Society had presented Job with the Pentateuch in Arabic, in Erpenius's edition, and reminding him that they had already given him, in addition, the New Testament

---

[1] Bluett, p. 32.
[2] Hoare is supposed to have been studying in Rome in 1734, but Bluett is specific in stating that Job's portrait 'was done by Mr. *Hoare*', and no other Hoare seems possible.
[3] Bluett, pp. 50–1.
[4] S.P.C.K. Minute Book, under 21 May 1734.

and Psalter in Arabic, printed by the Society itself. They are informed, Newman went on, that these works 'are as much as he will be able to understand, or make room for among his Baggage'.[1]

Job's ceaseless anxiety to further his own religion led him to persuade the Royal African Company to agree that in future, whenever a Mohammedan was bought as a slave by the Company's agents in the Gambia, he should be allowed to redeem himself upon application, in exchange for two other good slaves. The Company's rather surprising agreement to this request was not merely nominal and intended to placate Job, backed up as he now was by powerful friends, but they sent instructions to their agents in the Gambia that this arrangement should be put into effect.

The only Mohammedan whom Job himself could immediately help was his unfortunate servant, Loumein Yoai, still a slave in Maryland. When Job told him of his servant's plight, the Duke of Montagu agreed to arrange for his release and to pay the price of his redemption. Strange, that a man's fate should depend on such a set of improbable chances, linking such distant and different places as the burnt savannahs of the Gambia, the plantations of Maryland, and the drawing-rooms at Boughton, whose architecture copied the splendours of Versailles and whose treasure in pictures and furniture was immense.

The loading and victualling of a ship for the Gambia took time; in the case of the Royal African Company's snow, the *Dolphin*, which had been chosen as the readiest way of returning Job, more than a month was required. The *Dolphin* was a new ship of eighty-six tons, launched in 1731, and carried a crew of thirteen and an armament of ten guns.[2] Although it was not fitted out to sail until the end of June, the Company was paying William Smith 12s. 6d. for 'a suit of bedding' for Job's use on the *Dolphin* as early as 6 June.[3]

But more important precautions had to be taken on Job's behalf than clean bedding. Senegambia was a region contested by the English and the French, and Job was alarmed at what might happen to him were he to fall into French hands during his voyage home, having identified himself so completely with the English. He talked about this possibility one morning at Sir Hans Sloane's, in the company of Sir Randal Macdonald, who was on the point of returning to the French Court. Sir Randal promised to help by getting him a French passport, which would give him all the protection he could possibly

[1] ibid. under 5 June 1734.   [2] P.R.O., T.70/1193, p. 6.
[3] P.R.O., T.70/302, p. 102.

require. He was as good as his word and wrote to Sir Hans from Chantilly on 25 May telling him that he had approached the Secretary of State on Job's behalf. The Secretary 'told me', he continued, 'he wanted no passeport, the two nations being in peace, that he ensured him against any accident of being taken by any French Shipp: but that if he took his passage to Africa in a French Vessel, in that case he should have a passeport to carry him safe. If he goes in an English bottom it is plain he wants no French passeport.'[1] Sir Randal's letter did not reassure Job completely, but as it contained a categorical statement by the French Secretary of State that he personally insured him against 'any accident of being taken by any French Shipp', he asked if he could have it as a safeguard. Sir Hans took a copy for himself and noted on it that Job was given the original on 9 June.

June was a month of leave-taking. Job's baggage of assorted tools and goods, worth in value more than £500, all gifts from his well-wishers, was neatly and stoutly packed up in chests and carried down at a charge of 18s. 6d. to where the *Dolphin* was moored at Gravesend.[2] Job himself left Africa House on 27 June to board the vessel.[3]

The *Dolphin* was under the command of Captain Thomas Freeman, and having cleared his list of crew and passengers on 28 June, Freeman took her down river into the Downs and, on 2 July, began to sail along the coast to the Solent, the starting-point for voyages to West Africa. The Company was meanwhile preparing its final instructions to be handed over to Freeman by its agent in Gosport. The packet was dispatched from the London office on 5 July.

The covering letter from Richard Spence to Freeman began with a reprimand for his having omitted Job's name from his list of passengers, and having thus indicated at the outset the importance which the Company attached to Job's comfort and safety, Spence asked Freeman to give Job a letter to the Company's officers in the Gambia, which Job was to deliver to them himself. Freeman was first to read the letter over to him 'and make him as sensible of the contents thereof as you possibly can'.[4] The letter, dated 4 July and addressed to 'Messrs. Richard Hull, Charles Orfeur and Hugh Hamilton, Chief Merchants at Gambia', was signed by Sir Bibye Lake, the Governor, Charles Hayes, the Deputy Governor, and ten members of the Court of Assistants, and read as follows:

---

[1] B.M., Sloane MS. 4053, f. 219.
[2] P.R.O., T.70/302, p. 111.
[3] The Company paid James Forbes for lodgings for Job until that day.
[4] P.R.O., T.70/47, p. 131.

Gentlemen

This will be delivered to you by one Job, a free Black, and Son of a Mahometan Priest, he was formerly taken and sold to one of the private Traders and carried to Mary Land, where he was sold for a Slave, but by the Interest and good Offices of Mr. Oglethorpe, has been redeemed in order to be sett at Liberty and sent back to his own Country, he has been here in England for some time and appears to be a very Sober and Ingenious Person, and has met with many favours and civilities here from many Persons of great Rank and worth, who have bestowed upon him several Considerable Presents all which he carries along with him, and as we are very desirous that he should be well and kindly used, while he stays with you, and that all due Care may be taken to send him with his things safe home to his own Country, we do earnestly recommend him to your Care and Protection, and do hereby strictly direct and require you to consult with him about the most proper measures for sending him safe home, and for that Purpose to send him with all his things to such of our Factorys up the River as to be nearest to and most convenient for him to gett to his own Country under the Care of some discreet Person whom you can confide in to see these our Orders duely put in Execution. He has likewise requested of us, That if any of his Religion should at any time be Sold to any of our Factors, That upon application for their Redemption and upon paying two other good Slaves for one, they may be restored to their Liberty, which we have agreed to, and do therefore recommend it to you to give the Necessary Orders to all our Factors up the River to pay due Obedience to the Same; and as it will be a great Satisfaction to his Friends and Benefactors here to be informed by Letters under his own hand of the Treatment he meets with from you and of his Safe Arrival in his own Country, you are to desire him to write to us by all opportunitys. We are

Your Loving Friends
The Court of Assistants of the Royal
African Co. of England.[1]

Among the general instructions sent out at the same time by the Company there was a paragraph dealing with Job couched in more or less the same terms as those of the letter he himself was to deliver, but in the privacy of this correspondence the Company could be plainer about both their anxiety for Job's welfare and their intentions. After remarking, in order to leave no doubt of his importance, that Job had been taken notice of by 'the King and Queen', as well as by other prominent people, the Company asked particularly that care should be taken to save his goods from loss or embezzlement, and observed that by sending somebody up with him on his return to his own country 'a trade and Correspondence between the Nations of those parts and

---

[1] P.R.O., T.70/55, p. 224.

our highest Factory' might be opened up, a glimpse of the self-interest that underlay the Company's interest in Job. And that there should be no evasion of their injunction that Job should be well treated, the Company's agents were requested to see that Job himself should write by the *Dolphin* on its return, and confirm 'that he had been well used by Capt. Freeman as well as while he stays with you'.[1] Both the Company and Job's private benefactors had now done all they possibly could to protect him at such a distance: when the *Dolphin* finally sailed on 15 July,[2] he was once more entrusted to chance.

The *Dolphin*'s voyage was fortunate. The brisk seas of the Channel widened into the unconfined waters of the Atlantic; Teneriffe hove in sight, a perfect volcanic cone; and as the Canaries fell astern, the presence of the West African coast could be detected in the set of the currents and in a variation in the light, and in other special signs. The sea thickened and lost its luminosity as it met the brown streams discharged by the Gambia, and suddenly the low undistinguished shorelines of Barrah and Cumbo were to be seen on either side.

On 7 August one of the usual tragedies took place at James Fort. John Shuckforth, a writer, only eight months out from England, died and was buried in the evening at Gillyfree. The mourners had just returned to the fort when they saw a vessel coming up the river, but at such a distance, in the late light, it was hardly possible to see whether she was one of the Company's, carrying mail and supplies from home. The ship sent up its longboat at about midnight to announce that she was the Company's snow, the *Dolphin*, and the officers at the fort were later able to report back to London that Captain Freeman 'arrived here the 7th August with his papers, cargo and passengers agreeable to list, Invoice and Bills of lading, and all in good condition and order'.[3] The *Dolphin* stood off the fort the following day at noon and saluted with nine guns. Nine guns were fired in return. Captain Freeman, four writers, an apprentice to the Company, 'and one Black Man, by name Job ben Solomon, a Pholey of Bundo in Foota', then all went ashore.[4] Job had most improbably returned to the Gambia, in the space of four years.

Among the soldiers and civilians and Company slaves who crowded down at the jetty to see the newcomers step ashore was Francis Moore, who had noted in his journal the date of the *Arabella*'s sailing for

[1] P.R.O., T.70/55, p. 221.
[2] *Read's Weekly Journal*, 20 July 1734.
[3] P.R.O., T.70/4, p. 118.   [4] Moore, p. 202.

Maryland on 11 April 1731. Moore now learnt about Job's strange history for the first time and, like everyone else who had happened to meet him, took a great liking to him. The Company's officers closely followed their instructions to treat him well and when they found that he had no sheets to sleep on while he was living at the fort, they arranged for some to be made for him at a cost of £1. 10s. 0d.[1]

Job himself was intensely anxious to get news home to his father and wives of his safe arrival, and as messages could be more readily sent overland from places higher up the river than from the fort, it was decided that he should travel to Cower, where he had once been sold to Captain Pyke, in company with Francis Moore, who was taking up an appointment as chief factor at the Company's factory at Joar. Richard Hull and Hugh Hamilton, the Company's chief merchants, particularly required Moore in his instructions to use Job 'with the greatest Respect, and all the Civility you possibly can'.[2]

They left James Island in the evening of 23 August in a sloop, the *Flame*, heavily laden with the goods Moore needed to restock the factory at Joar. The *Flame* saluted the fort with five guns, receiving five in reply. The voyage up river was slow, the waters having already begun to rise with the rains, and the sloop did not make the opening to the creek at Damasensa until 26 August. Damasensa was the trading place not far from where Job had been kidnapped, and Moore agreed that they should put in to give Job a chance of meeting his friends and astounding them with his reappearance. Leaving the sloop moored in the river, they went up the creek in a yawl; as they passed under the trees they disturbed a troop of brilliantly blue and red-coloured monkeys, so agile that the natives believed they never set foot to ground.

They reached Damasensa and then there occurred an extraordinary coincidence. As they were sitting in the evening under the bentang tree, six or seven of the same men who had panyarred Job and his servant strolled past. Moore had thought Job to be a quiet-tempered man, but at the sight of his old enemies he was almost beside himself with rage and, clutching his pistols and broadsword, wanted to attack and kill them on the spot. Moore recognized at once the extreme precariousness of their position, but it was only with much ado that he could hold Job back, urging upon him the certain consequences to them of any rash action. He managed to quieten him down at last, and persuaded him to call the men over and question them about himself, without revealing his identity. The men answered willingly

[1] P.R.O., T.70/1451, p. 244.   [2] Moore, p. 205.

enough and told the truth, as far as Job was concerned. As for their king, they said, he was dead; killed most strangely. Among the goods he had been paid by Captain Pyke as the price for Job and Loumein Yoai was a pistol, which he had taken to wearing loaded, hanging from a string round his neck. One day it had gone off accidentally and lodged a ball in his throat, killing him instantly. When Job heard this he was so overcome that he fell to his knees and thanked Mahomet for using the king's ill-gotten gains as the means of destroying him. 'Mr. *Moore*, you see now God Almighty was displeas'd at this Man's making me a Slave, and therefore made him die by the very Pistol for which he sold me', he exclaimed, turning to his companion; 'yet I ought to forgive him,' he went on, beginning to explore the moral complexities of the situation, 'because had I not been sold, I should neither have known any thing of the *English* Tongue, nor have had any of the fine, useful and valuable Things I now carry over, nor have known that in the World there is such a Place as *England*, nor such noble, good and generous People as Queen *Caroline*, Prince *William*, the Duke of *Montague*, the Earl of *Pembroke*, Mr. *Holden*, Mr. *Oglethorpe*, and the Royal *African* Company.'[1]

After this highly satisfactory incident, Job and Moore crossed upstream to Joar, where they arrived on 1 September. Moore promptly found a Fula who knew Job's father and engaged him to deliver a message telling him of Job's return, but asking him not to travel from Bondou to meet him, for, as Job himself expressed it, 'it was fit for the Young to go to the Old, and not for the Old to come to the Young'.[2] Job also sent messages and presents to his wives by the same messenger and asked him to bring his favourite child back with him on his return.

Job had little to do while he waited for the messenger's return and passed the time going about the neighbouring villages with Moore as he traded. Moore found him particularly useful, for he not only spoke handsomely of the English and gave a good notion of their power, but 'what he said, took away a great deal of the Horror of the *Pholeys* for

---

[1] Moore, pp. 206–7. These sentiments greatly annoyed Thomas Green, the editor of Astley's *Voyages*, and he commented tartly (ii. 237 n.): 'The Folly and Vanity of this Man must have been very great, to suppose that God should punish this King merely to revenge the Injury done him, and yet let his having made Slaves of hundreds of others, go unpunished. *Job* had shewn more Humility, if not more sense, if he had imputed his own Slavery as a Punishment for dealing in Slaves himself, and selling his two Brother-Negros to the Whites; though believing, that they would be eaten or murdered: Which . . . was the *Fuli*'s Opinion.'
[2] Moore, p. 207.

the State of Slavery among the *English*; for they before generally
imagined, that all who were sold for Slaves, were generally either
eaten or murdered, since none returned'.[1] Job also traded on his own
account: he bought a woman slave—and two horses, in readiness for
his return. While at Joar, he made himself very popular by his devout-
ness and affability, and his generosity in giving away among the Fula
many sheets of the much coveted paper. But he could afford to be
generous, having brought back such a considerable wealth in goods.
He returned to James Island on 26 September to look after his goods,
sailing in the *Flame* which was carrying a load of corn to the fort.
Moore promised to let him know at once when the messenger returned
and to send out other messengers in case the first miscarried. Other
messengers were dispatched,[2] but Job was still kept waiting for news.
Nearly two months later, on 13 November, Richard Hull, Governor
at James Fort, was remarking at the end of a letter to Moore: 'I desire
you would send me a Line or two as to what *Fody Cojear* has done
relating to letting *Job*'s Friends know of his being here, and to desire
you to let me know if he has sent a Messenger, and when expected
back; in doing which you will oblige *Job*, (who gives his Service to you)
and, Sir, your humble Servant....'[3] But an answer had still not been
received when Moore himself, who had been ill with a heavy cold and
a sore throat, decided to travel down to James Fort in the *Flame*, with
twelve slaves. He arrived at the Island on 3 December.

Job had sent messages home, but he had also been writing to his
friends in England. On 8 December he wrote to Sir Hans Sloane in
Arabic, with an English version attached, dating the letter as from
'James Fort Rio Gambia'.

I give you my service greatly [he began]; You have done great favour ...
and are my best friend, and I wish you long life. I wish God may bless
you ... Mussulmen here love you very heartily, and pray for you. I
wish you ... happiness in this world and the world to come. I always
remember you ... Prayers both day and night. You have been as a Father
to me in my ... I wish from my heart all that you have may prosper. I am
very well ... sent me here to Gov. Hull and Mr. Orfeur and they take a great
deal of no[tice] ... and do any thing that lies in their power for me. I am
still here but have [sent] ... Letters into my own Countrey and wait for ye
messenger's return. I am wi[th] ... Respect, Sir, Your most obedient and
most humble...[4]

---

[1] ibid. p. 208.   [2] ibid. p. 219.   [3] ibid. p. 217.
[4] B.M., Sloane MS. 4053, f. 341. The MS. is damaged along the outer edge and
the omission points and readings within square brackets mark where the text is
affected.

The primitive simplicity of the sentiments contrasts as strangely with the formal salutation as the fort where the letter was written would compare with the Bloomsbury to which it was bound.

On 9 December the Company's snow, the *Success*, arrived from Holland with a good cargo. A young writer, Thomas Hilton, came out in the *Success*. He was at once attached to Francis Moore and they set out together for Joar in the *Flame* on 26 December, a speedy end to the Christmas celebrations. Job went with them, taking some of his goods. When they were lying off Elephant's Island, below Damasensa Creek, they heard the news that Boomey Haman Seaca had taken the field against his brother, the king of Barsally, and upon his advancing on Joar everyone had fled, including the servants at the Company's factory, which was now lying undefended. Moore took a canoe and straight away crossed over to Joar to find out what had happened. As Job had nothing to gain by once more endangering himself, he asked to be put ashore from the *Flame* at a village called Indea, about six miles above Damasensa, where he proposed to stay until it was safe to cross.

Moore found when he got to Joar that though the villagers had fled, the factory itself and its stores were untouched and in good condition. The Boomey was in the field, at Sanjally, a town about a half-day's journey away. Moore promptly sent him some brandy and a hanger as a present, and the Boomey returned his thanks with the expected assurance that he never meditated harming white men, especially his old friend Mr. Moore, whom he remembered so well from their meeting in 1731—a recollection which might not have reassured Moore of his intended kindness.[1] But Moore had other more immediate worries than the Boomey's intentions. Thomas Hilton, his new assistant, had already fallen ill of a fever; on 21 January he died, forty-four days after landing on James Island from England. Moore buried him with decent care under an orange tree in the garden of the factory.

While it was uncertain whether or not Boomey Haman Seaca would advance further towards Joar, Job wisely stayed in safety at Indea, but as soon as the campaign seemed about to end, he thought he might risk himself alongside Moore and travelled up to the factory. He had still not heard from home and the hostilities along the river suggested that conditions further inland might be too dangerous for travel; but at last and unexpectedly, on 14 February, one of the messengers Moore had dispatched to Bondou returned with news and letters.

[1] See above, pp. 36–7.

Job had not seen his home for four years and while the time had ended in unexpected prosperity for him, the news he now received was of misfortune and hard times. His father was dead, though he had lived long enough to get the letters Job had written to him from London; and one of his wives had married again, believing him dead. On learning of Job's arrival in the Gambia the second husband had absconded. But these personal griefs and irritations were as nothing to the fate that had overtaken his country. During his absence, an interregnum of civil disorder had been ended by the Sisibe family's successful attempt to reassert its authority, but Bondou had been devastated by a terrible war in the process.[1] Once it had been famous for its herds; now there was hardly a head of cattle left in the land. Several of his old acquaintances came down with the messenger to welcome him and these 'he was exceeding glad to see; but notwithstanding the Joy he had to see his Friends, he wept grievously for his Father's Death, and the Misfortunes of his Country. He forgave his Wife, and the Man that had taken her; *For*, says he, *Mr.* Moore, *she could not help thinking I was dead, for I was gone to a Land from whence no Pholey ever yet returned; therefore she is not to be blamed, nor the Man neither*. For three or four Days he held a Conversation with his Friends without any Interruption, unless to sleep or eat.'[2]

Now that he had had news from home Job began to make preparations for his return, but he agreed first to accompany Governor Richard Hull up river to the important trading centre of Yanimarew, and thence inland in the hope of opening up a trade in gum arabic. Hull arrived at Joar for this purpose on 16 March in the sloop *James*. Francis Moore was also about to return home. The Court of Assistants in London had written to the Gambia on 7 November instructing the Governor to allow Moore to return if he so wished, 'first settling his accounts with the Company'.[3] The Governor had brought up Thomas Johnson, Moore's successor as chief factor at Joar, with him in the *James*.

Moore was able to leave Joar at the beginning of April and Job took the opportunity of sending back letters to his English friends. He was not able to write in English himself, but his greetings—rather than letters—were taken down for him at his dictation. His letter on this occasion to the Duke of Montagu, dated Joar Factory, the 5th April, was probably taken down by Moore himself:

This comes to give my duty to your Grace [it begins], praying God to

---

[1] See Curtin, *Africa Remembered*, pp. 27–8.   [2] Moore, p. 224.
[3] P.R.O., T.70/55, p. 231.

bless you for what you have done for me. All the Mussulmen here pray for you. This comes by Mr. Moore, late a factor in the Company's Service, who came up hither along with me, and has taken a great deal of care of me, and used me as his Brother, for which I should be glad to hear of your doing good for him. I am still in Gambia; have heard news from Bundo that my Father is dead, and one of my Wives married, the Bearer will inform you more of my Affairs than anybody else, he having been here trading for the Company these six or seven months. My duty to the King and Queen and all the Royal Family. I heartily pray to God to bless your Grace . . . . P.S. I hope your Grace will not forget my Servant and fellow Slave who is in Maryland.[1]

Moore sailed three days later, on 8 April, in the *James*. Governor Hull came down to the wharf to see him off, and so did Job. Job had given him the letters to the Duke of Montagu and James Oglethorpe and to several more of his friends, and he particularly asked Moore to assure them that he would be later writing at length to report to them what happened to him after he at last reached home. He parted from Moore with tears in his eyes and as the sloop disappeared round the curve of the great empty river, so vanished his last immediate connection with his year as a guest in England.

Moore took four days to reach James Island and on 13 May, having cleared his accounts, he embarked for England in the *Dolphin*, still under command of Captain Freeman. One of his fellow passengers was Hugh Hamilton, one of the chief merchants, also fortunate in returning, and it was in his honour that the fort saluted the *Dolphin* with nine guns as she weighed anchor. The sea breezes were so strong that the *Dolphin* took two days to make the mouth of the river, but once they were out at sea the gales blew favourably and the voyage was speedy. The only untoward happenings were the death of James Ellis, the 'martyr to rum', and a chase by a man-of-war, the *Edinburgh*. The *Edinburgh* brought the *Dolphin* to with a shot and put a lieutenant on board. He took away the three best sailors and left three others in their stead.

Moore landed at Deal on 13 July, exactly two months after leaving James Island. He stayed that night at Deal and another at Gravesend and took a boat up to London the following day. He wrote from London to his mother in Worcester and by return of post he had a 'kind letter' from her, 'expressing the Joy and Satisfaction she received by hearing of the Return of her Son, whom she had for four or five Years past never expected to see again; and in the same Letter

---

[1] *Hist. MSS. Comm.*, xlv. 385.

she sent me the melancholy Account of my Father's Death, as likewise of two Brothers and a Sister, and several other near Relations,
since the Year 1730, of which I never before had received the least
Account.'[1]

Change and Mortality, the constant attendants on Time, had been
as active in Moore's absence as they had been in Job's. Moore's
gratitude for his unexpected return from a country 'which our *English*
People most of them think so unhealthy, that White People cannot
live there',[2] was as sincere as Job's at his redemption from what was
equally believed by his own people to be a certain early grave. After
settling his account with the Royal African Company, Moore went
down to Worcester in September, 'where I was kindly received by my
old Acquaintance, and returned GOD Thanks, who thro' so many
Dangers had brought me back in Safety to my Friends, Relations, and
native Country.'[3]

[1] Moore, p. 234.   [2] ibid. p. 233.   [3] ibid. p. 234.

CHAPTER FIVE

Savages: Noble or Accursed?

JOB BEN SOLOMON had hardly returned to the Gambia before his friend Thomas Bluett published a short account of him, in November 1734. *Some Memoirs of the Life of Job, the Son of Solomon the High Priest of Boonda in Africa* was, according to Bluett himself, written at Job's behest, expressly to acknowledge the Duke of Montagu's kindness to him. The pamphlet was therefore appropriately dedicated to the Duke.

Bluett's account provides most of the details of Job's stay in England, but it is too short and the last moralizing section could have been spared for the sake of more facts. In concluding, Bluett affirmed that as there is 'a divine Œconomy of Things', we must believe that all events are directed by Providence towards an ultimate good, a view that Job himself found consoling in adversity. The good that might be arrived at by way of Job's strange and apparently unfortunate adventure could be the improvement of his people's condition, by the application of what he had learnt of practical use during his visit, and also the expansion of English trade through his goodwill and influence. A further advantage that had certainly been enjoyed by those who had helped him had been the opportunity of exercising hospitality, a mundane reflection of Divine benevolence. The simplicity and sincerity of Bluett's views show the qualities that made him such a fervent and disinterested friend to Job.

A noticeable and even surprising feature of Bluett's account of Job, given his evangelical and pious views, is his uncritical acceptance of slavery. He clearly believed that Job was unjustly sold into captivity and suffered some unwarrantable inconveniences while a slave in Maryland, but though regretting what had happened in this particular instance, he gives no sign of considering slavery as being in itself a deplorable and outrageous institution. He may have felt himself to be in an awkward position, since Job himself trafficked without scruple in slaves, but if such were his feelings, they ought to have come through in a touch or two of irony, if not in outright disapproval. No one need be expected necessarily to be in advance of his age, but one might think that Bluett's religious views and personal kindness would have inclined him to condemn slavery, especially as Job's stay in England coincided with the beginning of the anti-slavery movement.

Thomas Clarkson himself dated the rise of the movement from 1735, when John Atkins's *A Voyage to Guinea, Brasil, and the West-Indies* was published. But Atkins, a surgeon in the Royal Navy, was describing a voyage that he had made more than ten years before and was probably encouraged to publish when he did by the popular interest that had suddenly begun to be taken in Nigritia and its notorious trade. Of course, protests against slavery were not being raised for the first time in the 1730s. Such a blatant offence against humanity and liberty had long been condemned on sentimental, philosophical, and religious grounds. Aphra Behn's interpretation of the African character may have been theatrical rather than real, but Oroonoko's motives and feelings are sufficiently plausible and natural to make the tale of his humiliation and excruciating fate a powerful means of persuading the uncommitted to view the trade with horror, especially when it was given a more tolerable form by Southerne in his popular play.

Stories like Oroonoko's were frequently told as though they were fact, but while the cruelties they retailed could undoubtedly have happened, they often read like fiction. One account widely printed was of a slave arriving in Virginia to find a planter about to administer three hundred lashes to another slave for attempted escape. The newcomer recognized in the culprit his old companion and saviour in some African war and begged the planter to spare him, or allow him to be beaten in his place. In a fury of challenged authority, the planter ordered each in turn to whip the other, and when they nobly refused, prepared to punish them himself. At this, the new Negro drew a knife, stabbed the planter to the heart and afterwards stabbed himself, 'rejoicing with his last Breath, that he had reveng'd his Friend, and rid the World of such a Monster'.[1]

Such heroics may seem too obviously intended as propaganda to please us, suspicious as we have had to become of the timely disclosure of atrocities, but the story John Atkins had to tell of the punishment Captain Harding inflicted on the courageous and determined Negro, Captain Tomba, and his companions, cannot be dismissed as one of the progeny of Mrs. Behn's fervent imagination. The lashes

[1] *London Magazine*, 1745, pp. 495–6.

that scarified Tomba's shoulders were lashes indeed, described by a ship's surgeon who had had a long professional experience of bloody backs. Nevertheless, when Atkins's anecdote was read, the significance that Oroonoko had acquired was transferred to Tomba, elevating him to a figure of representative proportions.

But the idea of Oroonoko had advanced by Atkins's day far beyond Aphra Behn's original conception. In spite of all her heroics, Mrs. Behn's view of the character is strangely matter-of-fact. The royal African may sigh and languish after the fair Imoinda in too fashionable a manner to square with the behaviour and sentiments of the Dark Continent, and when his virtue is put to the test he may respond as an ancient Roman might have done, but Mrs. Behn's imagination had a literalness which allowed her to describe courage and pain as they are, and the reader of today finds himself struck by her realism. As Mrs. Behn presents them, Oroonoko and his fate were too bold and harsh to persuade all her readers to sympathize with him and want to champion his cause.

Southerne did much to make Oroonoko a popular figure by his play, but it was Steele and Addison who were largely responsible for making the character a tolerable and potent symbol of his race, in spite of their never actually citing Oroonoko by name. Two of the *Spectator* papers bore directly on the West Indies and slavery. The first paper, Number 11, by Steele, is the more important, though none of the characters in its story is an African. 'Inkle and Yarico' is the most famous of the tales in the *Spectator*. It was turned into poems and novelettes and plays and translated into all the European languages, in one or more of these forms, and its influence was continuous and widespread throughout the century.

The story tells of how Thomas Inkle, a disingenuous and handsome young English merchant, is saved by an Indian girl, Yarico, from massacre at the hands of her tribe. Yarico hides and protects him and together they escape to Barbados. But when Inkle considers how much money he must be out of pocket after being idle for so many months, he sells Yarico to a Barbadian merchant, in spite of her pathetically declaring that she is with child—indeed, 'he only made use of that information, to rise in his Demands upon the Purchaser'. The elements of the story are immoral and brutal, but Steele made them acceptable at the tea-table by his remarkable literary tact and skilful infusion of sentiment. Yarico could be discussed and wept over where the names of other women, who found themselves in her condition for like reasons, were unmentionable; and Inkle could be openly reprobated as unusually horrid, by people who would never have admitted that the common practice of planters' selling their offspring by slave women could be decently introduced into general conversation. The story was actually supposed to have been told to Mr. Spectator by Arietta, a fashionable woman of 'gaiety and prudence', who was pleased that Yarico's misfortune should bring tears to her listener's eyes. Steele enabled the moral implications of slavery, as they affected the feelings, to be examined under the guise of a pleasing fiction.

Yarico is an Indian, not an African; but as Inkle sells her into slavery in the West Indies where only Africans were slaves—the native Indians earlier enslaved having failed to survive—her story hinted at the desperate condition of the Negroes and directed sympathy where it could still be useful. But Steele's indirect approach was strongly reinforced by Addison's open defence of the African character in a later *Spectator*, Number 215. Unfortunately, while this paper is an issue of Addison's charitable heart and refined sentiments, and, given the extraordinary and profound influence of the *Spectator* throughout the century, cannot but have helped the Africans' cause, it carried moral and cultural implications that helped to do almost as much harm as good.

Addison begins the essay in his usual ingratiating and philosophical manner by reminding his reader of Aristotle's theory of realization and his notion 'that a Statue lies hid in a Block of Marble; and that the Art of the Statuary only clears away the superfluous Matter, and removes the Rubbish'. Compare education with sculpture, Addison urges, and we see that it brings out the proper man lodged in the rude mass, especially in the instance of savage peoples, where implicit in their wild qualities are heroic and civilized virtues; looking at these children of nature with a reflective eye, must we not remark 'Courage exerting itself in Fierceness, Resolution in Obstinacy, Wisdom in Cunning, Patience in Sullenness and Despair'.

The African slaves in the West Indies offered Addison the exact illustration he required. They would hang themselves out of grief on the death of their masters, or upon changing their service, and who could forbear admiring such fidelity, and similar instances of a 'Savage Greatness of Soul'? 'And what Colour of Excuse can there be for the Contempt with which we treat this Part of our species; that we should not put them upon the common foot of Humanity, that we should only set an insignificant Fine upon the Man who murders them; nay, that we should as much as in us lies, cut them off from the Prospects of

Happiness in another World as well as in this, and deny them that which we look upon as the proper Means for attaining it?'

At this point, where he seems to threaten a sermon, Addison tells a story that in its horrible detail resembles Oroonoko's murder of Imoinda. Two Negroes on the Leeward Islands were friends and in love with the same girl. As neither could bear to give her up, they walked with her into the woods and stabbed her to the heart, before turning their knives on themselves. 'Though the Action which I have recited is in itself full of Guilt and Horror,' Addison admonishes, 'it proceeded from a Temper of Mind which might have produced very noble Fruits, had it been informed and guided by a suitable Education.'

The paper is an excellent example of Addison's tact; of his skill in calling in turn upon the mind and the heart, so that once a principle is asserted the appropriate feelings are introduced for its nourishment. The bland and varied style does not allow the reader time, or give him an occasion, to demur. Slavery—or, rather, the conditions of slavery—are condemned; not openly, but implicitly, by showing that the Negroes are essentially superior to what they seem, and that they deserve to be pitied and helped to rise above themselves rather than to be treated to blows. Addison's motives were good and his means effective, but by emphasizing the slave's supposed fidelity to his white master as a reason for sympathy and by describing his character as inchoate, he helped to establish the image of the African as a servant and a child, to be morally and culturally condescended to; an attitude that has helped to destroy the harmony that ought to have been maintained between whites and blacks. The thrashings and tortures that were applied to Oroonoko were a brutal compliment paid to his indomitable spirit, and if you are a man it may be better to be beaten like one, rather than to be led forward by the hand like a child.

The story of Inkle and Yarico and the account of the Negro friends' savagery in love were the only *Spectators* addressed directly at the slave trade, but all the *Spectators*, in helping to curb brutality and encourage tolerance, in refining manners and fostering sympathy, made it impossible to accept atrocities in silence. But feelings are changeable unless there are principles to which they can adhere, and those stimulated by Addison and Steele might have proved to be merely fashionable, had they not been supported by certain stern assumptions.

The Christian conscience, Roman Catholic and Protestant, employed several arguments to allay the qualms that slavery caused it.

The Negroes were enslaved justly in their own sovereign countries by being taken prisoner in their own national wars, or incurred slavery as punishment for crimes, or became slaves by voluntarily putting themselves up for sale. As they could be freely bought and sold, the European was also entitled to deal in them. But even had slavery been forbidden at law, it could still be defended on the principle of *salus populi suprema lex*—so many interests essential to the physical and moral welfare of so many different people depending entirely on its maintenance. In the case of Great Britain and its colonies, the slave trade had become an integral part of the system's whole economy; abolish slavery and the economy would collapse. And should these arguments smack too much of compromising with the world, slavery could not be condemned as breaking God's law, the Bible nowhere expressly forbidding it.[1]

Such arguments, developed with skill and easily referable to matters as they stood in all their complexity, convinced many Christians—at first, the majority of Christians. The Society for the Propagation of the Gospel, one of the few vital parts of the Established Church at the time, had no hesitation in accepting in 1710 a plantation in Barbados under the terms of Colonel Codrington's will, with its injunction that the Society must continuously employ at least three hundred Negro slaves. 'The laws of God do not forbid the keeping of Christian slaves', declared Bishop Fleetwood, preaching on the subject in 1711; 'nor do the laws of the land. Therefore, in the words of St. Paul, "Let every man abide in the same calling wherein he was called." '[2] But the Bishop left it in no doubt that the Society's slaves would become Christians and that they were 'equally the workmanship of God, endued with the same faculties and intellectual powers, bodies of the same flesh and blood and souls certainly as immortal'.[3]

The argument that because slavery had not been condemned by the Gospel it ought to be tolerable to Christians was one, however, that a growing number of Christians began to find increasingly unacceptable, as the facts about the slave trade became more widely known. The way in which the Gospel was instinctively construed as opposing slavery is shown in the belief that once a slave was baptized he could no longer remain a slave, a belief as widespread in Maryland, for instance, and the West Indies, as in London. In the American colony, the Act passed in 1671 'to Encourage the Importation of Negroes',

---

[1] I am summarizing the argument as it is outlined by H. A. Wyndham in *The Atlantic and Slavery*, 1935, pp. 233–7.
[2] Quoted by Wyndham, p. 236.   [3] ibid.

specifically affirmed that, even if baptized, slaves and their issue were always to remain slaves;[1] but in spite of such reassurances, and the comfortable doctrine of ecclesiastics like Bishop Fleetwood, many planters declined evangelizing their slaves out of self-interest. At home, where self-interest in the maintenance of the slave trade was not so easily recognized, the 'mob', under the impression that to christen a Negro was promptly to set him free, would gang up to prevent runaways from arrest by their masters.[2]

The hostile and highly emotional interpretation of the Gospel put the slaveholders in a dilemma. If they helped towards the conversion of their slaves, they might be destroying their right in their property; but if they deliberately kept them in ignorance, they seemed to be admitting the power of the Gospel to set men free, in addition to laying themselves open to the charge of wilfully and selfishly endangering the salvation of countless human souls. The consequences of flouting the sensibilities and questioning the assumptions of a Christian society were so serious that the slaveholders and their associates began to justify the trade as a gigantic rescue operation on behalf of Christianity.

Such an excuse was as old as the slave trade itself. The Negroes may lament that they have exchanged freedom for servitude, exclaimed the Portuguese chronicler, Eannes de Azurara, in 1450, but they ought rather to consider that they were then the captives of sin, to 'the perdition of their souls'.[3] Eannes de Azurara's simple argument was refurbished in the eighteenth century and was put forward most fully and unambiguously by John Barbot. The slaves' condition in their own countries was so appalling, Barbot affirmed, that it was a kindness to ship them to the West Indies and more considerate masters; not to mention', he goes on, 'the inestimable advantage they may reap of becoming Christians, and saving their souls, if they make a true use of their condition; whereof some instances might be brought: tho' it must be owned, they are very hard to be brought to a true notion of the Christian religion, and much less to be prevail'd on to live up to its holy rules; being naturally very stupid and sensual, and so apt to continue till their end, without the least concern for a future state of eternal bliss, or misery, according as they have lived in this

---

[1] See Elizabeth Donnan, *Documents Illustrative of the History of the Slave Trade to America*, 1935, iv. 9–10.

[2] See J. Fielding, *Penal Laws*, 1768, pp. 144–5; quoted by George, p. 135.

[3] Gomes Eannes de Azurara, *The Chronicle of the Discovery and Conquest of Guinea*, trans. C. R. Beazley and E. Prestage, 1896, ii. 201.

world.'[1] Barbot admits that the Protestant slaveholders were shirking their Christian duty—the Roman Catholics had always maintained extensive missions—but he alleged in excuse the difficulty of teaching slaves English as a necessary preliminary to their conversion, as well as the fear that baptism would set them free, a view that Barbot most strongly opposed. But he urged the planters to discharge their obligations, if only with an eye to getting more tractable slaves. 'The maxims of Christianity would doubtless be a curb to their rude temper, and the planters might expect the blessing of heaven on their plantations, as a reward of their charitable endeavours to convert those gross pagans from their deplorable state of depravation in all malice and vileness towards God and man.'[2]

Barbot's argument was too coarse and cynical to bear exact repetition, but in a modified form it was useful in quietening those who opposed the trade on Christian grounds. 'For, by purchasing, or rather *ransoming* the Negroes from their *national Tyrants* and transplanting them under the benign Influences of the *Law*, and *Gospel*,' a writer in *Common Sense* argued in 1740, 'they are advanced to much greater Degrees of Felicity, tho' not to absolute Liberty.'[3] But while such ideas might satisfy the temporizing Christian, they were dismissed with contempt by the scrupulous, who asked whether the usual means of conversion were men whose behaviour would fit fiends from hell. Daniel Defoe, in his satire *The Reformation of Manners*, reflected bitingly on the hypocrisy of the argument. The cruelty of the Spanish *conquistadores* was as nothing to the slaveholders':

> Blood quench'd *their* Thirst, and it suffic'd to kill:
> But these the tender *Coup de Grace* deny,
> And make Men beg in vain for leave to die;
> To more than *Spanish* Cruelty inclin'd,
> Torment the Body, and debauch the Mind:
> The ling'ring Life of Slavery preserve,
> And vilely teach them both to sin and serve.
> In vain they talk to them of Shades below,
> They fear no Hell *but where such Christians go*;
> Of *Jesus Christ* they very often hear,
> Often as his Blaspheming Servants Swear;
> They hear and wonder what strange Gods they be,
> Can bear with Patience such Indignity:
> They look for Famines, Plagues, Disease and Death,
> Blasts from above, and Earthquakes from beneath:

[1] Churchill, v. 270.   [2] ibid. p. 271.
[3] Quoted in *London Magazine*, 1740, p. 493.

> But when they see regardless Heaven looks on,
> They curse our Gods, or think that we have none.
> Thus thousands to Religion are brought o'er,
> And made worse Devils than they were before.[1]

The sedate Quakers, with charitable eye fixed fast on justice, would not accept a convenient interpretation of the Gospel; nor would the growing body of Methodists, who swamped the slaveholders' subtleties as they sang of the universal democracy of those redeemed by their dear Saviour's blood:

> The servile progeny of Ham
>   Seize as the purchase of thy blood!
> Let all the Heathens know thy name:
>   From idols to the living God
> The dark Americans convert,
> And shine in every Pagan heart.

But the ordinary Christian, the conservative churchman, was just as appalled as his brothers at extremes. The consequences of Henry the Navigator's discoveries have been so awful, Dr. Johnson averred, introducing a collection of voyages, that he himself would have wished they had never been. 'The *Europeans* have scarely visited any coast, but to gratify avarice, and extend corruption; to arrogate dominion without right, and practice cruelty without incentive.' The only happy consequence might be the conversion of these unfortunate peoples to Christianity, 'though its progress cannot but be slow, when it is so much obstructed by the lives of Christians'.[2] Barbot's argument had some strange and dangerous consequences, as Wesley's verse and Johnson's sombre observation ought to suggest.

The Christian objection to slavery was reinforced by the civil. A word can as easily be a metaphor as a token, and while 'slave' might denote no more than a particular class of persons, it also came to represent in English idiom not only those Englishmen who fawned on holders of political power and could be bought with a pension, but all those peoples who had not the good fortune to enjoy the native rights of a true-born Englishman. 'Slavery is so vile and miserable an estate of man,' wrote John Locke in his *Treatise on Civil Government* in 1690, 'and so directly opposite to the generous temper and courage of our nation, that it is hardly to be conceived that an "Englishman," much less a "gentleman," should plead for it.'[3]

---

[1] *Collected Writings*, 1703, pp. 77–8.
[2] *The World Displayed*, 4th. ed., 1774, i. xvi–xvii.
[3] Quoted by R. Coupland, *The British Anti-Slavery Movement*, 1933, p. 41.

Locke's view was increasingly to prevail until it became absolute.

Locke expressed himself with the certainty of a theorist who assumes that the law is on his side, but in fact the law was ambiguous,[1] and it was on account of this ambiguity that Yorke and Talbot were enabled to reassert, in their notorious opinion of 1729, the right of masters over slaves introduced into England. The opinion maintained uncertainty as to the state of the law, but it had no effect on lovers of liberty. Ephraim Chambers categorically asserted in the second edition of his great *Cyclopædia* of 1738 that slavery is 'absolutely abolished in England', and added, 'It is said, that the moment a *slave* steps on English ground, he becomes free.'[2] William Blackstone, in his *Commentaries* of 1765, did not entirely confirm Chambers's view, but he acknowledged that 'The spirit of liberty is so deeply implanted in our constitution and rooted even in our very soil, that a slave or Negro, the moment he lands in England, falls under the protection of the law and so far becomes a freeman, though his master's right to his servitude may possibly still continue.'[3] But even Blackstone's qualification did not stand long. In 1765 the country had been singing for nearly thirty years the most famous of national odes, James Thomson's 'Rule, Britannia', and assuring themselves time and again to the tune of Arne's music that 'Britons never will be slaves'. The term 'slave' had become so opprobrious that it could no longer be decently attached to anyone under British rule. The famous Somerset case of 1771 and 1772 made it a truism that 'the moment a *slave* steps on English ground, he becomes free'.

The Negro gained a legal status at the expense of his national character. Montesquieu remarked on slavery in 1748, with his usual keen wisdom, that 'It is impossible for us to suppose these creatures to be men, because, allowing them to be men, a suspicion would follow that we ourselves are not Christians.'[4] The denigration of the Negro can be traced back beyond Christ into antiquity, and those who wished to show that his moral complexion was as unchanging as his skin were always ready with appropriate classical tags,[5] but such prejudices were not elevated into deliberate opinion until the slave trade had to be justified.

William Bosman, a Dutch factor on the Guinea coast, published in 1705 *A New and Accurate Description of the Coast of Guinea*, an account that was generally accepted for a long time as 'the most per-

---

[1] See George, pp. 135 and 361, n. 78.   [2] Chambers, *s.v.* 'slave'.
[3] Quoted by George, p. 361, n. 78.
[4] Quoted by Coupland, p. 41.   [5] See above, p. 7.

fect' and useful history of West Africa.[1] Bosman dismissed the Negro character out of hand, and his view became a commonplace. In 1732 two very important books on West Africa appeared. Thomas Phillips's journal of a slaving voyage made in 1693 and 1694 was then first published in a new edition of Churchill's *Voyages*, and John Barbot's extensive survey of the whole length of the West African coast—in part observation, in part compilation—also appeared in the same collection. Phillips was not as specific in his dismissal of the Negroes' character as Barbot, but his description of African society gives the unambiguous impression that in his opinion, too, the Negroes were 'generally extremely sensual, knavish, revengeful, impudent, lyars, impertinent, gluttonous, extravagant in their expressions, and giving ill language; luxurious beyond expression, and so intemperate, that they drink brandy as if it were water; deceitful in their dealings with the *Europeans*, and no less with their own neighbours, even to selling of one another for slaves, if they have an opportunity; and . . . so very lazy, that rather than work for their living, they will rob and commit murders on the highways, and in the woods and desarts . . .'[2]

The cruelty with which they treated their own people was unbelievable. After a battle, Barbot affirmed, prisoners would be slaughtered in the most horrid ways—men, women, and children. Pregnant women would be ripped open up the belly, and, of equal horror, the lower jaw of the male captives would be torn off, leaving the victim 'to perish and starve'. Barbot must have guessed that his word alone might hardly have seemed enough to establish the truth of such an unbelievable atrocity as the second, for he brought forward an authority: 'A *Commendo* man assured me', he claimed, 'he had done so by twenty-three men after a battle; first laying the man down, then cutting his face from the ears to the mouth, and setting his knees on the stomach of the unfortunate wretch, with both hands tore off the under jaw, leaving him in that miserable condition, wallowing in his blood, till he expired; taking the jaws of them all home with him, as testimonies of his bravery. . . .'[3]

An extraordinary account which seemed to confirm Barbot's description of atrocities appeared in 1734, the year of Job ben Solomon's return to the Gambia. Captain William Snelgrave had arrived with the *Katherine* at Whidaw on the Slave Coast at the end of March 1727, only to find that the small and prosperous kingdom had been recently devastated by the highly disciplined and ruthless armies of the martial king of the inland and widely feared kingdom of Dahomey, to the

---

[1] See Snelgrave, p. a4[r].   [2] Churchill, v. 34.   [3] ibid. p. 296.

complete ruination of trade. 'It was a lamentable Story to hear,' Snelgrave observed, 'and a dismal Sight to see, the Desolation of so fine a Country, lately exceeding populous, now destroyed in such a manner by Fire and Sword. The Carnage of the Inhabitants was, above all, a most moving Spectacle, the Fields being strewed with their Bones.'[1] As there was no trade to be found under the circumstances at Whidaw, Snelgrave sailed on down the coast to Jaqueen, a tributary port of the kingdom of Ardra and now of the king of Dahomey, who had also conquered Ardra and was in camp about forty miles inland from Jaqueen.

No sooner had he arrived, in the first week of April, than Snelgrave received a message from the king of Dahomey inviting him to attend him at his camp and making it plain that he would not be allowed to trade if he did not comply. Snelgrave set out in a party on 8 April and they arrived at the king's camp the following morning, travelling all the way in hammocks, the customary mode, or occasionally on horseback for relief. The landscape was desolated by war. When they arrived at the camp, which was pitched beside the ruined capital of Ardra, Snelgrave and his party were greeted by a guard of honour and escorted to the huts prepared for them. The people were a nuisance, crowding around to examine them, never having seen a white man before. Another nuisance was the flies, which made it difficult to eat. 'These Flies, it seems,' Snelgrave almost casually remarks, 'were bred by a great number of dead Men's Heads, which were piled on Stages, not far from our Tent, tho' we did not know so much at that time.'[2]

They passed the stages on their way to court; two large stages heaped with the heads of four thousand Whidaws sacrificed by the Dahomeys to their god, so Snelgrave was told. The Dahomeys liked skulls and their appurtenances. The king's guard—his 'Heroes' or 'Worthies', as they were styled, forty in number—'had about their necks strings of dead Men's Teeth, reaching as low as their middle, both behind and before, in such Quantities, as might furnish all the Barber-Surgeons Shops in *Europe*'. The punishment for their daring to string a tooth of someone they had not killed in battle was death. Snelgrave was greatly impressed. Tell them, he asked the interpreter, that 'they appeared to be a Company of brave Gentlemen, and that I was their humble Servant'.[3] The common soldiers were paid at the rate of five shillings for each of the enemy's heads brought into camp, and as the heads were thrown into a common heap it was thought

---

[1] Snelgrave, p. 19.   [2] ibid. p. 31.   [3] ibid. pp. 2–3.

that the king intended to build a monument to his victories with the accumulated skulls.[1]

While Snelgrave was in the camp about eighteen hundred prisoners were brought in from a country called Tuffoe, which had been devastated by the Dahomeys in revenge for the Tuffoes having dared to attack and slay a convoy in which some of the king's wives had been travelling. The king himself separated the prisoners into three groups: some were to be kept as slaves for his own use, others were to be sold as slaves to the Europeans, and the rest were to be sacrificed to his fetish. Snelgrave watched the sacrifices, which were by decapitation. The head was supposed to be for the king, the blood for the fetish, and the body, which was dragged away out of sight, for the common people. The men seemed unmoved by their fate, but the cries of the women and children were very disturbing. Why were so many old men sacrificed, Snelgrave asked? To deprive the subjected Tuffoes of the advantages of wisdom, came the answer. And the young men, who might have been sold advantageously to the Europeans? To attend in death on the king's wives slain by the Tuffoes.

The peculiar horror of these sacrifices lay in the belief, widespread along the coast, that the Dahomeys were cannibals. On the evening of the sacrifices, Snelgrave passed two great heaps of bodies, amounting to about four hundred in all. The next morning he was told by one of the Negroes who had accompanied him from Jaqueen that the bodies had been taken away by the common people, 'who had boiled and feasted on them, as holy Food'.[2] Snelgrave deliberately went with his interpreter to where the bodies had been and found them gone, except for the blood. When he asked how they had vanished, the interpreter said, with a smile, that the vultures had eaten them. '"That was very extraordinary indeed to swallow Bones and all"', Snelgrave remarked. Snelgrave was under no doubt as to what had happened to the bodies. A ship's surgeon called Robert More, who visited the king's camp shortly after Snelgrave, told him that he had seen human flesh sold publicly in the great market-place. Snelgrave was anxious not to claim anything he had not seen and he had not himself visited the market, but 'I don't doubt but that I should have seen the same, had I gone into that place', he remarked.[3]

Snelgrave's stories of the Dahomeys' cruelty were largely about victims from among the neighbouring tribes, but he had a short and telling anecdote of their cruelty to a European—an Englishman. The Governor of the Royal African Company's factory at Whidaw in 1729

[1] ibid. p. 38.   [2] ibid. p. 52.   [3] ibid. p. 53.

was an imprudent fellow called Testesole. Testesole foolishly schemed
with the deposed king of Whidaw against the king of Dahomey, and in
other ways offended him. The king had him ambushed while he was
visiting the French factory and took him prisoner, though he tried to
escape by hiding in a chest. The king later denied having given orders
to have him put to death, but his gaolers, in spite of having received a
large ransom for him, executed him in the most fearsome manner.
They tied him to the ground, 'where, spreading him on his Belly, they
with sharp knives cut open his Arms, Back, Thighs and Legs in
several places, and filled the Wounds with a mixture of Limejuice,
Salt and Pepper mixed together; which put him to inexpressible
Torment. However, they soon after put him out of his pain, by cutting
off his Head. Then they cut his Body in pieces, broiled them on the
Coals, and eat them.'[1] Snelgrave learnt of Testesole's terrible fate
when he returned to Jaqueen in 1730.

Snelgrave was an ordinary trader engaged in slaving and he recounted the most extraordinary and horrible scenes with a matter-of-
factness that made them even more telling; like a sailor, he had an
excellent natural sense of the virtues of a good story. The report on
his visit to the king of Dahomey's court is told directly and with an
instinctive skill in the introduction of the detail necessary to a complete effect. His style is easy and colloquial, without pretence or
decoration, but he could occasionally bring a scene effortlessly to life
in a way beyond a self-conscious stylist. When the Whidaws fled in
panic before the invading Dahomeys, he remarked that 'the Fields were
covered with them many Miles round, and their black Colour made
them the more conspicuous in a clear sunshiny Day, on a fine flat
champaign Country'.[2] On account of his manner, which seemed to
square with a bluff, decent, shrewd character, Snelgrave's narrative
greatly helped to establish the view of the Negro character as being
thoroughly luxurious and morally corrupt on the coast and cruel and
superstitiously debased inland, away from any ameliorative effect of
European influence.

Snelgrave also immeasurably strengthened the arguments in
favour of the slave trade. He himself remarked to one of the captains
in the Dahomey army that he was surprised so many people were
sacrificed who might otherwise be profitably sold as slaves to the
Europeans. It is the custom, the captain replied, and were the sacrifices to be omitted success would no longer attend on the armies. But
the traders were quick to take Snelgrave's point: surely it was better

[1] ibid. p. 133.   [2] ibid. p. 14.

to work on the peaceful plantations of the West Indies and North America than fatally to co-operate in augmenting the king of Dahomey's mound of whitening skulls? Slavery was, in this view, a great migration of refugees.

Snelgrave also helped the cause of slavery by telling two pathetic anecdotes illustrative of the Negroes' extraordinary callousness towards their own slaves; anecdotes that were to be constantly repeated by the defenders of slavery. The first, which he recounted in his Introduction, a most effective place, belonged to an earlier date, to 1713, when he was trading to Old Calabar. The king invited him to visit him ashore and Snelgrave accepted, but knowing that the tribe had a reputation for being 'fierce brutish cannibals', he went with a guard of ten well-armed sailors in attendance. At one point in the exchange of mutual civilities, Snelgrave suddenly noticed a child of about eighteen months tethered by the leg to a stake and covered with flies. When he asked what the child was there for, he was told that it was to be sacrificed that night to the king's god, Egbo. Mixing a show of force with arguments about human sacrifice being an affront to Heaven, Snelgrave managed to buy the child for the price of 'a bunch of sky-coloured Beads, worth about half a Crown sterling'. On returning to the ship and handing the child over for nursing to a woman, purchased the day before, with milk still in her breasts, Snelgrave found that he had unknowingly given it to its own mother, to their mutual joy. The three hundred Negroes on board were all jubilant when they heard what had happened and sang a song in praise of Snelgrave. 'This affair proved a great service to us,' Snelgrave continued, 'for it gave them a good Notion of white Men; so that we had no Mutiny in our Ship, during the whole Voyage.'[1] And to crown his kindness, Snelgrave sold the mother and child together to a good master in Antigua.

Snelgrave's second anecdote concerned another almost miraculous rescue. When he returned from the king of Dahomey's camp to Jaqueen and began loading the slaves which the king had supplied him with, he was brought two women by the interpreter with the injunction that they were not to be parted or redeemed, at the king's express command. One of the women was about twenty, but the other was past fifty, and suspecting that he was being put upon by the interpreter, Snelgrave refused to purchase them as a pair, whereupon they were led away. The next day, Snelgrave learnt to his horror that the older woman had been sacrificed to the sea. She had been taken out about half a mile in a canoe and dropped overboard tied hand and

[1] ibid. p. a3ᵛ.

foot, to be devoured by the notoriously voracious sharks. But a boat from Snelgrave's ship, happening to put off for shore at almost the same time, saw the woman floating on her back and spouting water out of her mouth. The crew dragged her on board and revived her. Once again Snelgrave benefited, for the woman, who was as sensible as she was grateful, went about among the Negroes saying, 'That as we had shown such kindness to her, first in saving her Life, and since in taking care of her, who might be reckoned an useless Person to us, on account of her Age; so they had all the reason in the World to believe we were much better people than their own Countrymen; and that the strange Stories they had been formerly told of white People, must be false.' She proved especially good at keeping the women quiet, who could make themselves great nuisances. Snelgrave could never learn what her offence had been, but he thought she might have assisted 'some of the King's Women in their Amours'. Once again, he sold her to a good master; again, in Antigua.[1]

The moral of Snelgrave's two pathetic and most cleverly told anecdotes was to illustrate further that the Negroes' treatment of their own slaves was so inhuman that it was a mercy to purchase and transport them. Barbot had urged the same lesson as Snelgrave. The slaves were so 'severely and barbarously treated' that when they were sold to Europeans their bodies were usually found to be covered with scabs and wounds. 'The barbarous usage of those unfortunate wretches,' Barbot roundly affirmed, 'makes it appear, that the fate of such as are bought, and transported from the coast to *America* or other parts of the world, by *Europeans*, is less deplorable than that of those who end their days in their native country.'[2] And since an anecdote is so telling, Barbot capped his argument by relating how he had once bought separately and at different places a whole family: man, wife, three young boys, and a girl. Their joy at being reunited was excessively touching and on arriving at Martinico Barbot sold them all together to a good master, contenting himself with the necessarily lower price.[3]

The pathetic images of the child sacrifice, the rescued woman, and the reunited family were constantly called up to throw an air of charity over the trade, but if these unusual instances seemed too few to exonerate a traffic that was now running into many thousands of slaves a year, the defenders of slavery could readily fall back on the argument that the brutishness and stupidity of the Negro made him fit only to be a slave. The most philosophic statement of the view that the Negro

[1] ibid. pp. 97–106.   [2] Churchill, v. 270.   [3] ibid. pp. 271–2.

was suited rationally only for hard labour was put forward by David Hume in a footnote to his essay 'Of National Character':

I am apt to suspect the negroes, and in general all other species of men [Hume ruminated] . . . to be naturally inferior to the white. There never was a civilized nation of any other complexion than white, nor even any individual eminent either in action or speculation. No ingenious manufactures amongst them, no arts, no sciences. . . . Not to mention our colonies, there are Negroe slaves dispersed all over Europe, of which none ever discovered any symptoms of ingenuity; though low people, without any education, will start up amongst us, and distinguish themselves in every profession. In Jamaica indeed they talk of one negroe as a man of parts and learning; but 'tis likely he is admired for very slender accomplishments, like a parrot, who speaks a few words plainly.[1]

Snelgrave was too ordinary a man ever to have entertained these generalizations, but even he might have queried Hume's assertion that the Negroes lacked anyone eminent even in action; at least, he had thought that the king of Dahomey looked 'very taking, and withal majestick', and felt bound to comment on him as 'the most extraordinary Man of his Colour, that I had ever conversed with, having seen nothing in him that appeared barbarous, except the sacrificing of his Enemies', which, he added, appeared 'done out of Policy'.[2]

Hume's view was no more than an interesting speculation, but when it was referred to what was actually happening, it could be used to justify the slave trade on the grounds that the commodity fell short of full humanity. The most extreme statement of this view was made by Edward Long, the historian of Jamaica. Slaves, Long argued in the course of a lengthy justification of the trade, are to be considered as being to Africa 'actual *staple products*, as much as wool and corn are to Great Britain'.[3]

Long's arguments in defence of the trade appeared at the height of the first phase of the anti-slavery agitation and, ranging from the crude to the sophisticated, only rehearsed what had been frequently aired. The most telling argument had long since been advanced. The trade flourished, Snelgrave affirmed, because of its advantages. 'In a word, from this Trade proceed Benefits, far outweighing all, either real or pretended Mischiefs and Inconveniences. And, let the worst that can, be said of it, it will be found, like all other earthly Advantages, tempered with a mixture of Good and Evil.'[4] The 'advantages' were shared by the whole British people and, as a writer in *Fog's*

---

[1] *Essays and Treatises*, 1768, i. 235.   [2] Snelgrave, p. 75.
[3] *History of Jamaica*, ii. 390.   [4] Snelgrave, p. 161.

Journal put it in 1737, one of the causes of the trade was 'the good People of *England*, who protect and encourage this Trade, because all the Gain, both of it and the *Sugar Trade*, always centers among themselves'.[1] Whether by theory or self-interest, the trade, it seemed, could be completely justified.

William Snelgrave was answered in part the following year, 1735, by another seaman, John Atkins. Atkins may have been a better-educated man than Snelgrave—he was certainly far more pretentious intellectually—but he lacked his unselfconscious narrative skill. He was clearly disinterested, however, in his views on the Negro and the slave trade, which Snelgrave certainly was not—his book was warningly inscribed to 'the Merchants of London'—and, as a surgeon in the Royal Navy, with a textbook on practical surgery to his credit,[2] his opinions were bound to carry weight.

Atkins took issue with Snelgrave for asserting that the Dahomeys were cannibals, by pointing out that he had seen only the prisoners being slaughtered, a fairly common practice among certain peoples, however awful: he was depending on rumour for proof that they were subsequently eaten. But Atkins was not a polemicist. He described the people as they were, poor and primitive and superstitious, but, he argued, these were insufficient grounds for transporting them into slavery. 'When the Nakedness, Poverty and Ignorance of these Species of Men are considered; it would incline one to think it a bettering their Condition, to transport them to the worst of Christian Slavery; but as we find them little mended in those respects at the *West-Indies*, their Patrons respecting them only as Beasts of Burthen; there is rather Inhumanity in removing them from their Countries and Families; here they get Ease with their spare Diet; the Woods, the Fruits, the Rivers, and Forests, with what they produce, is equally the property of all.'[3] Atkins returned later to the specious argument that the Negroes somehow benefited by their transportation. 'They live indeed, according to our *European* Phrase, very poor and mean, destitute almost of the common Necessaries of Life; but never starve, that is peculiar to trading Republicks; then who is to judge of their Wants, themselves, or we? Or what does Poorness mean? more than a sound, to signify we have that which another does not want.'[4] Atkins roundly concluded, with equally telling effect, that to 'remove *Negroes* then from their Homes and Friends, where they are at ease, to

---

[1] Quoted in *London Magazine*, 1737, p. 191.
[2] *The Navy Surgeon: Or, A Practical System of Surgery.*
[3] Atkins, pp. 61–2.   [4] ibid. pp. 177–8.

a strange Country, People, and Language, must be highly offending against the Laws of natural Justice and Humanity'.[1]

Atkins also drew upon his experience of the coast to answer those who claimed that the only slaves dealt in were prisoners of war, or cast criminals, or the destined victims of cannibalism or sacrifice. 'By war,' Atkins exclaimed, 'for the most part is meant Robbery of inland, defenceless Creatures, who are hurried down to the Coast with the greater Cruelty, as it is from a contented, tho' a very poor Life.'[2] He thought that very few slaves were sold as a punishment for crimes; and as for the view that it was a charity to buy those who might otherwise have been sacrificed or eaten, and give them a chance of Christian salvation, he thought it too hypocritical to be worth his consideration. Atkins is brief in considering the source of slaves, but he left it in no doubt that in his opinion the principal source was war —war waged only for that purpose.

Atkins was as sympathetic to Negro superstition as he was to Negro poverty. 'It is impossible', he argued, 'to expect in such a State of Nature as theirs, naked of Education and Science, that they should be able to form any refined Notions of a Deity; which, we experience among our selves, receives the Improvement with our growing Understanding, purely the Effect of Art and Study; the Philosopher and Countryman being at as much distance in their Explanation of divine Points, as it is possible the Christian Sailor and the *Negro* can be.'[3] Atkins tried to explain the elements of Negro fetish worship and animism by imagining the human species newly created and faced by a mysterious universe. Good nature may be more evident than anthropology in his remarks, but he does nevertheless conclude with some degree of plausibility that the 'original Gods, obvious to the first and darker days of Reason, were in my opinion, *Stocks* and *Stones, Serpents, Calves, Onions, Garlick,* &c. Not that these things appeared to them in the exalted Attributes of Spirit, Creator, Omniscience, &c. then inconceivable: No; they only could observe that all the parts of Nature were mysterious in their Essence and Operations, and therefore attracted their Esteem and Worship.'[4]

These sensible observations led Atkins to conclusions that may have surprised a contemporary reader. He believed that the Negro was as perfectly capable of moral and intellectual development as any other people; 'as it is, their Actions demonstrate that the Soul wants a proper Nurture as well as the Body, and will hardly, without a

[1] ibid. p. 178.　　[2] ibid. p. 176.　　[3] ibid. pp. 80–1.
[4] ibid. pp. 84–5.

Miracle, increase its Knowledge to any degree above what at present it appears; but when the Seeds and Principles are laid by letter'd Nations, it is not then nigh so difficult to improve.'[1] He constantly affirmed that the 'grossest idolatries are not a proper Subject of Laughter', but rather require 'the Pity of greater Light and Knowledge', since they represent some attempt to understand the mystery surrounding all men. And he concluded by asking the awkward question, if the inland Negroes are ignorant equally of good and evil when they are brought down to the coast, and once there rapidly develop in evil, whose religion is at fault, theirs or Europe's?

John Atkins wrote as 'a Christian sailor', but as he was singularly free from cant and pietism, he compelled his contemporaries to read Bosman and Barbot and Snelgrave far more critically and to understand the moral issues that were being obscured. He was not as brilliant an anecdotist as Snelgrave, but his account of 'Old Cracker' and Captain Tomba was more than enough to balance Snelgrave's pathetic sketches of the infant sacrifice and the rescued *gouvernante*. Captain Tomba's bloody back, and the monstrous punishment meted out to his fellow conspirators, strengthened the image of the Negro as Oroonoko and changed what Snelgrave would have to be a matter of trade to a question of principle.

Snelgrave himself claimed to have usually avoided mutinies among his slaves by treating them with understanding and kindness, and no reader would be inclined to dispute him, but even he had had to cope occasionally with a mutinous cargo and take the necessary measures. On one occasion he was driven to punish a ringleader in such a way as to intimidate all the other slaves on board both his own vessel and the other ships in the fleet. He had the man hoisted up on the foreyard-arm and shot to death by a firing squad. 'The Body being let down upon the Deck, the Head was cut off, and thrown overboard. This last part was done, to let our Negroes see, that all who offended thus, should be served in the same manner. For many of the Blacks believe, that if they are put to death and not dismembered, they shall return again to their own Country, after they are thrown overboard.'[2] Snelgrave's stories of this kind are made tolerable by his calm assumption that terror was occasionally necessary to maintain order, in the same way as a drover might, without a touch of malice, beat a recalcitrant brute. But after reading about Captain Tomba, Snelgrave's assumption could not pass unchallenged; nor could the suspicion be suppressed that he was concealing other degrees of atrocity. John

[1] ibid. p. 82.　　[2] Snelgrave, pp. 183–4.

Barbot, for instance, protested as much as Snelgrave that he did all he could for his cargoes of slaves, but he had to admit that when they refused to eat out of despair, 'naturally compassionate' though he was, he had 'been necessitated sometimes to cause the teeth of those wretches to be broken, because they would not open their mouths, or be prevail'd upon by any intreaties to feed themselves; and thus have forced some sustenance into their throats'.[1]

The critical reading which Atkins encouraged would reveal other discrepancies in Snelgrave's and Barbot's accounts of the trade. Snelgrave asserted that slaves were obtained by the voluntary sale of children by their parents, but he had to admit that this could be practised only by the inland people. He had never known it to be done by the people on the coast, except on the occasion of the sacking of Whidaw by the Dahomeys. The Whidaws were then in such a starving condition that they did sell their domestic slaves and children, and Snelgrave's friend Captain Dagge of the *Italian*, for one, filled up his complement of slaves in double-quick time.[2] Barbot had a similar story to tell. He illustrated his description of how the African continent was periodically swept by the most devastating famines by recalling the time he arrived at Goree, shortly after the terrible famine of 1681. Thousands of people had already died and many of them were selling themselves as slaves, 'only to get a sustenance'. The situation reminded Barbot of the seven years' famine in Egypt, when the exhausted Egyptians and Canaanites sold themselves as slaves to Pharaoh and to Joseph.[3] A reader might conclude that a people afflicted by such a calamity would have been more properly a subject for charity than for cruel exploitation.

The other ways in which slaves were said to be obtained could be equally called into question. Snelgrave affirmed that all the avenues were legitimate and approved by native custom, but he disingenuously let fall that on the Windward Coast both French and English slavers had kidnapped so many natives who had come out in canoes to trade with them, that the Coast had become exceedingly dangerous. Snelgrave's remark was an implicit condemnation of the morality of the European slavers, and many even more unguarded comments could be found in Barbot. 'I cannot but observe,' he remarked, 'that if the *Negroes* be generally crafty and treacherous, it may well be said, the *Europeans* have not dealt with them as becomes *Christians*: for it is too well known, that many of the *European* nations, trading among these people, have very unjustly and inhumanly, without any

---

[1] Churchill, v. 272.   [2] Snelgrave, p. 70.   [3] Churchill, v. 33.

provocation, stolen away, from time to time, abundance of the people. . . .'[1]

The same spasmodic inclination to be fair made Barbot acknowledge that if the Negro women were extremely wanton, the Europeans living on the coast were equally 'a loose sort of people; it is easy to guess what a scene of leudness and debauchery is continually acting there'.[2] And at the conclusion of a thoroughly hostile analysis of the Negro character he was compelled in all honesty to admit in compensation that Europe had its share of 'pride, vanity, and envy'.[3] 'Fortune never exerted more cruelly her empire over mankind,' remarked a later and sterner commentator, 'than when she subjected those nations of heroes to the refuse of the gaols of Europe.'[4]

The moral consequences of the slave trade could also be seen, as Barbot suggested, in the demoralizing effect on its agents. Captain Thomas Phillips's account of his singularly unfortunate voyage in 1694, on which he lost fourteen crew and three hundred and twenty Negroes, ended with his own 'unhappiness' at being seized with 'convulsions' in his head. After spending about a hundred guineas among the London doctors in an attempt to cure the deafness that followed on the convulsions, he returned, a broken man, to live out his days among relations in Brecknock.[5] Phillips was one of the casualties of a dirty trade, and it was these casualties that Thomas Clarkson was later to use with such effect in the first of the sustained anti-slavery campaigns.

John Atkins's *Voyage* struck the first effective blow at the trade, but it was followed only three years later, in 1738, by a far more notable work, by Francis Moore, Job ben Solomon's friend. As well as being the best and most intimate description of life in West Africa written in the eighteenth century, and the chief authority on the region until the end of the period, Moore's *Travels into the Inland Parts of Africa* was also the most important source of evidence for the impact of the slave trade on African society, which was, in the nature of things, very difficult to obtain. Elsewhere on the coast the Europeans were prevented from travelling inland, with the exception of such a remarkable excursion as Snelgrave's to the king of Dahomey's camp; but even if they had been admitted, self-interest might have censored, or ignorance obscured, what they could have seen.

Moore had kept a careful journal during his residence in the Gambia, but when he came to publish it, while claiming not to have

---

[1] ibid. p. 110.　　　[2] ibid. p. 36.　　　[3] ibid. p. 236.
[4] Adam Smith, quoted by Clarkson, i. 85.　　　[5] Churchill, vi. 254–5.

revised it, in the belief that his readers would prefer 'to read real Facts told in the plainest way, than beautiful Works of Imagination',[1] he added to it as appendices a journal kept by Captain Stibbs of his attempt to discover the source of the Gambia in 1723, and extracts from the writings of classical and modern geographers on the river and its region. These additions helped to make Moore's book even more useful and interesting, as well as showing his scholarly and inquiring turn of mind.

The information given in the *Travels* is invaluable, but its other great merit is that it puts African life into an ordinary perspective. Of all the writers on Africa in this period, only Moore had lived for a considerable time on an intimate and equal footing with the Negroes; often he had been the only white person in a district and entirely dependent on them for both protection and society. The others were at best observers, without a chance of getting to know any Negroes unaffected by European civilization, and as a result they were unable to relate whatever facts they may have picked up to a comprehensible society. The Negro who appears in Barbot's pages may be reasonably well documented, but he is completely foreign and unintelligible; and even in Atkins's sympathetic account, we feel it is an act of Christian faith and charity to assume that the Negro is really a man. Moore is ready enough to point out what he thinks are the Negroes' characteristic faults, but rather than being the marks of another species, these are the local aberrations of a common human nature. After reading Moore's description, the people became, in spite of all differences of colour, religion, and social organization, individuals with whom it was possible to sympathize. In terms of their pain and misery could be measured the enormities of the slave trade.

Moore himself accepted the slave trade. He bargained for slaves at the factories to which he was posted, but like all the servants of the Royal African Company he wanted the trade to be conducted properly and deplored the predatory behaviour of the interlopers. Because he was not opposed to the traffic, his incidental remarks on how slaves were obtained, and the state of undeclared war that consequently existed between the interlopers and the natives along the river, were more effective in stirring the English conscience than they would have been if advanced by an avowed opponent of the trade. But even more telling were his illustrations of how the Africans themselves levied slaves, especially his account of the king of Barsally's setting fire to one of his own villages and enslaving the stricken villagers in

[1] Moore, p. vi.

order to raise funds to squander on drink. The incident proved that the supposed prisoners of war were more likely than not the victims of similar raids, and that the European traders' insatiable demand for slaves, and their readiness to buy without serious question all that were produced, incited and maintained an appalling state of fratricidal warfare.

Moore's account of the king of Barsally's raid became as common an illustration in the anti-slavery arguments as Snelgrave's anecdotes in defence of the trade. Anthony Benezet, the Philadelphian Quaker, referred to it in his brief *Historical Account of Guinea*, a work in which he drew heavily throughout on Moore's *Travels*, and it was in Benezet that Thomas Clarkson first learnt the story. Benezet's tract, for it was written expressly in the Negro cause, became for the young Clarkson a 'precious book', in which he found all that he wanted.

The way in which Moore's matter-of-fact account of the raid became charged with sentiment and emotion in the course of its use by the opponents of slavery can be seen perfectly by comparing Moore's account with Clarkson's version of it.

It is to that insatiable Thirst of his after Brandy [Moore wrote] that his Subjects' Freedoms and Families are in so precarious a Situation; for he very often goes with some of his Troops by a Town in the Day-time, and returns in the Night and sets fire to three Parts of it, and sets Guards at the fourth to seize the People as they run out from the Fire; he ties their Arms behind them, and marches them to the Place where he sells them, which is either *Joar* or *Cahone*.[1]

At the beginning of his *History of the Abolition of the Slave-Trade* Clarkson sketches in a number of scenes the horrible effects of the trade on African society, and one of these is based on Moore's simple and effective recital of facts. 'And whither shall we go now?' he demands;

The night is approaching fast. Let us find some friendly hut, where sleep may make us forget for a while the sorrows of the day. Behold a hospitable native ready to receive us at his door! Let us avail ourselves of his kindness. And now let us give ourselves to repose. But why, when our eyelids are but just closed, do we find ourselves thus suddenly awakened? What is the meaning of the noise around us, of the trampling of people's feet, of the rustling of the bow, the quiver and the lance; Let us rise up and inquire. Behold! the inhabitants are all alarmed! A wakeful woman has shown them yon distant column of smoke and blaze. The neighbouring village is on

[1] ibid. p. 87.

fire. The prince, unfaithful to the sacred duty of the protection of his subjects, has surrounded them. He is now burning their habitations, and seizing, as saleable booty, the fugitives from the flames.[1]

The transformation Clarkson has worked suggests how the fervent imagination of a political reformer can falsify with the best of intentions; in this instance by fantasticating the harsh and actual.

Francis Moore dedicated his *Travels* to Job ben Solomon's friend and protector, the Duke of Montagu. 'Benevolence is the distinguishing Character of your Grace', Moore declared; 'In the *Wilds* of *Africa* your Humanity is praised, and the grateful *Arabs* pray for you in the Deserts.' The prayers raised in the wilds on the Duke's behalf were those of Job ben Solomon, and Job's story figured so prominently in the *Travels* that in the synopsis on the title-page it was stated that the book included 'a particular Account of Job ben Solomon, a *Pholey*, who was in England in the Year 1733, and known by the Name of the *African*'.

Moore's account of Job's return to the Gambia supplemented Thomas Bluett's biographical sketch. Bluett had gathered from Job himself some details of African manners and society, but as he was unfamiliar with Africa he could only report what he had been told, without in any way drawing out the significance of the facts. Moore's information about the kind of society Job came from allowed the sympathetic reader to understand him much more clearly. Moore also held as high an opinion of Job as Bluett had done. He makes his liking and admiration for him perfectly plain and discusses him without a touch of condescension.

Because of Moore's and Bluett's accounts, Job became a significant figure in the battle against slavery. The slaves shipped from Africa were an undifferentiated mass. When they were put up for sale, with their naked bodies specially greased and their heads shaven, they could be told apart only by their physical condition; and in their sale and purchase only their condition counted. They were never able to assert their individuality again, except by acts of rebellion, for which they were executed or thrashed back into conformity. The more pliant might become overseers on the plantations or domestic servants, but however favoured they were by their masters, their characters were scrutinized only in their new capacities. The colour of their skins alone reminded their masters, who were entirely ignorant of their language and culture, that they hailed from Africa.

Job was the first African who could be appreciated as a person. As

[1] Clarkson, i. 12–13.

a Muslim, he offered a complete and intelligible contrast to the super-stitious worshippers of snakes and fetishes who seemed to populate Africa; and as a devout Muslim, who zealously fasted and prayed even in the inclement atmosphere of London and without fellow worship-pers to encourage him, he challenged the Christians' lax beliefs. Neither was he ignorant and unlettered. His knowledge may have been circumscribed, but anyone who could write out the whole Koran from memory and discuss its precepts was an unusual guest in an England where illiteracy was commonplace. And mixing in very good English society, he held his own in a way that showed he had been taught to appreciate good breeding, although ignorant of English manners—this '*African* Gentleman', Bluett called him. He was alto-gether different from the impression of the Negro that could be gathered from seeing him as an uprooted slave, or from reading about him in ignorant reports.

Job's character was sympathetic, but it was also paradoxical. He owned slaves himself, and, what was worse, he dealt in them; and though he prayed, his usual prayers were strictly partial to members of his own faith. When Francis Moore's *Travels* was reprinted in summary in Astley's *A New General Collection of Voyages and Travels* in 1745, the account of Job was abstracted and combined with Thomas Bluett's to make a separate biographical sketch, and Thomas Green, the critical and irascible editor of the *Collection*, took occasion to com-ment sharply on Job.[1] But whatever scorn such a man as Green may have felt for aspects of Job's character and beliefs, Job was the only contemporary Negro whose life was known in any detail. Astley's *Collection* helped greatly to make Job better known in both England and abroad.[2] He appeared also later in the century in John Newbery's very popular collection of voyages and travels, *The World Displayed*, in twenty duodecimo volumes, with a general Preface by Samuel Johnson. Newbery abridged Francis Moore's *Travels*, and the necessary rearrangement of the material helped to make Job even more of a legendary figure.[3]

But the chances were that Job would be as well known to literary scholars and antiquaries as to readers of travels. Because he had been elected a member of the Gentlemen's Society of Spalding, his name appeared in the list of members given in an appendix to an account of

---

[1] See above, p. 113.
[2] Astley's conflation of Moore's and Bluett's accounts of Job was included in J. J. Schwabe's *Allgemeine Historie der Reisen*, 1747, iii. 127–39.
[3] See above, Introduction, p. v.

the Society published by John Nichols in 1784, with a biographical account, compiled from Moore and Bluett. Nichols later included this account of the Gentlemen's Society in his invaluable collection of *Literary Anecdotes of the Eighteenth Century* and Job's name again appeared, with a carefully revised biographical note.[1] Job's name was included by Alexander Chalmers in his *General Biographical Dictionary*, published in 1816, and his inclusion in the great *Biographie Universelle* helped equally to ensure that he was not forgotten abroad.

Job was among the first and the most notable, though not the last, visitor of his kind.[2] In June 1750 the engraving of him by William Hoare, which had been published as the frontispiece to Bluett's biography, was reproduced in *The Gentleman's Magazine* as the companion piece of a portrait of the prince of Annamaboe. This young prince arrived in London by means almost as circuitous as those which had earlier brought Job.

Annamaboe (Anomabu) was one of the most important of the Royal African Company's forts on the Guinea Coast, on account of its easy communications with the interior. The town itself and its fifteen square miles of dependent territory were governed by a Braffo, or chief, who, in the 1740s, was a man known to the English traders under the name of John Corrente. John Corrente was very much courted by both the French and the English, and the French, who tried to make up by diplomacy and generous dealing for their weakness in numbers, persuaded him to allow one of his sons to visit France. After a little hesitation, the Braffo agreed. The boy spent some time in France and in due course returned home, dressed in the height of French fashion and full of wonderful stories of French power and hospitality. And his usefulness to the French was not confined to Annamaboe and its neighbourhood, for all 'the Inland Traders coming from the most distant Part of *Africk* to bring their Gold and Slaves to *Annamaboe*, had an Opportunity of seeing the

---

[1] *Literary Anecdotes*, 1812, vi. pt. i. 90–1.

[2] Apart from the many unrecorded visits by Negroes that must have taken place, Job seems to have been immediately preceded by the shadowy Adomo Tomo who is supposed to have arrived in London in 1731 as an envoy from the king of Dahomey to the king of England, accompanied by one of the Royal African Company's agents, Bullfinch Lambe. The story was told in some detail by Snelgrave, but Donnan, who reprints the relevant passages from Snelgrave and other material, pertinently asks whether Snelgrave has not confused the story of Job ben Solomon with that of Adomo Tomo (see Elizabeth Donnan, *Documents Illustrative of the History of the Slave Trade to America*, 1935, ii. 345–8; also H. A. Wyndham, *The Atlantic and Slavery*, 1935, pp. 65–6). Such a confusion seems highly probable, to say the least.

L

young *African* in all his *French* Finery,' and hearing about France
from the youth himself.[1]

John Corrente was equally pleased. The complaisance shown by
the French to his son had greatly enhanced his own standing, and the
son's experience of France and knowledge of the language were a
great advantage in his commercial dealings with the French. John
Corrente saw similar and even greater advantages in having another
of his sons taken to England, and he at length entrusted his favourite
son to an independent trader, with whom he thought he was on the
friendliest terms. The youth, who was known among the English at
Annamaboe under the name of Cupid, 'as most expressive of his
sweet and amiable Temper',[2] had already learnt some English from
living for a time as a boy in the Company's fort. Cupid sailed for
London with the friendly captain by way of Barbados. He was very
well treated on the voyage out, but the captain promptly put him up
for sale the moment the ship docked at Bridgetown. He later tried to
justify his conduct by claiming that John Corrente owed him money.

The fortunes of the Royal African Company were on the ebb during
these years. At Annamaboe the fort was in a state of almost complete
disrepair, and the French took advantage of this weakness to win John
Corrente over to their side and by his means almost to exclude British
trade. Luckily for the Company, the English fleet won command of
the seas during the naval engagements of 1747, and when a frigate
appeared off Annamaboe the Company's agent went on board and had
the town bombarded until John Corrente was brought to terms. The
complete exclusion of the French traders was the main article of the
agreement, but in return the Company agreed to find John Corrente's
missing son, Cupid.

The Company's agent sailed soon after for the West Indies and
home, taking with him a son of the English caboceer—that is, the
native officer in charge of English trading interests—as a companion
for the young prince as soon as he was found. The boy was quickly
tracked down, redeemed, and brought to London, where both he and
his companion were handsomely entertained. A notice in the journals
shows them at Covent Garden Theatre, at a performance, appropriately enough, of *Oroonoko*, 'with which they were so affected, that the
tears flow'd plentifully from their eyes; the case of *Oronooko*'s being
made a slave by the treachery of a captain being so very similar to
their own'.[3]

---

[1] *The Royal African*, p. 29.   [2] ibid. p. 37.
[3] *London Magazine*, February 1749, p. 94.

The prince was treated, like Job ben Solomon, to a biographical pamphlet, though the very competent author of *The Royal African: or, Memoirs of the Young Prince of Annamaboe*, which came out in 1749, preferred to remain anonymous.[1] The author may not have been on the coast himself, but he was clearly well informed about it at first hand and familiar with Barbot and Atkins and Snelgrave, by then the standard authorities. He was not himself opposed to the slave trade, or at least did not come out openly against it, but he unhesitatingly condemned 'so flagrant a Breach of Trust, as selling a *Free-man*, and a Person of Consideration, whatever his *Complexion* may be, for a *Slave*'.[2] And his sympathies were entirely with the Negroes in their relations with Europeans. He defended their character in general, by putting it on a level with human nature as a whole elsewhere; and in answer to the specific charge that they demonstrated their depravity by selling their own children into slavery for gain, he angrily replied that they did so only when driven to it by famine, and then to save the lives of the children, as much as their own: 'Hunger and the Sword', he roundly affirmed, 'are very pressing Arguments with white People as well as black; and therefore, what they compel Men to, can never be taken for the Custom of any Nation.'[3] He wished to admonish his readers that in view of England's stake in African trade and its possibilities, 'to fancy that superior Power or superior Knowledge gives *one* Race of People a Title to use *another* Race who are weaker or more ignorant with Haughtiness or Contempt, is to abuse Power and Science, and in spite of both to shew ourselves worse Men than those who have neither'.[4]

The misadventure of the prince of Annamaboe inspired not only the biographical pamphlet but also two verse epistles by the parson and poet William Dodd, later to be hanged for forgery. The first epistle, which came out in *The Gentleman's Magazine* for July 1749, was supposed to be addressed by the prince in England to Zara, his betrothed, at Annamaboe. He describes his fortunes after taking leave of Zara and his father beneath the palms on Afric's strand. He tells how he was basely sold into slavery and had imagined for a time that

[1] Wylie Sypher, *Guinea's Captive Kings*, 1942, seems for no good reason at all to consider this account to be a novel. The prince's real name—with the addition of the Christian name given to him on his baptism on 30 November 1749 (see *Gentleman's Magazine*, November 1749, p. 522)—was William Ansah Sessaracoo—or Sesarakoo. On his return to Africa he was taken on the books as a writer at the English factory at Cape Coast Castle and was later sent down to Anomabu. He sent an extremely interesting report back from there to the Earl of Halifax on 20 February 1752, describing French activity on the coast (P.R.O., C.O. 267/5).

[2] *The Royal African*, p. iii.   [3] ibid. p. 28.   [4] ibid. pp. vii–viii.

he could have borne the horror of his new state, if only Zara had been
by his side. He threw off the languor of this amorous contemplation by
sternly asking himself,

> Could I, a slave, and hopeless to be free,
> Crawl, tamely recent from the scourge, to thee?
> Thy blooming beauties could these arms embrace?
> My guilty joys enslave an infant race?

Instead, he was redeemed and brought to London, and now, after
enjoying the wonders of the metropolis, he trusts that Providence,
permitting his safe return,

> Shall bless the love, that's built on virtue's base,
> And spare me to evangelize my race.

The poem was sufficiently popular to encourage Dodd to publish
in the August number of *The Gentleman's Magazine* an epistle from
Zara in answer to the prince. He drew heavily on Pope's *Eloisa to
Abelard*, but his attempts to unravel Zara's erotic meditations entirely
lack his master's perception and show the lusciousness that is one of
Dodd's most unseemly characteristics. Both the poems are marked as
much by vulgarity of sentiment as by metrical competence, but they
are among the earliest verses to exploit the pathos and drama of the
Africans' plight and were reprinted several times during the century.

If a movement of sympathy is to be sustained and become a cause,
images must be found that can powerfully strike the popular imagination with more or less uniform effect. The anti-slavery movement, as
it was beginning to emerge at about the time of Job ben Solomon's
stay in London, had already adopted some of the images that were to
fire it emotionally for a century. In Africa, the king of Barsally setting
fire at night to one of his own peaceful villages; on the slaveships, the
heroic figure of Captain Tomba, bloody but unbowed; on the plantations, Oroonoko, the prototype of all such martyrs, dying by fire, the
mutilated victim of the white planter's lust and greed: these were
some of the scenes and characters that became, in a manner of speaking, the cells that discharged the energy needed by the movement.
Dodd's verses hardly added to the number. He was far more interested in using 'Cupid's' misadventure to titillate the fancy than to
impress the imagination with the brutal reality of the slave's plight;
at the most, his service to the Negro was the maintenance of general
goodwill. But an earlier poet had already and almost casually provided
what was to become one of the most obsessive of these images.

A common attendant on the slaveship was the shark. Sharks abounded in the waters off the Guinea Coast; Snelgrave describes how the woman offered to him and later thrown as a sacrifice into the sea was expected to be dispatched by their voracity. They were popularly supposed to accompany the slavers all the way across the Atlantic, feasting on the bodies tossed overboard when mortality ran high among the cargo, which happened especially in bad weather. The Negroes who leapt overboard to escape being shipped before the vessels sailed were often 'eaten by the sharks, of which a prodigious number kept about the ships in this place [Whidaw], and I have been told,' Captain Phillips went on, 'will follow her hence to *Barbadoes*, for the dead Negroes that are thrown overboard in the passage. I am certain in our voyage there we did not want the sight of some every day, but that they were the same I can't affirm.'[1] Such information as this was seized on by James Thomson and introduced by him into a revised and enlarged edition of *The Seasons* published in 1744.

Thomson's excuse for introducing such a horrific element into a pastoral poem was his need in 'Summer' to describe the season at its extreme, in the tropics. When the poem was first published he had been content with drawing a general contrast between the clement sun of Britain and the tyrannical sun of Africa, but on enlarging it he added several scenes descriptive of the climatic violence of the southern zones; on land the overwhelming sandstorm, the hurricane at sea. The precipitous hurricane—

> a mingled Mass
> Of roaring Winds, and Flame, and rushing Floods[2]

—can defeat the most skilful sailors and drown the finest vessels in 'the black Abyss'. Yet the worst fate is not simply to be drowned:

> Increasing still the Terrors of these Storms,
> His Jaws horrific arm'd with threefold Fate,
> Here dwells the direful Shark. Lur'd by the Scent
> Of steaming Crouds, of rank Disease, and Death,
> Behold! he rushing cuts the briny Flood,
> Swift as the Gale can bear the Ship along;
> And, from the Partners of that cruel Trade,
> Which spoils unhappy *Guinea* of her Sons,
> Demands his share of Prey, demands themselves.
> The stormy Fates descend: one Death involves
> Tyrants and Slaves; when strait, their mangled Limbs
> Crushing at once, he dyes the purple Seas
> With Gore, and riots in the vengeful Meal.[3]

---

[1] Churchill, vi. 235.   [2] ll. 984–5.   [3] ll. 1002–14.

Thomson was able in this passage to associate the consequences of the slave trade with most aspects of the sublime: fear, mystery, power, infinity, solitude, obscurity, and death, which both repel and attract the imagination, leaving it in a state of mingled terror and exaltation. When Immanuel Kant tried later in the century, in his *Critique of Judgment*, to illustrate the sublime in nature he included in his list 'hurricanes with their track of devastation; the boundless ocean in a state of tumult'; to these Thomson had united the further sublimity of moral retribution. The passage came to haunt the imagination because it combined the humanitarian and the romantic, and as its ultimate effect it inspired the great and terrifying image of Turner's 'Slave Ship', the work John Ruskin affirmed that he would choose to rest Turner's immortality upon: 'Purple and blue, the lurid shadows of the hollow breakers are cast upon the mist of night, which gathers cold and low, advancing like the shadow of death upon the guilty ship as it labours amidst the lightning of the sea, its thin masts written upon the sky in lines of blood, girded with condemnation in that fearful hue which signs the sky with horror, and mixes its flaming flood with the sunlight, and, cast far along the desolate heave of the sepulchral waves, incarnadines the multitudinous sea.'[1]

Thomson's protest against the slave trade, in this lurid description of one of the horrors of the 'Middle Passage', was disseminated as widely as *The Seasons* itself, the most popular of eighteenth-century poems, and was particularly effective because it occurred in a work which appealed throughout to the reader's sympathy and charity. 'Guinea's sons' were only one of the objects of the 'benevolence of soul' which Thomson tried to promote, but by not being exceptional they stood a better chance of falling under its kindly surveillance.

While Thomson's heart might bleed for the miseries of the slave, he was far from translating the Negro into the 'noble savage', an ideal abstraction that shared as greatly in the romantic imagination as the sublime. 'Summer' is a poem of contrasts and the primary contrast is between liberty and tyranny, which, in terms of nature, becomes a contrast between the temperate and the tropical zones. Liberty and moderation dwell in Britain, their favoured home, and these he celebrates with fervent patriotism; and after he has concluded a rapid and romantic survey of the 'Wonders of the *torrid Zone*', he has to ask himself, to what do they amount, compared with the moral virtues of the northern clime? The passage in which he answers his question is

---

[1] Ruskin, *Works*, iii. 572; quoted by T. S. R. Boase, *English Art, 1800–1870*, 1959, p. 122.

long, but it is worth quoting because it shows clearly how the images of heat and vegetable luxuriance determine the social and moral characteristics of Africa.

> What all that *Afric*'s golden Rivers rowl,
> Her odorous Woods, and shining Ivory Stores?
> Ill-fated Race! the softening Arts of Peace,
> Whate'er the humanizing Muses teach;
> The Godlike Wisdom of the temper'd Breast;
> Progressive Truth, the patient Force of Thought;
> Investigation calm, whose silent Powers
> Command the World; the LIGHT that leads to HEAVEN;
> Kind equal Rule, the Government of Laws,
> And all-protecting FREEDOM, which alone
> Sustains the Name and Dignity of Man:
> These are not theirs. The Parent Sun himself
> Seems o'er this World of Slaves to tyrannize;
> And, with oppressive Ray, the roseat Bloom
> Of Beauty blasting, gives the gloomy Hue,
> And Feature gross: or worse, to ruthless Deeds,
> Mad Jealousy, blind Rage, and fell Revenge,
> Their fervid Spirit fires. Love dwells not there,
> The soft Regards, the Tenderness of Life,
> The Heart-shed Tear, th' ineffable Delight
> Of sweet Humanity: These court the Beam
> Of milder Climes; in selfish fierce Desire,
> And the wild Fury of voluptuous Sense,
> There lost. The very Brute-Creation there
> This Rage partakes, and burns with horrid Fire.[1]

The 'full-form'd Maids of *Afric*' might lave their 'jetty' limbs in the waters of Thomson's Niger, but except in their appearance, and then rather in their contour than in their colour, there is little to be discovered in them or their brothers of the 'noble savage', that stately figure from the Golden Age of classical mythology, who was believed to live in an innocent state of nature somewhere in the world.

The domains of the 'noble savage' lay in America rather than in Africa. Oroonoko, in Aphra Behn's romance, is noble and a savage, but a savage only to the extent that savagery consists in passionate virility. He is not a 'noble savage'. The 'noble savage' in *Oroonoko* are the Indians of Surinam. These people may walk quite naked, Mrs. Behn provocatively affirmed, but they are 'extreme modest and bashful, very shy, and nice of being touched'. The very sight of them

---

[1] Ed. 1744, ll. 862–86.

represented to her 'an absolute idea of the first state of innocence, before man knew how to sin: And 'tis most evident and plain, that simple Nature is the most harmless, inoffensive and virtuous mistress. It is she alone, if she were permitted, that better instructs the world, than all the inventions of man: religion would here but destroy that tranquillity they possess by ignorance; and laws would but teach them to know offences, of which now they have no notion.'[1]

Mrs. Behn's idea of innocence and the convenience of the state of nature may be rather strictly confined to 'full nakedness', but her exclusion of Oroonoko himself from this world indicates how the idea of the 'noble savage' was attached to America rather than to Africa. The pre-eminence of the Indian in this respect was confirmed by the spectacular visits of Indian chiefs to London. A famous visit of four Indian 'kings', emissaries of the six tribes, took place in 1710,[2] but they were obscured in the popular memory by the embassy of ten chiefs or 'kings' who arrived from Georgia accompanied by Oglethorpe at almost the same moment as Job ben Solomon sailed for the Gambia.

Oglethorpe brought these Creek Indians to England with the intention of cementing the Indian alliance, which was of special importance in helping to defend the new colony against the menaces of the Spaniards in Florida. They were led by Tomochichi and his wife Senauki and arrived in London on 28 June 1734. They were presented at Court, they waited on the Archbishop of Canterbury, they visited Eton College and requested a half-holiday for the boys, and as they wore Indian dress, suitably adapted to the climate and the English sense of propriety, and, on ceremonial occasions, painted their faces in a surprising manner, some half black, others triangular, or with bearded arrows instead of whiskers, they roused a great deal of attention and interest wherever they went.[3]

The only unhappiness during their visit was the death of one of their number, the brother of Senauki, from smallpox. He was buried according to Indian rites in the burying ground of St. John the Evangelist, Horseferry Road. The scene was described in the journals of the day: 'The Deceased being sew'd up in two Blankets with one Deal Board under and another over him, and tied down with a Cord, was placed upon a Bier, and carried to the Place of Interment; there were only present at the Time of his being put into the Grave, the

---

[1] *Novels of Aphra Behn*, pp. 3–4.
[2] These visitors are the subject of R. P. Bond's *Queen Anne's American Kings*, 1952.
[3] See *London Magazine*, August 1734, p. 446.

Emperor *Tomo*, some of his Domesticks, the Upper Church-Warden
of the Parish, and the Grave-Digger. When the Corpse was laid in the
Earth, without any Rites or Ceremony, the Cloaths of the Deceased
were thrown into the Grave; after this a Quantity of Glass Beads
were cast in, and then some Pieces of Silver: For the Custom of those
Indians is to bury all their Effects with them.'¹ These sad rites, which
brought together the extraordinary combination of an English grave-
digger and an Indian chief, had been credited in anticipation with a
comprehensible and touching metaphysical significance by Alexander
Pope in his famous passage on 'the poor Indian' in *An Essay on Man*:

> Lo! the poor Indian, whose untutor'd mind
> Sees God in clouds, or hears him in the wind;
> His soul proud Science never taught to stray
> Far as the solar walk, or milky way;
> Yet simple Nature to his hope has giv'n,
> Behind the cloud-topt hill, an humbler heav'n;
> Some safer world in depth of woods embrac'd,
> Some happier island in the watry waste,
> Where slaves once more their native land behold,
> No fiends torment, no Christians thirst for gold!
> To Be, contents his natural desire,
> He asks no Angel's wing, no Seraph's fire;
> But thinks, admitted to that equal sky,
> His faithful dog shall bear him company.²

A contemporary, reading the account of the interment in Horseferry
Road, could have believed that it was in simple beliefs like these that
Tomochichi and his band found consolation. Such a childlike trust in
the poetic justice of immortality was appropriate to 'noble savages'—
and 'noble savages' the Creeks had proved themselves to be, by the
instinctive courtesy and dignity of their behaviour during their visit.

The subject of Pope's lines is the American Indian, but the Negro is
associated with him in his noble savagery by the charitable reference
to the slave torn by Christian greed from his native land. The subsidiary standing of the Negro in this connection was the one generally
and unconsciously accepted at the time: the Negro could never be
entirely excluded from the myths of primal innocence and the Golden
Age. One of the clearest statements of the Negroes having once, at
least, enjoyed a state of nature undefiled, and an interesting explanation of how it came to be lost, is given in the 'Letter to the Publisher'
prefixed to Francis Moore's *Travels*. 'Before the *Moors* mix'd amongst

¹ ibid.   ² Epistle I, ll. 99–112.

them,' this correspondent argued, 'the *Negroes* were entirely ignorant of Arts and Letters, and of the Use of Iron; They lived in common, having no Property in Lands nor Goods, no Tyrants, nor superior Lords; but supported themselves in an equal State upon the natural Produce of the Country, which afforded plenty of Roots and Game, and Honey made by Bees in hollow Trees: Ambition or Avarice never drove them into Foreign Countries, to subdue or cheat their Neighbours. Thus they lived without Toil or Superfluities. And this the *Greeks* and *Romans* believed to be the First State of Mankind, which they describe in the *Golden Age.*'[1] The Negroes' loss of Eden may be conveniently blamed here on the Moors, but as it is civilization rather than race or creed which is at fault, the argument could easily be extended to making the Europeans responsible for corrupting and enslaving Africa. The ideal and mythical standing of the Negro was often unconsciously, and sometimes deliberately, obscured by Europeans out of a sense of guilt. If they were naturally depraved and corrupt and if, as Thomson strikingly suggests, this was the consequence of being born in a torrid zone, then they deserved their fate, or, at least, there was nothing about them to warrant any unusual show of sympathy.

But glimpses of this lost Eden could not be entirely obscured. Even in John Barbot's account there are occasional suggestions that the people and the country were not always as bad as they seemed. He occasionally remarks on the natives' cheerful industry, or indicates a splendour in the landscape. A far more attractive impression of the African character and African life was given by Francis Moore. He described a society that might have been entirely peaceful and stable had it not been subjected to the rapacity of princes, whose vicious conduct was encouraged if not caused by European greed. But it was hard to graft any such ideas as the state of innocence and the 'noble savage' on to Moore's account of the Gambia, he was too much the trader; and until the Negro could be more successfully identified with these abstractions, he was cut off from a source of feeling that might have worked powerfully in favour of his cause.

In 1749 Michel Adanson, a young French botanist, sailed from Port l'Orient for the French factory at St. Louis on the Senegal. Adanson had determined to make his name as a botanist, and having concluded that the possibilities for original work had been almost exhausted in France, he turned to West Africa, a virgin field. He had the right connections and was able to get a place at St. Louis through

[1] Moore, p. iii.

the director of the French East India Company, who realized that there could be advantages in Adanson's work to the Company, as well as to science.

Adanson spent more than four years botanizing on the Senegal, with an important excursion to Albreda on the Gambia, and three years after his return, in 1756, he published an account of his experiences and observations. Adanson had sailed out to Senegal after the signing of the treaty of Aix-la-Chapelle, which had opened the seas to French shipping once again, but Aix-la-Chapelle proved to be only a truce and widespread hostilities between England and France hardly ceased, though the Seven Years War was not formally begun until 1756. One of the most strikingly successful of Pitt's schemes in the early stages of the war was the capture in 1758 of all the French factories on the West African coast, including Goree and Senegal, by the naval forces under Commodore Keppel.

The capture of Senegal was one of the reasons for the prompt translation into English in 1759 of Adanson's *A Voyage to Senegal, the Isle of Goree, and the River Gambia.* As the translator remarked, the trade with Senegal was now in English hands and Adanson gave an excellent picture of the natives with whom it would have to be conducted. But he also acknowledged that Adanson was a most unusual adventurer in those parts, 'former adventurers having had no notion of improving their minds, but their fortunes; so that their relations are confined to the *auri sacra fames*, the purchase of slaves, teeth and dust, with other materials of gain. Our author is the first philosopher, who adventured to visit the torrid zone, for the propagation of knowledge.'[1] Adanson, he concluded, was as observant as he was courageous, and from 'so exact and judicious a narrative, one may therefore form a just idea of this part of Africa; a country', he went on, with the complacent arrogance of Lombard Street, 'overspread with misery, the natural consequence of laziness'.[2]

The translator was blinkered. As he knew very well, and partly admitted, Adanson describes a very different country from one wallowing in misery and idleness. He had no more faults to find in Africa than he might have found in Provence, or, for that matter, in Kent. But the translator was correct in distinguishing the philosophic Adanson from the traders. He had nothing to do with slavery and his pages, unstained by brutalities, are wonderfully refreshing in their account of his strenuous but untroubled pursuit of flowers, after the flagrancies of Snelgrave and Barbot, even after the decent and

---

[1] Adanson, pp. iv–v.   [2] ibid. p. vii.

sympathetic journalizing of Moore. *A Voyage to Senegal* is one of the most delightful books on Africa ever written.

Its importance lay in its delight. Adanson did not sentimentalize the Negroes; he admits to a degree of misery and idleness; but he describes them as they could fairly be said to be, when not corrupted or victimized: a peaceful and cheerful people, held together by close social ties, kind by nature and hospitable if it was in their power. Shortly after he had landed, in May 1749, he made an excursion to the near-by village of Sor: 'Which way soever I turned my eyes on this pleasant spot,' he wrote, 'I beheld a perfect image of pure nature: an agreeable solitude, bounded on every side by a charming landskip; the rural situation of cottages in the midst of trees; the ease and indolence of the Negroes, reclined under the shade of their spreading foliage; the simplicity of their dress and manners; the whole revived in my mind, the idea of our first parents, and I seemed to contemplate the world in its primeval state.'[1] On this occasion he dined on couscous with the headman of the village, thrusting his hand into the communal bowl. He made it a practice always to follow native customs and manners, and his kind reception and all that he observed convinced him 'that there ought to be considerable abatements made, in the accounts I had read and heard every where, of the savage character of the Africans'.[2]

Adanson not only exonerated the Negro character, but also, to some extent, the climate and the nature of the country. He was astonished by the heat, and the violence of the rains, but he was able to live, and though the ground along the river banks where he tramped looking for plants was often a morass, it could usually be crossed. Snakes and crocodiles and wild beasts abounded, but were a hazard only when provoked. The countryside was far from being the fiery and stricken arena of Thomson's visions, where

> sublim'd
> To fearless Lust of Blood, the Savage Race
> Roam,

but, rather, a difficult region of fields and marshes and dense woods which began to appear ordinary once it was explored; a country that could be lived in comfortably in spite of its fevers, if you watched your health and avoided debauch. When he visited Albreda, Adanson found that the native huts were too dark for his experiments, so he built a shelter of straw under a tamarind tree in his garden, 'which,

[1] ibid. p. 54.   [2] ibid. p. 58.

besides affording me a cool retreat,' he wrote, 'invited the feathered choristers to warble out their notes. In short, it was a real cabinet of natural philosophy, and I question whether so rural a one was ever seen before. For my part, the memory thereof is still dear to me, because of the knowledge I thereby acquired of an infinite multitude of new and curious plants, the growth of this country, which is doubtless one of the finest spots of all Africa.'[1]

Adanson's interest in going to Africa was innocent and he found innocence; he went as a botanist, and the people themselves, finding no harm, took on the same character as his search. A more striking contrast between his report on Africa and Snelgrave's and the others' —though, once again, an exception has to be made in favour of Moore, whose daily life at Joar shared something of the pastoral quality of Adanson's at Albreda—could hardly have been devised. By never once referring to the slave trade he had shown up completely its bestiality and turpitude. The eye sees according to the beholder's interest.

Adanson's was the last evidence that was needed to set the anti-slavery campaign irresistibly in motion. While the true humanity of the Negro was in doubt, or the impression of his rapacity and depravity was sufficiently strong and unchallenged, his enslavement could be made to appear either natural or just, but Adanson's delightful account revived and seemed to justify the classical notion of Africa as the scene of the Golden Age. Once the Negro could be reconsidered as a 'noble savage', Christian morality and philanthropy received the active addition of sentiment. In combination, they were as strong as they could be without the final reinforcement of political power.

When Thomas Clarkson was considering how to go about writing his Latin dissertation in 1785 on the theme set by the Vice-Chancellor of Cambridge, Dr. Peckard, 'Anne liceat Invitos in Servitutem dare?' or, 'Is it right to make slaves of others against their will?',[2] his researches led him by way of Anthony Benezet's *Historical Account of Guinea* to 'the great authorities of Adanson, Moore, Barbot, Smith, Bosman and others'.[3] Clarkson approached the writing of his dissertation simply as a literary exercise, with his reputation as a Latinist at stake, but once he had plunged into his subject, he felt overwhelmed by the facts. 'It was but one gloomy subject from morning to night. In the day-time I was uneasy. In the night I had little rest. I sometimes never closed my eye-lids for grief.' But he persisted. He submitted his essay. He was awarded the first prize and, according to custom, he read his essay publicly in the Senate House.

[1] ibid. p. 164.   [2] Clarkson, i. 205.   [3] ibid. pp. 207–8.

The event that followed Clarkson's reading, which determined his own future and affected the future of hundreds of thousands of other lives, witnessed to the extraordinary power of the books he had studied with such care. Clarkson recalled that he became 'very seriously affected' as he travelled back to London after reading his essay:

I stopped my horse occasionally, and dismounted and walked. I frequently tried to persuade myself in these intervals that the contents of my Essay could not be true. The more however I reflected upon them, or rather upon the authorities on which they were founded, the more I gave them credit. Coming in sight of Wades Hill in Hertfordshire, I sat down disconsolate on the turf by the roadside and held my horse. Here a thought came into my mind, that if the contents of the Essay were true, it was time some person should see these calamities to their end.[1]

Clarkson speaks with the conscience at last fully awake and alert to its duties, half a century after Job ben Solomon had been returned to the Gambia. Since his return the lamentations heard in Joseph Warton's ode 'To Liberty' had never ceased:

> And Guinea's captive Kings lament
> By Christian lords to labour sent,
> Whipt like the dull, unfeeling ox.

[1] ibid. p. 210

CHAPTER SIX

The Return to Bondou:
Gum and Gold

THE Royal African Company's kindness to Job ben Solomon while he was their guest in England and their concern for his safety after his return showed foresight as much as altruism. It was remarked even of James Oglethorpe that he redeemed Job either 'out of Tenderness, or thinking he might be usefull'.[1] The Company was in serious competition with the French for trade, and one of the means used with great effect by the French to gain the goodwill of the natives and confirm them in the French interest, was to send some of their chiefs to France and return them overwhelmed with the splendours of French civilization. They followed this policy with the Indian chiefs of North America and the English tried to copy it,[2] and the unfortunate venture of bringing William Ansah Sessarakoo of Annamaboe to England in 1749 was initiated as a reply to the successful visit to France of his brother.

The Company hoped that Job would repay their kindness, and in the letter they sent to their officers at James Island at the time of his return, they were quite specific in their expectations. 'We do further recommend it to you,' they wrote, 'to consult with him about the most proper and safest way of sending him home to his own Country and for this purpose to give him all the Assistance that lies in your Power and if the person you shall send up the River with him should be willing to accompany him into his own Country, possibly by that means he might be able to do the Company good Service by opening and settling a trade and Correspondence between the Nations of those parts and our highest Factorys.'[3]

The Company was extremely anxious in these years to exploit the Gambia and the hinterland more fully and systematically than they had done in the past, both as a source of raw materials and as an

---

[1] See above, p. 89.   [2] See Bond, p. 33.
[3] P.R.O., T.70/55, pp. 221–2.

unlimited market for manufactured goods.[1] When Francis Moore was appointed factor at Joar in January 1732 he was instructed to procure as large quantities as he could of cotton, indigo, malagueta pepper, hides of various kinds, Palma Christi seeds, and different sorts of wood:[2] 'And to induce the Company's servants to be vigilant in opening new Trades, they gave Twenty *per Cent.* Encouragement to those who should discover any new Goods, out of the Gains that should arise from them.'[3] The commodity most eagerly sought for after gold was gum.

Gum senegal was first imported into Europe by the Dutch at the beginning of the seventeenth century from their factory at Arguin, on the coast to the north of the Senegal. After the French had dispossessed the Dutch, under the terms of the treaty at The Hague in 1727, the whole of the gum trade fell into French hands, giving them a monopoly in all the markets of Europe. Before the importation of gum senegal, gum arabic, brought in through Marseilles from Arabia, had been in general use, but gum senegal was quickly found to have not only similar but superior properties and came to be preferred to the other. The gum was put to a multitude of uses: 'it is indispensable in almost every process of dying, and in the manufacture of printed cottons; it is used in silks, ribbons, lawns, gauzes, cambrics, and hats; it is also necessary in medical and confectionary preparations; the painter and the gilder are compelled to use it, as well as many other trades too numerous to mention.'[4]

The importance of the gum trade increased with the development and rapid growth in the eighteenth century of the industries to which it was necessary, and England and France were competitors in many of those industries, in that of silk and other printed textiles especially. The silk-weavers of Spitalfields were always claiming protection against French silks and as it was in dyes and designs that the English weavers were markedly inferior, the damage that might be inflicted on their rivals by denying them the gum that was essential to giving their silks their unsurpassed finish, or punitively raising its price, was

---

[1] In 1733 the Company 'proposed, in order to increase their assortments of goods at their factories, and for the purpose of carrying on a large inland trade with their vast countries behind their forts and factories, to create bonds under the common seal, to the value of twenty thousand pounds, bearing four per cent. interest; to which their general court agreed'. (Adam Anderson, *An Historical and Chronological Deduction of the Origin of Commerce*, 1801, iii. 196–7.)

[2] Moore, p. 10. (of App. II).   [3] ibid. p. 93.

[4] S. M. X. Golberry, *Travels in Africa*, 1803, i. 138. Golberry's account of the gum trade is the fullest I have found and, unless stated otherwise, my remarks are based on him.

one of the reasons why the trade was endlessly squabbled and fought over.[1] But the trade was sufficiently lucrative in itself to encourage the African Company to try and share it with the French, or to discover an alternative source of supply.

The gum—white or red, but similar in properties whatever the colour—comes from two species of the acacia. The main source was the three forests of Lebiar, Sahel, and Alfatak, lying inland and to the north of the Senegal, on the edge of the Sahara. At the end of the rainy season, about the middle of November, when the dry and keen harmattan begins to blow, the sap rises in the acacias and exudes through natural fissures in the smooth bark, where it congeals as drops of gum, round or oblong, or sometimes vermicular in shape, of a clear colour, red or white. Each of these forests was harvested by a tribe of nomadic Moors, who moved southwards from the wilderness at the beginning of December: 'an immense army, the disposition of which is equally confused and savage; it is a wild assemblage of men, women, young girls and boys, children at the breast, and an innumerable number of camels, oxen, and goats'.[2] The harvesting of the gum took six weeks, and after being packed into immense sacks made of tanned oxhide, it was carried down to market at a place significantly known to the French as the Desert, on the bank of the Senegal between St. Louis and the fort at Podhor. The sale was transacted in a shrill hubbub of unscrupulous and savage bargaining.

Only the capture of St. Louis could have given the English immediate access to the trade of the three forests,[3] but there were always the

---

[1] The French determination to maintain their monopoly of the trade in gum and their efforts to defeat the English challenge is fully discussed and illustrated by André Delcourt, *La France et les Établissements Français au Sénégal entre 1713 et 1763*, Dakar, 1952, pp. 179–358. The silk-masters of London petitioned the Commons in January 1752 to do something to improve supplies, now seriously threatened by the decline of the Royal African Company, or else 'the French will certainly be able to undersell us at foreign markets, with respect to all printed silks, calicoes, linens, and cottons; and if they should, we hope it will not be imputed to the extravagance or luxury of our people, but to our allowing them to get a monopoly of the material so necessary in that sort of manufacture' (*London Magazine*, June 1752, p. 267). An interesting expression of the great importance of the gum trade is given in a memoir written *c.* 1755, after the loss of Senegal, urging upon the French government the reasons why it must press for the restitution of its rights in the Senegal (Bibliothèque Nationale, 'Memoire sur le Sénégal', pressmark, Fr. 12079).

[2] Golberry, i. 162.

[3] Several English traders tried trading directly with the Moors at Portendick, a bay on the coast to the north of St. Louis, but they could only do so in safety under the protection of the Royal Navy. The coast was patrolled by French cruisers during the season. See Delcourt, pp. 273–91.

possibilities of another route to it, or of an alternative source of gum, and the Company had been searching unremittingly for them at the time of Job's return to the Gambia. When Francis Moore was serving at the factory at Brucoe in May 1733, he was ordered particularly by the Governor, Richard Hull, to obtain as much as he could of the gum from a tree called *Pau de Sangue*, 'which is of great value'.[1] The gum from this particular tree was known as gum dragon, but it was unfortunately inferior to gum senegal.

The Company's efforts in finding an alternative supply were not, however, entirely unsuccessful. Richard Hull encouraged one of the best-known of the native merchants, Jonco Sonco, a Joloff from Yanimarew, 'a stirring man',[2] to search for gum, and two Moors of his acquaintance, Malacai See and Malacai Con, eventually brought back with them from the country lying to the north of the river about a pound of a 'very fine white gum', which proved to be of the right kind. Moore sent the sample down to James Fort but forgot to explain where it had been obtained, and was ordered by Hull to supply the details immediately so that the information could be promptly sent back to the Company in London by a vessel about to sail. Moore was too ill himself to interview the Moors, but he sent John Westwood, a writer under him, and Captain John Brown, the master of the *Flame*, one of the sloops, and as a result of their inquiries he was able to report to Hull, on 20 November 1734, the approximate position and extent of the forests where the gum had been collected.

The forests lay about five days' journey north of the Gambia, setting out from Yanimarew, and seven or eight days' journey south of the Senegal. They were about sixteen days' journey long and six days' journey wide, amply stocked with rich gum trees, and uninhabited. They were shared by the people of Yany, the Grand Joloff, and Futa Toro. Moore saw at once the importance of this information. 'I began now to hope, that the Gum-Trade might be enlarged and made considerable, since *Job's* country, which is called *Foota*, lay on the Edge of the Forest, and was but four Days Journey from *Fatatenda*, and by his bringing that People into a good opinion of the *English*, they might be prevailed upon to trade with us, and bring Quantities of that Commodity to *Fatatenda*, from whence it might be carried by Water with small charge to the Fort.'[3] Hull was so elated by the information that he wrote to the Company in London on 5 December, telling them that he had now succeeded 'in my Attempt for the Discovery of Gum *Senegal*, or rather Gum *Gambia*, and for bringing the Whole of that Trade in the Company's Hands only'.[1]

Richard Hull was so convinced of the importance of the opportunity that had now presented itself that he decided to travel to the forest himself with Job, who was at the time of his writing his dispatch to London living in James Fort with him. When Francis Moore embarked from Joar on 8 May on the first leg of his return to England and was seen off by Hull and Job, they were on the eve of leaving for Yanimarew and the gum forest.[2]

They set out for the forest, but they did not reach it. When they arrived at the capital of Yany, they were held up by the two great obstacles to travel in those parts, warfare and drought. The king and all his great men agreed, however, to allow only the Company to have the gum produced in their part of the forest. Messengers had also been sent with similar proposals to Futa Toro and the Grand Joloff, but Hull returned before their answers. He had planned to set up a factory on the borders of the forest, as the most effectual way of securing a monopoly of the trade for the Company, and in order to facilitate its establishment he sent a man to buy four camels from the Grand Joloff and to load them with gum from the forest on his return. The camels were brought back safely, but the forest had not been reached on account of 'there being so universal a Scarcity of Corn, that a Famine was caused in those Parts, and which reaches even to *Yanimarew*, and Places adjacent on the North of this River'.[3]

The sudden extension inland of the Company's operations on the Gambia gave considerable concern to the French, who treated them as an infringement of their assumed privileges. At the time of his visit to Yany, Hull would have pressed on to the forest as soon as the rains had begun and broken the drought, had the French 'not offered some Proposals, and attempted to dispute the Rights of this River'.[4] The proposals offered by the French led to an agreement being tentatively reached between Governor Richard Hull and Peter Felix David, the Director of the French East India Company, whereby the French agreed to supply the Royal African Company annually with from 200,000 to 400,000 or 500,000 lb. weight of gum, taking payment in slaves, in return for the Company's ceasing to trade in the commodity direct. The Court of Assistants in London congratulated

---

[1] ibid. p. 19 (of App. IV).
[2] They probably set out on 12 May. 'Job a great Fooley' was included in the list of those who shared in the £39. 16s. 3d. spent at Yanimarew on presents and liquor from 10 April to 12 May (P.R.O., T.70/1452, p. 94).
[3] Moore, p. 20 (of App. IV).   [4] ibid.

the Governor on the arrangement and earnestly recommended him 'to encourage so valuable a branch of Trade all that you possibly can, by the most punctual complyance of your agreements with them'.[1] A contract intended to last for ten years was finally signed between David and Hull's successor, Charles Orfeur, on 14 May 1740. By its terms the French East India Company agreed to furnish the Royal African Company annually with 360,000 lb. of gum in return for three hundred 'prime slaves', the men all to be between fifteen and thirty, and the women between fourteen and twenty-five years old.[2]

Richard Hull and Job ben Solomon returned from Yany at the end of May. Hull went down immediately to James Fort and Job began preparations for his journey home. He had already been in the Gambia for almost a year, but the distracted and famished state of the country, which had made it impassable as Hull had already experienced, prevented him from risking himself and his valuable cargo of goods on the road. The reports coming in were that it was now safe to travel and on Saturday 14 June 1735 he set off for Bondou, accompanied by Thomas Hull.

Thomas Hull, a nephew of the Governor, Richard Hull, had arrived out from England as a writer in May 1733 and, after serving first at James Fort and later at Brucoe, was at the time of his journey with Job in charge of the factory at Joar. He may have been chosen to accompany Job because of his connections, but he was himself eager to explore the interior parts of Africa. He was at least qualified physically for such a strenuous enterprise, but intellectually he was an incurious, phlegmatic man, and this was to have at least one unfortunate consequence.

Hull was being offered a better opportunity for exploration than any that had yet been granted to an Englishman. He was travelling in company with a native, who, if not quite as important in his own country as his English hosts had supposed, was certainly a notable, and whose influence and sincere gratitude to the Company for his deliverance would help to allay the suspicions and avoid the open hostility that would otherwise have made such a journey impossible. And the rewards might be great. Job's country was supposed to border on the fabulous gold mines of Bambuk, which had been a lure to Europeans for four hundred years.[3] But more was at stake than gold. Could a factory be set up with Job's help in Bondou and firm

[1] P.R.O., T.70/56, p. 24.
[2] P.R.O., T.70/1424, p. 174. See also Delcourt, pp. 341–2.
[3] Bambuk was the long-sought-after country of Wangara; see Bovill, pp. 248–9.

communications be maintained between it and the Gambia, it was easy to hope that all the trade that the French now enjoyed could be diverted from the Senegal, and those vast interior densely populated territories become a market for English manufacturers. The alternative was sufficiently alarming also to inspire action. When Cornelius Hodges was on the Faleme and Senegal in 1690, he learnt to his consternation that the French were already as high as Dramanet and might, if they became established, 'frustrate us' on the Gambia 'of the greatest part of our trade for slaves'.[1] Since then the French had actively tried to consolidate their position with exactly this purpose in mind, setting up new factories where they could, though with little permanent success, and attempting, in 1730 and 1732, to survey the mines at Nettico. Rumours of these plans had almost certainly been brought down to James Fort by the African slave traders. Unfortunately for the French, their surveyor was killed by the natives in Bambuk.[2] Consequently the object of Hull's mission was so important that he was ordered to keep a journal so that his steps might be retraced and the possibilities more fully appreciated and understood.

Hull left the factory at Yamyamacunda at 7 o'clock in the morning on Saturday 14 June. He began by sending his horses and asses across the river and at midday he crossed himself with his goods, which he loaded on to one of his horses and one of his two remaining asses, the other being sick. He had with him two guides, sent down to him by Endeney Seca, the Governor of Congcord (Cauncade), one of the principal towns in the kingdom of Woolly, three messengers, and a butler—a hired native servant—who had been recruited for him in Sutamoe (Sutema) by John Cooper, the factor at Yamyamacunda. The party proceeded three or four miles that afternoon to the village of Cobas (Covas) where they were joined by 'Mr. Job', who had been waiting there for them. As it was too late in the day to travel further, they spent the night in the village, where they were visited by some of the local chiefs. They heard that a girl in a near-by Fula village had been killed by lightning the night before; the rainy season had begun.

The next morning they were ready to start at 6 o'clock, but the weather looked so black that they were afraid to stir. After a 'tornado of rain', it cleared up and by 10 o'clock the whole party, now increased to eighteen, were on the road to Moncodaway, about ten miles distant, which they reached in the late afternoon. Moncodaway had been a

---

[1] *English Historical Review*, xxxix. 94.
[2] See J. Machat, *Documents sur les Établissements Français*, 1906, pp. 36–46 and *passim*.

'large strong town', but it had been destroyed by fire the year before. They passed the night there.

They were on the road again by 6 o'clock the next morning, 16 June, and by travelling hard they made the twelve miles to a large town called Suncabar by noon. Between Moncodaway and Suncabar they passed a great hill 'with large plain Stones upon the top, with a great many places like the Marks of peoples feet, which I was inform'd was done formerly by a King of Cabbah who came thither to fight'—one of Hull's few topographical notes. The Alcaid's name was Manjama Size. Hull rested in a house belonging to a man called Marramormodue until 3 o'clock in the afternoon, when he and most of the party pushed on another six miles to Congcord. Job and two of his people had to be left behind at Suncabar because one of his asses was too sick to go on.

Congcord—'formerly a Town of force, but now . . . decay'd'—was ruled by Endeney Seca, the Governor appointed by the king of Woolly, and as Hull could not proceed through the kingdom without permission, he was delayed for three days in the town. As the entries for these days are among the most continuously interesting in his journal they are worth giving in full.

As soon as he arrived in Congcord, at 6 o'clock, he went to the Tabaubo Mansa's house. The term Tabaubo Mansa meant 'white men's king' and the office went back to the days of the Portuguese, when a native was specially chosen in the large trading centres to see that the white merchants were protected and justice done to them. He then sent

the Messengers Mr. Cooper and the People of Sutamoe sent with us to this great Man, to give the Governor's and Chief Merchants' service and to acquaint him of the business they had sent me upon, but thought it too late to go myself that night.

About 8 had a hard Tornado of Thunder and rain.

17th

At 8 this morning came Mr. Job and his People, who we left at Suncabar last night.

At 9 we all went to the Palavouring house where this great Man Endeney Seca, Nackwood and Sambo his younger Brothers and all the People of the Town was ready to receive us. I saluted him with 7 Gunns and gave him the present Mr. Cooper sent for the King of Wooley.

At 11 I telling all my Palavour I was sent upon, broke up and went home.

About 3 this great Man himself came and told me how proud he was to think that the Company would settle a Factory in this Country and every body that brought Trade thro' this Country should be well used and that he would send a Man of Note with them as a Safe Guard to Yamyamacunda.

Corn and Rice is so scarce at this place, I can't get it for any Money.

18th

About 9 this Morning came the Master of the Town to me and return'd the Company thanks for the present and promis'd a Cow.

This Day entertain'd a Butler in the Company's Service at 6 Months for a Tradeing Gun.

This Evening had the pleasure to see all the Young Girls of the Town dance.

This Night went and spent about an hour with the Master of the Town, he is a little old Man, but very good Natur'd. I'm inform'd here is in this Country large quantities of Elephants, as likewise Teeth.

19th

This Morning went to see the Master of the Town and desir'd to know when he thought he could dispatch us? His Answer was, either to Night or to Morrow Morning.

Here is great plenty of Goats and Guanous, the latter are so plenty and tame that they run about the houses in the Town, no one being suffer'd to hurt them.

I'm inform'd that the Natives of Tinda are on the Way for the Company's Factory of Yamyamacunda, with Teeth and Gold.

Here Mr. Job bought an Ass.

This Evening sent for the Master of the Town to come to Supper with me, which he did, and at the same time inform'd me we should set out to Morrow morning.

Every traveller in this part of Africa was to learn to his chagrin how much time he must waste and how many presents he had to give before being allowed to proceed beyond administrative towns such as Congcord. Hull was fortunate. Endeney Seca was as good as his word and Hull and Job, with a party of fifteen, were able to set out again at 7 o'clock on the morning of 20 June.

They travelled for two days without interruption in a north-easterly direction, making about fifteen miles each day. One of the towns they passed, Sowro, had been 'burnt in the last fight of Wooley'. Their supply of grain was beginning to run low, and there was little to be found in the neighbourhood. Hull was able to buy some rice, in a village called Canophy, only by paying in silver. He had to open one of his 'caggs' (kegs) specially, and he had also to lend Job two 'Zellots' to buy rice for his people. The whole of 22 June was spent at Canophy cleaning the rice.

They were only able to make eight miles the next day because they had to wait for permission from Cassa Cadong, the Master of a large town called Casong, before they could proceed. But they made up somewhat for the delay by travelling sixteen miles on 24 June, crossing a large creek which, Hull was informed, flowed from the Senegal into the Gambia through the Samy River. They reached a town called Calore at 1 o'clock in the afternoon and decided to stay there the night in order to let Job buy some corn. 'About 4 came all the people of the Town to the Bantaba, Drums beating, the men acting as tho' fighting and a great deal of merry-making; this was on Account the Master of the Town never saw or heard of white Men's being here before.' The women were so afraid of Hull's colour that they refused to come near him. The Master and everyone else in the town were slaves belonging to 'the late king of Wooley'. The weather was now so bad that they spent the whole of 25 June at Calore.

After the rain had cleared up, they were able the next day to reach a large town called Cambey, the last town in Woolly; ahead, lay the four days' journey across the Wilderness that separated Woolly from Bondou; an uninhabited region of woods and sandy scrub, tracked by herds of elephants. They spent a day in Cambey making their preparations and trying to hire a guide. All the men were hard at work in the fields and none was willing to accompany them, but Job was at least able to replace with another ass a horse he had had to leave behind. The party, now fourteen strong, set off at 9 o'clock in the morning of Saturday 28 June and travelled hard, in spite of the rain. 'I thought we might as well travell in the rain as set still in it,' Hull wrote, 'as having nothing to cover us, and that we must not expect to sleep in a house for these 3 Nights, so must make the best of our Way.' They slept that night in shelters made of boughs, native style.[1]

They travelled hard all day on Sunday and on Monday they were on foot before dawn, in order to take advantage of the brilliant moonlight. Hull was almost entirely concerned with distances and directions and stopping places, but he at least noticed on this day that they crossed 'a sort of a large Creek but little water in it, with large trees about it'. They ate their last fowl with that evening's meal.

The rain held them up the next morning, but they were still able to set out at 5 o'clock. Before stopping at another large and wooded creek to dress rice for their midday meal, they passed a broad pond of

---

[1] Hull's route from Woolly to Bondou across the Wilderness was the one followed, more or less, by Daniel Houghton in 1791 and Mungo Park in 1795, the explorers sent out by the African Association.

water called Sittadella, which was supposed never to dry up. They continued again in the afternoon and within six miles came to the banks of a small river called, according to Hull, the Ynere or Yarico— actually, the Nerico. 'The people inform me,' Hull reported, 'it rises between the Grand Jolliffs and Futa and comes away here, so thro' Tinda into the River Gambia, it is but small here and runs from North to South, they acquaint me it's much larger to the South and that here is water enough for a sloop in the Rains.' They could see a mile beyond the river the houses of Goodery, the first town in Bondou.[1]

Job was at last almost within reach of his home, after more than four years' absence, but the laconic Hull does not give even an inkling of what Job must have felt. He only reports that at Goodery 'Mr. Job dispatch'd a Messenger to Bundo to acquaint his friends of our Arrival in these parts', and that while they were waiting in the town for the messenger's return, the people of the district came crowding in to welcome Job and congratulate him on his return, after adventures stranger and more improbable than any other that can ever have befallen another of their compatriots.

The people were all Mohammedans, Hull noted, and were subject to Bondou and governed by 'a sort of Farrong'—which, in Hull's terminology, was 'a sort of King or Emperor'—called Bubacar Tombadoe, who lived some distance away. The countryside was rich in cattle and goats, wildfowl were plentiful, and elephants and swarms of bees, 'but these people have no Notion of making Wax, for they have very little if any Correspondence with White Men, but sell their Elephant's teeth for little to the Merchants as they pass for the river Gambia'.

They spent two whole days, 2 and 3 July, waiting at Goodery for the messenger's return. Hull whiled away the time as best he could; at least their provisions were more plentiful, the master of the house where they were lodging having made them a present of a cow. He spent the morning of 4 July taking an observation and found that the town lay in the latitude of 14' 33" degrees north.[2] The weather was appallingly hot, hotter than Hull had ever known it on the Gambia.

---

[1] Goodery is the present-day Goudiry Foulbé, a provincial centre, not the neighbouring provincial centre, Goudiry, which, as Professor Curtin has informed me, came into existence with the railway. By following on the map the distances and directions entered by Hull each day in his journal, we arrive within a mile or two of Goudiry Foulbé, but in spite of this accuracy I am unable to identify any of the places he passed with any certainty, except for the river Nerico.

[2] He was out in his calculation; the correct latitude would have been 14' 10", to within seconds.

Later in the day, when Job's messengers had still not returned, they could bear the delay no longer and at 4 o'clock in the afternoon set out for a small town called Wild, about five miles from Goodery. In the evening Hull had a bout of fever, brought on, he thought, by taking the observation under such a grilling sun.

They were not able to press on the next day until 2 o'clock in the afternoon because of the rain, but once they were started they march-ed hard and made the fifteen miles to the next town, Bullabuck, by 9 o'clock in the evening, which was very good for a man with a fever. They were now within five miles of Job's own town, which was called Chambey, the present-day Diamweli.[1] The gently rising countryside, a later traveller observed, was 'beautifully diversified by hill and dale, and thickly covered in every direction with small villages'.[2] The country must still have been suffering from the devastating effects of civil war, but in more settled times it showed signs of Fula industry everywhere and appeared 'opulent in a high degree'.[3]

The morning of Sunday 6 July began with a little rain, but by 9.30 they were on the road to Job's home. Job dressed himself splendidly for his return and was wearing 'a silk Damask Gown made after this Country['s] fashion, a black Velvet cap and Mundingo breeches', the most voluminous of breeches. The gown may have been the one that had been specially made in London for him, before his presentation at Court. When he came within sight of his house all his relatives and friends poured out to welcome him, dancing and singing, and Job himself galloped his horse wildly up and down firing off guns and pistols. He rode so furiously that his horse 'drop'd down under him, being not able to stand no longer'. Only on this occasion does Hull catch any of the excitement and drama of the moment, though the sight of Job's house had a very different effect on him than it had on the exile: 'I with much ado arrived at Mr. Job's house,' Hull observed sourly, 'had I not known it to be a Mahometan Town, should have thought it to be a Hogg house.' But Hull was now seriously ill with fever.

Job's joy was inexpressible. 'I must leave you to guess... the Raptures and pleasure I enjoy'd', he told a friend; 'Floods of Tears burst their way and some little time afterward we recover'd so as to have some discourse, and in time I acquainted them and all the Country how I

---

[1] By Hull's directions alone Chambey must be in the neighbourhood of Youpé-Amadi, but Professor Curtin has pointed out to me that on the grounds of pro-nunciation Diamweli is clearly the correct place.

[2] Gray and Dochard, p. 122.
Park, *Travels*, p. 61.

had been redeem'd and Conducted by the Company from such distant parts as are beyond their Capacity to conceive. . . .'[1] Immediately on his return Job began to keep a month's strict fast, in gratitude to God for his restoration.

Thomas Hull spent five months in Chambey, from 7 July to 3 December; five whole months. He stayed there under the most favourable of circumstances, protected by a man of rank who owed great obligations to the English and was eager to repay them. He could have reported in detail on the domestic and economic life of an interesting people and tried to explain the internal revolutions of the Fula who, especially in Bondou, were on the eve of a great period of national and religious expansion. Instead, he entered in his journal day after day such pointless comments as 'Last Night had a Tornado of Thunder and Rain', followed by 'Nothing remarkable', or, simply, for the entire day, 'Nothing remarkable'. 'Nothing remarkable' sums up Hull's Journal. What a chance was missed! Had Job's companion only been someone like Richard Jobson or Francis Moore, we might have had the most remarkable account of Africa of the century.

The only excuse that can be offered for Hull is that he was ill with malaria for at least the first month of his visit. He suffered severely from attacks of 'fever and ague' and treated himself by taking a 'vomit' on at least one occasion and regularly and heavily dosing himself with the 'bark', or quinine. He ran out of his own supply of bark and had to buy more from Job. The season was also unhealthy for horses and Hull remarks on one of the Company's horses or asses being ill almost as often as he refers to his own poor health.

Hull may have been sick and incurious, but he was not entirely idle. He had come to establish if possible a factory for the Company in these parts and he used for this purpose all the contacts Job could offer him. Job's house may have seemed at first glance to resemble a hog's house rather than the palace Hull was expecting, but Job was clearly a man of standing and considerable influence. Rank was seldom reflected in domestic architecture among the Fula of Bondou, and their houses of whatever shape were undistinguished, some 'entirely composed of clay and rough timber, are square and flat roofed', wrote a later observer; 'others are round, having the walls of the same material as the former, but are covered with a conical roof, formed of poles and thatched with long dry grass; the third and last are entirely composed of wood and dry grass, in the form of a half splaire. The doors of all are

---

[1] Job to Jacob Smith, 27 January 1736, see below, p. 184.

inconveniently low, particularly the latter, which is rendered the more unpleasant by its serving, at the same time, as door, window and chimney.'[1]

The king of Bondou, as Hull styles him—more correctly, Eleman; head of both Church and State[2]—had his capital at a large town called Phenah about eight miles south of Chambey,[3] and on the evening of the day they arrived, he sent a messenger to welcome Hull and Job to the country. Hull sent the man back the following morning with the message that he himself would wait upon the king as soon as he was able and explain his purpose in visiting the country.

Phenah and the villages round about had become the refuge of the exiled Siratick of Futa Toro and his adherents. The Siratick was Job's old schoolfellow, Sambo—Sambo Clajo[4]—who had been recently overpowered by his younger brother, Conco, and forced to flee the country. The rivalry and wars between these brothers is one of the great themes of the legends and epic poetry of Senegal. Sambo called to see Job and Hull four days after their arrival, in company with two of Job's elder brothers. One of the princes of Futa, also an exile, called to see Job on 1 July, and four days later one of Sambo's sisters came to try and sell Hull some gold. He was unable to purchase it for want of amber, one of the most coveted articles of exchange in this part of Africa. The last reference to these refugees from Futa and the only indication of what they were plotting comes under the entry for 31 October. 'Came here Sambo Clajo, late King of Futa,' Hull noted, 'to take his leave of Mr. Job for he is going to try for the Capp once more.' What could be more exasperating? Hull must have been told about Sambo's plans to recover power and the means at his disposal, but he allows it to pass unremarked, along with so much else.

Hull paid his first visit to Eleman Maccah, the ruler of Bondou, on Monday 14 July, accompanied by Job and a linguister. He arrived at Phenah at about midday and as he approached Eleman, he saluted him by firing off his guns and pistols; unfortunately one of the pistols burst, but without doing harm. The palaver lasted until 3 o'clock and at the end Eleman Maccah promised 'that the Company

---

[1] Gray and Dochard, pp. 126–7.

[2] The Eleman—strictly, Eliman, i.e. *el-iman*—was Maka Bubu Malik Si, who had regained power in 1728 or 1731; see *Africa Remembered*, ed. Curtin, pp. 27–8. The greater title of Almamy was taken by the rulers of Bondou later in the century.

[3] Phenah was most probably the old ruined town of Féna, lying on the road between Koussane and Sanbakalo, as Professor Curtin has suggested to me.

[4] Sambo Clajo in Hull's Journal; Sambo Guelaye was the contemporary French version of the name. He is the Samba Geladio Jegi of the Denianke dynasty; his brother was Konko Bubu Musa; see above, p. 66 n. 2.

should meet with the best of Usage he could help them to'. He insisted on accompanying them part of the way home, which he did riding on the largest horse that Hull had seen since he had arrived out in the Gambia. It rained so hard that they were very thoroughly drenched. Eleman showed the sincerity of his goodwill by sending one of his brothers to call on Hull the following day and by calling himself two days later, when he invited Hull to stay with him for a time and go shooting. Hull did not take up the invitation, though one of his occasional diversions was to go wildfowling with Job.

Eleman was the head of an oligarchy rather than an autocrat, and although he may have been ready himself to support the Company, the other leaders had still to give their assent. An assembly was called for 9 September and Hull understood that they were to consider 'some extraordinary Affairs concerning the Country's good and concerning my Message from the Company for promoting Trade, and as to the bad and good fortune and usage of Job'. Hull was invited, but as he was unable to go, being now without a horse, Job went alone.

Hull's absence on this occasion is specially to be regretted, as even he might have left some account of the proceedings, particularly of Job's manner of recounting his trials and adventures. He did not even record the name of the place where the assembly was held, but Job was away for four days, returning on 13 September. During his absence Hull had 'nothing remarkable' to report, except for a 'dry Tornado'. On his return Job 'brought the news of all the Countrys being well pleased with the Company'; a satisfactory decision.

But Job also returned with some less pleasing news. Hull's arrival in Bondou had been noticed with alarm by other strangers in the region. Chambey lay about six miles from the Faleme River, and near its junction with the Senegal, about twenty-two miles downstream, the French had an important fort, St. Joseph's, at Macanet on the Senegal. News travels with surprising speed between communities as closely connected as those of Bondou, and shortly after he had arrived in the country Hull was astonished to find himself being questioned by a native interpreter in the employ of the French. Hull told him that if his employers wanted to get in touch with him they had better not try to do so in French, for he was unable to understand a word. A little later, on 28 July, Hull was again met by 'the French Linguist belonging to Maccana [Macanet] or St. Joseph's Fort in Gallam', this time 'with a Letter wrote in French, so the contents I can't tell, but gave him another wrote in English'.

Hull may not have been able to read the letter, but he preserved it, so the courtly and civil address of M. De Balmauir, the Governor of Galam,[1] was not lost entirely.

Je viens d'apprendre Monsieur qu'il est arrivé des blancs Etrangers, dans le Païs de Bondow; dans l'incertitude ou je suis, s'ils pourront lire le François, je hazarde cette Lettre; pour leur offrir en cas qu'il en est besoin, les Secours qui dependront de Moy, et que les François donnent toujours avec affection à tous les Etrangers qui peuvent être apportée de les recevoir d'Euxs.

Si vous pouvés [*sic.* pouvez] lire ces Caracteres, je Vous prie de me faire reponse, et d'être persuadé que si Vous me marqués vos besoins, je Vous rendray tous les Services qui dependeront de Moy, je Vous prie si Vous pouvés le faire de me marquer les Motifs de Vôtre Voyage dans ce Pais-cy. Si c'est le Com[m]erce qui Vous y mêne Vous ne divés pas craindre que j'en sois jaloux ni que je Vous nuize en rien. Si c'est quelque malheureux Accident, Vous pouvés compter sur tous les Services qui dependront d'un bon françois et d'un Chretien.[2]

Hull could not read a word of this epistle, but since the linguister who had brought it assured him of M. De Balmauir's goodwill and anxiety to help him, he promptly replied in something as like the same style as his bluntness would allow. Hull at least knew De Balmauir by name, for he was aware that he had a brother trading in the Gambia. De Balmauir appears to have thought Hull might have been the bearer of a letter from his brother. Hull's 'answer' was dated 'Bundo, July the 28th 1735' and addressed to 'Monsr. Belmore', a splendid anglicization:

I just received Yours of the 21st ult. but as to the Contents therein am uncapable of knowing, by reason, as I desir'd your Messenger when here before, to acquaint You that I could not read French; But as to your Linguist telling me any thing You have got at your Fort is at my service, I return You my best thanks.

---

[1] M. De Balmauir's is not a name that occurs among the names of the French India Company's officers given by Delcourt, *La France et les Établissments Français au Sénégal*, but the contemporary records are far from complete. De Balmauir subscribed himself as Governor 'de Galam pour la Compagnie'.

[2] I have kept the spelling given in Hull's Journal.
    'I have learnt, Sir, that some Europeans have arrived in Bondu, and although I cannot know whether or not they can read French, I am writing on chance to offer them, in case of need, whatever help I can. The French are always ready to offer help to strangers who are in a position to receive it.
    'If you can read this letter, I must beg you to reply and make known your needs. I shall do all that I can to help you. May I ask you to tell me what your purpose is in this country? If it is trade that has brought you here, you need not fear that I shall be jealous or do anything to interfere with you. If you are here by accident you can rely on the help of a Frenchman and Christian.'

I was sent here by the English Company's Governor and Chiefs of James Fort, with one Job, a Native of this Country, who was made a Slave about 5 Years since and afterwards carried in to England, made free and sent back into his own Country by the Royal African Company, to see that he nor his things was not abused by the Natives in the River Gambia.

As to your Brother's sending You a Letter by me, is what he did not, for he did not know of my coming into those parts tho' he was in a large ship in the river Gambia when I came away.

If you have got anyone with You that could write English, should be glad you would do me the favour of letting me receive a Line or two from You.

I hope You will excuse this, being very much out of Order, so conclude, wishing you health, tho' unknown.

'Belmore' was greatly touched by his messenger's account of how he had found Hull sick and completely without any European comforts and he immediately sent two laptots—free blacks in service with the French—to him with a rather handsome parcel of goods and a letter complaining that he also was unable to read the other's letter.

Je Vous envoye Monsieur 20 Biscuit, 5 pintes de l'Eau de Vie, 2 pintes du Vin rouge, 1 pain de Sucre, 1 pinte d'huile, du Vinaigre et quelques autres bagatelles, sur le rapport que mon Laptots m'a fait que Vous manqués de touttes ces Choses.

Je n'ay peu malheureusement lire Vôtre Lettre et pense de même, que Vous n'avés peu lire la mienne, je suis faché que Vous ne puissiés apprendre combien je voudrois etre aportée, de Vous procurer ce que Vous pouvés avoir besoin pour la Vie; si les Chemins et vos affaires Vous permettent de Venir jusques icy, Vous me fairés un Grand plaisir de le faire.[1]

The Frenchman's letter and present, carried by the laptots, reached Hull on 14 August, but of all the goods listed by De Balmauir in his letter, only the twenty biscuits and a bottle of brandy were actually delivered. The messengers told Hull that 'the Governor had pack'd up a great deale of provisions, but could not get people to bring it for fear of the Natives of Bundo'. The suspicion is that the rest of the things disappeared on the road. The messengers left to return to St. Joseph's the same evening, taking Hull's letter of thanks back to 'Monsr. Belmore':

[1] 'I am sending you, Sir, 20 biscuits, 5 pints of brandy, 2 pints of red wine, 1 sugar loaf, a pint of oil and one of vinegar and a few other luxuries, acting on my Laptots' report that you are in need of such things.

'Unfortunately, I cannot read your letter any better than you can mine and I am distressed that you cannot know how much I should like to supply you with what you must need to survive. If the route is open and your business allows you to come here, it would give me great pleasure to welcome you.'

I just received yours of the 16th ult. as likewise the 20 Biscakes and bottle of Brandy for which I return you my best thanks; But as to the Contents of Your Letter am unsensible of, which is no small uneasiness to me, for did I know the Contents, I then might perhaps be capable of sending You an Answer suitable to this which I received.

I have no more to add than that I am perfectly recover'd of the Fever which I had on me, when Your last Messenger was here and that I return you many thanks for these and all other favours, which you are so kind as to bestow on, Sir, Your most obedient and most humble Servant.

De Balmauir might assure Hull of his goodwill and express the hope that it would be put in his power to entertain him, but the reports that Job brought back from the meeting of the council on 13 September gave a very different idea of his intentions. The council agreed to stand by the Company 'against the French or others, and that the Company should have all possible Security and encouragement for their Servants and Effects', but the French were trying hard to prevent this new alliance. Job was told at the meeting, and repeated to Hull on his return, 'that the French Governor at Gallam had made offers to any that would deliver me [Hull] into his hands. To which Job replyed that they were fools they did not take the Money offer'd and then to deceive them.' Hull cannot help but have thought that such cheats and counter-cheats were dangerous, especially since he was soon to discover that the French were closer at hand than he might have supposed, at least within distance to have him kidnapped. At about 7 o'clock in the morning of 14 September, the day after Job's return, Hull unexpectedly 'heard the great Gunns fire at Maccanah or Gallam Fort, so conclude the French Vessels are arriv'd at that place'. And to confirm that the noise was indeed guns and not thunder, he heard them fire again—sixteen in all[1]—at 1 o'clock in the afternoon. The vessels arriving were the fleet of shallow draught boats that were sent up to the fort each year with supplies and trading goods, when the annual floods made the river navigable. The proximity of the fort gives much more point to Hull's observation on 10 November: 'I have been several times inform'd of the great Summes of Money being bid by the French of Gallam or Maccana for my life, or that any one would drive me out of this Country, for they are very sensible that had the English Company a Factory any where hereabouts, their Trade would be very much lessen'd and to their Sorrow and great Shame Ours very much enlarg'd.'

The French were the more alarmed because, as they quickly learnt,

---

[1] The fort—a mud fort—'est monté de 16 canons', in 1725 (see Machat, p. 27).

Hull did not intend only to try and established a factory in Bondou; he wanted to push across the Faleme River into Bambuk and divert the gold trade into the Company's hands. The natural route into the country was up the Sanonkolé—or the Rio di Oro, as it was significantly called on European maps—which flowed into the Faleme only a few miles away from Chambey. The French fort of St. Pierre, founded by André Brüe in 1714, but since abandoned, had been tactically sited on the Faleme at Kaynoura, near the confluence of the two rivers. Hull hoped to travel himself to Nettico where the richest gold mines were, making arrangements in advance through his connection with Job and relying on Eleman Maccah to provide him with guards for protection, but just as he was starting to lay plans in September, he heard that fierce hostilities had broken out between Bambuk and its hereditary enemy to the north of the Senegal, the kingdom of Kassan—or Cassa, as Hull calls it. He was told by Hamman Sambo,[1] one of the great men of Bondou, who called on him with a man from Nettico on 24 September, that the fight was over, but ten days later, on 5 October, he heard that 'the People of Cassa are a coming again to take away some more of the People of Bumbuck'. The long trek to the coast for many natives and the horror of the Middle Passage and perpetual exile were about to begin.

While Hull was waiting undecided how next to proceed, a messenger arrived for him on 10 October from 'one Tommamy Yaule[2] a great slattee or king of Furbana [or Farbana or Ferbanna]', one of the most important towns in Bambuk; but Hull now learnt that for no evident reason, except possibly on account of the outbreak of hostilities, 'the Governor or Chief and every body else deserted it suddenly in the night and went to Gallam'. One of the reasons behind Tommamy Yaule's approach to Hull, quite apart from interests of trade, may have been the one mentioned by Hull, that the 'French are not at all liked by any of the Natives because they are too proud and insulting and abusive to the Blacks'.

Hull was eager to take up this invitation, especially when he learnt later that Tommamy Yaule was willing to send him on to Nettico and the mines, and on 24 October he sent Job to Eleman Maccah to learn when he would be ready to provide him with an escort to Furbana. But it was easier to make requests than to get them granted, especially when they meant helping a European towards the interior of the country, even the good friend of such a man as Job; and Hull now

---

[1] Hull also calls him Hammade Sambo.
[2] Hull also spells his name Tomamy Ynale.

became involved in a series of excuses and delays. He went with Job on 4 November to a trading town called Conjure[1] on the Faleme River to talk with a chief merchant—a slattee, or slatty—Slattee Cabalie, about travelling to Furbana. The next day Slattee Cabalie returned the call and promised to take him to Furbana and even beyond, to Nettico; but four days later, on 9 November, a messenger came from the Master of Nettico himself, begging him 'to stay till the rains are near at an end, because of the fight between them and the People of Cassa, which would make the Roads very dangerous for a white man to travel'. But it was not Hull's intention to travel unprotected and on 13 November, after reporting at Phenah, he was told by Eleman Maccah 'that Tomamy Yanalie [*sic*] had sent to him to let me come to Furbana, and if I would go, he would send his People with me'. Hull promptly asked him to let his people continue on to Nettico with him; 'at first he denied me, but when I made him sensible, that it would be for his Country's good he consented, that they should go with me, but not as yet, by reason of the Warrs.'

But Hull was not prevented from travelling to Furbana or Nettico by reason of either the wars or native diplomacy. He gave up his plans voluntarily upon running out of trading goods and losing all his horses. He had sent back to Yamyamacunda for more horses almost as soon as he had arrived in Bondou and found how essential they were, and how subject to mortality, but it took his messengers three months and four days to go there and back. When they did return, on 27 October, they brought only one horse; the other had had to be left at Cohunt. The new horse was seriously sick of 'gripes in his belly' within three weeks and did not last long. When another invitation was extended to him to travel to Nettico he was forced to decline. On 22 November he noted: 'Came here a great Man from Nettico with a small ring of Gold sent by the Master of that place, to acquaint me he should be glad to see me there: As for the Warrs he believes it is over for this Year; My Answer was, my Money was gone, besides my horse sick, so that it was impossible for me to go as yet, but I would go down the River and acquaint the Governor and Chief, and if they thought proper, I would be back again in less than 2 Months.'

The principal subject of Hull's laconic Journal is naturally the

---

[1] Hull describes Conjure as 'almost close to Fallam River', and according to his directions this would place it more or less where Sénoudébou is shown on the present-day maps. It may very well have been Kaynoura, where the French had had their fort of St. Pierre. In the chapel of this fort Job must have seen the religious pictures, to which Bluett refers (see above, p. 96).

writer himself, but he occasionally allows us to catch a glimpse of Job. Two of Job's elder brothers came to see Job, and his sister visited him, bringing him a present of a goat; but his most surprising visitor was the second of his two wives, the one who had married again during his absence, believing him dead. She came with her daughter by Job and stayed for three days. Job was also reunited with his faithful wife and rewarded her, in part at least, by having nine bars' worth of small silver coins made into two manillas, or bracelets, for her. Job also gave presents to Hull. When he was able to buy a horse from a trader with four to sell, each for the price of four slaves, he gave Hull 'a present of his old sick one', which soon died, but he also gave him a present of 'about 10 Barrs of Gold', which Hull credited to the Company in his accounts.

Job had brought some, but by no means all, of his English presents home with him, and since Hull was going down to the Gambia with the intention of returning to Bondou and proceeding on to Nettico within two months, Job decided to travel back with him. But he decided first to move his family from Chambey to Conjure, the town on the Faleme River where many of his friends lived.

In the most exasperating manner, Hull gives no reasons for anything he reports Job as doing, nor does he ever attempt any description: the people—their dress, houses, and customs—the appearance of the landscape; nothing is described. The women liked to wear a light French gauze which set off their handsome figures, but however good-looking they were, their manners were rough and greedy; they were always asking for presents. The houses were surrounded by a high mud wall and resembled a citadel. The banks of the Faleme River were covered towards the end of the year with splendid and extensive fields of corn, and the rapid shallows of the clear river were ingeniously fished with woven baskets, often as much as twenty feet long. The small fish resembling sprats were pounded to a paste, which was kneaded into loaves and dried in the sun. But these are details that have to be collected from the journal of a later and famous traveller in these parts—Mungo Park.

Hull was ready to set out on 4 December. He had a hard journey ahead and a dangerous one. As he said, having no horse he was forced to 'trudge it afoot to Yamyamacunda', and the country through which he had to travel was greatly disturbed. Civil war had broken out in Woolly and one of the pretenders to the throne, beaten by Endeney Seca, the Master of Congcord, had fled to Bondou. Hull had warned the people of Bondou not to harbour him for fear of 'spoiling

Friendships with the great Men' of Woolly, but he was no doubt also frightened of jeopardizing his own relations with Endeney Seca.

Hull left Bullabuck at 7 o'clock on the morning of 4 December and covered the fifteen miles to Wild by 2 o'clock in the afternoon, arriving there 'very much tir'd'. Job, who was travelling on horseback, caught up with Hull's party there and together they pushed on a further five miles to Goodery, where they spent the night. In order to travel fast they travelled light, without even burdening themselves with water, but when they came to the Golore River the next day, after a march of seven miles, they were alarmed to find it dry. Hull acted promptly and with the presence of mind which shows how well equipped he was in certain respects to be an explorer. He knew that not too far ahead of them lay the pool at Sittadella which was supposed never to run dry, so 'I took Mr. Job's horse and went full speed before to Settadella and took water and went back to meet them which saved some of their lives, who were almost dead with drought'.

They spent three days and two nights crossing the Wilderness, taking a different route from the outward journey, but on Monday 8 December they reached Cohunt,[1] a large strong town, the first in Woolly. The second of the two horses that had been sent up to Hull from the Gambia had fallen sick here and died, and now the master of the town, Madey Setta, begged Hull to give him the bridle and saddle as a present. Hull's butler was ill and had to be left behind at Cohunt when they set out the following morning, but the rest of the party travelled fast and made the sixteen miles to Casong, the next town, by late afternoon. The butler was determined not to be left behind and walked into Casong at 9 o'clock, five hours after the others.

After Casong, they rejoined their outward route. At the next place, Canophy, they were met by 'Tarrong Walley, Mr. Johnson's Butler, who was seiz'd on Mr. Lawson's Palavour, who insisted upon my paying him or otherwise I should not pass this town. After a long palavour did persuade him to go with me to Yamyamacunda and that I would pay him there, which he agreed to.' Hull also had trouble passing through the next town, Sowro, where the king of the country demanded a present, on the excuse that Hull had not given him anything on his way out. Hull satisfied his importunity with some 'Arrango small Corral', a popular kind of bead. But the following day, 13 December, they arrived at Congcord and felt that they were at last among friends; Endeney Seca and his people were 'overjoyed' to see

[1] This is not the same Cohunt he passed through near the beginning of his outward journey.

Hull safely back. They stayed for two days at Congcord, Endeney Seca entertaining them well and killing a cow in their honour, and while they were there they learnt the serious news that the pretender to Woolly, who had been beaten by Endeney Seca and fled to Bondou, 'was on the Road with a great number of People belonging to that place to try for this Country'. Hull's advice to Job's friends before leaving had not been taken seriously to heart.

Hull left Congcord on 16 December and reached Moncodaway late in the evening. The next day, a Tuesday, was his last day on the road and the entry under this date, 17 December, is the last in the Journal:

About 6 set out and about 2 arrived at Yamyamacunda, which I was very glad to see, it being 6 Months and 3 days since I saw a White Man. Deliver'd Mr. John Cooper the remains of my Cargo having bought in all but $11\frac{5}{16}$ Oz. Gold and received in presents $\frac{15}{16}$ Oz. which makes $12\frac{1}{4}$ Oz. Had I had large fine Coral and more goods I could have bought a great deal more at 40,, Country Money per Oz., which I am inform'd is the price the French Give for all the Gold they buy, which is very large Quantities. We were 22 days in going from Yamyamacunda to Chambey in Bundo which is about 185 Miles distance and is one day with another about $8\frac{1}{2}$ Miles a day, which as it was in the raining Season and that our People were well loaded, was hard travelling, but in coming back we travell'd about 14 Miles a day and reach'd Yamyamacunda in 13 days.

Hull's penetration into Bundo under Job's protection had immediate political repercussions. Whether or not De Balmauir, the Governor at St. Joseph's, had really tried to have Hull assassinated or kidnapped, as Hull was given to suppose, he certainly reported to his superiors in Senegal the unwelcome presence in Bondou of an agent of the Royal African Company. The Council of Directors at St. Louis dispatched a letter to Hull in Bondou on 18 December, the day after he had actually arrived back in Yamyamacunda, ordering him to leave the country. A copy was sent to the Governor at James Fort. The letter, even in its attached translation, left the strength of French feeling in no doubt.

We have see, Sir, with wonder how the Governor of Fort James have send you for make Establishment at Bondo Country beelonging of the River of Senegal and the Country of Bambouc which Country the french India Compagny have since long time in possession; as the English Company can't expect no Traffick or Commerce in that Country, we make You declaration that we see Your enterprise like Attempt upon Our Right.

We summon you in consequence to take off Your Establishment and to go off the Country of Bondo. Iff You dont we shall do with the ne[ce]ssary

N*

Voice [i.e. 'Voyes' = means] and permitted against the Interlooper and trangressors against the rights of the Nation.

We are perfectly
The Chief Consil of Directors
Your most humble and
obedient Servants.[1]

Anglo-French relations in the Gambia were already severely strained. Contrary to earlier agreements, which permitted them only one post on the Gambia, the French had recently attempted to maintain an agent at Vintain as well as their factory at Albreda. They had withdrawn from Vintain in the face of protests from James Fort, but they had successfully competed with the English by trading from ships in the river, even though they were supposed to sail no higher than Albreda. De Balmauir's brother had served in one of these vessels.[2]

The French, in their turn, had been greatly alarmed by Governor Hull's attempt to reach the gum forests lying between the Senegal and the Gambia, and they became even more concerned when they learnt of Thomas Hull's arrival in Bondou. The Council of Directors at St. Louis wrote to the Governor at James Fort on 3 February 1736, sending a copy of their letter to Hull in Bondou, and roundly charging the English Company with trespass. If you have sent your agent into Bondou, they wrote, 'to set up a factory in that country, we believe that you have overlooked the fact that it is situated on the River Faleme, which is part of the Senegal, on whose banks we have long had a fort and have now a market for trading in supplies. We have in neighbouring Bambuk, two small forts and our trade extends into both it and Bondou, which are dependencies of Galam and Futa Toro respectively. As we were in those regions before you we definitely cannot allow you to set yourselves up in territory to which we have the exclusive commercial rights. We are counting upon you recalling your agent, now that we have made the position clear.'[3]

---

[1] The original and the translation were both appended to the official copy of Hull's Journal.

[2] These matters are the subject of an exchange of letters between the French and English. The letters are in the Archives Nationales, Paris, pressmark, Colonies, C6[11].

[3] '. . . si vous l'avés envoyé pour former un établissement dans ce Païs, nous croyons que vous avés jgnoré qu'il est scitué sur la Riviere de Feleme qui fait partie de celle du Senegal et sur les bords de laquelle nous avons eu un Fort et ou nous avons actuellement une Caze pour la traite des Vivres, nous avons dans le païs de Bambouc qui luy est limitrophe deux Fortins, et nous étendons notre commerce dans ces deux Contrées qui sont de la dépendance de Galam et du païs des foules; c'est pourquoy nous vous prévenons que nous ne pourons point souffrir que vous vous établissiés sur des terres ou nous avons le droit éxclusif

This letter did not reach James Fort until 23 May and lay unanswered until 3 July, when Governor Hull returned from Yanimarew to the fort. The English began by levelling against the French a charge of bad faith. The agreement between the two Companies provided that Albreda and James Fort should both offer the same price for slaves, which, at the moment, should stand at forty bars, but the French were actually and unscrupulously offering fifty bars, the going price up river at Joar. This charge was so extravagantly unjust that one is left wondering how Richard Hull and his colleague Charles Orfeur had the effrontery to bring it: as they alone set the price at Joar, if it was fifty bars a slave there, the French would not stand a chance of buying any at ten bars a head less lower down the river. After running through one or two other similar charges, they came to the crux of the letter—the happenings in Bondou. They did not intend to say much at the moment about Bondou, except to affirm that they had no intention whatsoever of surrendering or discontinuing their rights to it, a riverain country, belonging to the Gambia; and as for Bambuk, they simply reversed the argument the French had brought forward in favour of their own rights. They believed that the English had preceded the French into those parts and based their claim to it on priority. 'We formerly maintained Factories at Nettico and Cambredou,[1] as the remains yet standing will prove', they went on; 'and there are natives still alive to swear to our having employed several factors in this trade. Although our operations there have been discontinued for several years, owing to the negligence of the previous officers of the Company, our rights to resume them have not thereby lapsed.'[2] They warned the French that they intended to re-establish

---

de Commerce, et sur notre déclaration nous comptons que vous rapellerés votre Commis.' (Archives Nationales, pressmark, Colonies C6[11].) The two forts referred to would seem to be those at Farabanna and Samarina, but the French hold was so weak and uncertain that it was a large claim to refer to these outposts even as 'fortins' (see J. Machat, p. 45).

[1] I am unable to find Cambredou on the maps.

[2] 'Nous avons eut autrefois une facture a Nettico et a Cambredou, comme les restes jusqu'a ce jour le prouvent, et encore il peut etre prouvé que plusieurs personnes ont été autrefois emploiés comme facteurs pour y faire le commerce plusieurs des natives le peuvent testiffier quoique par la negligence des Agents precedents pour la Compagnie, il a été pour plusieurs années omis, mais telle ommission ne peut jamais faire ou cause la confiscation d'un tel droit. . . .' (Arch. Nat., loc. cit.) The English claim was not altogether unsound. Cornelius Hodges had reached Bambuk, as we have seen (see above, pp. 27–8), but others had followed him. Le Sieur Charpentier, writing in 1725 about the gold mine at Tambaoura in Bambuk, remarked: 'Elle a été reconnue par le capitaine Ache, [or is this also 'Hodges'?] Anglais . . . qui vint pour découvrir la source de la rivière de Gambie . . .' (quoted in Machat, p. 34).

their factories and begin trading again, and they also expressed the hope that nothing might be done to harm any of their agents in those parts. In order to make the last point, with its implied threat, as plain as possible, they enclosed with their letter a copy of their letter to the French Governor at Galam, in which they asked him to treat Thomas Hull, or any other of the Company's agents, with the same kindness that they would show to agents of the French Company.

The letter from the 'Consil' of the French Company to Hull in Bondou, written after he had in fact left the country, and the belated exchange of letters between them and James Fort, illustrate exactly the difficulties that hung on every correspondence in those parts and the confusions that must follow any attempt to establish a chronology on their evidence. Job had begun to write back to his friends in England as soon as he had returned to the Gambia and to send them some of the curiosities they had asked for. Sir Hans Sloane told one of his correspondents on 16 September 1735 that he had already received a gift of some poisoned arrows from Job and that they were to be tried for their efficiency on dogs at the first opportunity.[1]

Unfortunately, none of Job's letters to Sir Hans appears to have survived, and, with the exception of the note he sent back with Francis Moore for the Duke of Montagu, the first of his extant letters to an English correspondent is one addressed to Jacob Smith, the drawing master at St. Paul's School and a friend of Joseph Ames, the antiquary.[2] Job wrote to him shortly after his return from Bondou, on 27 January 1736, giving his address as 'Yanimarow in the River Gambia', where he had gone to confer with the Governor, Richard Hull, who was still engaged in setting up a factory there in order to tap the trade from the neighbouring gum forest.[3] The letter, which may have been drafted for Job by the Governor himself, but certainly by some Englishman, is especially interesting because it complements the bare account of Job's return given by Thomas Hull in his Journal. The letter seems to have been turned by the amanuensis in several places with a view to enhancing the reputation of the Company, but it bears more clearly the marks of Job's deep piety and subtle address.

This is to acquaint you of my safe arrival at and return here from Bundo, being conducted safe and used with great Civillity all the Way, which was

---

[1] B.M., Sloane MS. 4068, copy of the draft of a letter from Sloane to an unnamed correspondent.
[2] Job's letter is addressed to 'Mr. Smith' and for want of any other candidate I am assuming that this Smith is Ames's friend—see Joan Evans, *A History of the Society of Antiquaries*, Oxford, 1956, p. 97.
[3] Thomas Hull's Journal under 16 December 1735.

owing to the respect and regard all the Natives in every part have for the Company and by being conducted by one white Man only which was the Governor's Nephew on the Company's behalf, which made no little Noise and was of much service to me. One of my Wives had got another husband in my Room and the other gave me over. My Father died soon after my Misfortune of being seized and sold for a Slave, but my Children are all well. My Redemption was so remarkable and surprizing that my Messengers and Letters sent on my behalf on my first arrival here were not Credited, but how elevated and amazed they were at my Arrival I must leave you to guess at as being inexpressible, as is likewise the Raptures and pleasure I enjoy'd. Floods of Tears burst their way and some little time afterward we recover'd so as to have some discourse, and in time I acquainted them and all the Country how I had been redeem'd and Conducted by the Company from such distant parts as are beyond their Capacity to conceive, from Maryland to England, from thence to Gambia's Fort, and from thence conducted by them to my very house, the Favours done me by the Queen, Duke of Montague, and other Generous persons I likewise acquainted them of, and all with me praised God for such his providence and Goodness, and as a more publick acknowledgement thereof I kept from arrival a Months Fast. I should think my self very happy in your Company in these parts if your Inclination continues to come in the Company's service.[1]

The poisoned arrows that Job had earlier sent to Sloane could have worked on the unfortunate dogs, for he asked Smith in a postcript to give his service to Joseph Ames, Dr. Oxley, and 'Mista Sail'—George Sale, dead by the time the letter reached England—and to assure them that while the book he had promised to send had been burnt in the wars, he would send the anti-poison at the first opportunity.

Thomas Hull's announced intention before leaving Bondou was to return and continue on to Bambuk and the gold mines as soon as possible, and, with the encouragement of the Governor, he began immediately to make preparations. Job had declared his willingness to accompany him and pay off his indebtedness to the Company by being useful in this way, but he had first to make arrangements for sending up to Bondou the bulk of his English presents, now that he had ascertained the state of his family and set them up at Conjure. The most convenient route was the one that he and Hull had just travelled, the recognized route for traders from the interior making for the Gambia, but the hostilities that had now broken out, between Endeney Seca and the forces raised in Bondou in support of the pretender to the kingdom of Woolly, made that road unsafe. The chances of moving so valuable a consignment of goods without its being greatly reduced by

---

[1] The original letter and a copy are in the library of the Royal Society. The copy is printed in Donnan, ii. 455–6.

the rapacity of local governors, or entirely lost through plunder, were too slight to justify the attempt. Job decided to risk his luck another way. As the French fort in Galam, St. Joseph's, was only a short distance from his home, if he could load his goods on a French sloop sailing from the Gambia he could ship them almost to his own door. He was able to make such an arrangement with the help of the Company, whose officers were individually often on good terms with the French officials and traders in the river, but in order to insure himself against a total loss, he stored part of his goods in the English factory at Yamyamacunda.

Thomas Hull did not travel as the only white man on this second journey. In spite of his having had Job with him on his visit to Bondou, he must clearly have felt the want of another Englishman to talk to, and on this further attempt to reach the gold mines he took with him John Kenn, one of the Company's soldiers.[1]

Hull was again ordered to keep a diary of his journey inland to 'Tombo Ouro or the Gold Country', as his destination was described, and to keep it more fully and observantly than his disappointing record of his residence in Bondou; but as such a diary, if it was kept, does not appear to have survived,[2] the only source of our knowing that the journey was successful in reaching Bambuk is a letter written by Job to Sir Hans Sloane immediately upon the party's return. Sir Hans promptly communicated it to the Royal Society on 4 November 1736 and a précis of it appeared in both the *Gentleman's* and the *London Magazines*. In this letter, the world could read, Job

very gratefully acknowledges the Favours he receiv'd in England; and in answer to some Things desir'd of him when here, says, he has been in the country where the Gum Arabick grows, (which at present we get chiefly from the French settlements) and can assist the English in that Trade: That he has been up the Country as far as the mountains from whence the Gold Dust is wash'd down, and that if the English would build flat-bottom'd boats to go up the rivers, and send persons well skilled in separating the Gold from the Oar (with which they may soon, and with ease, load their boats) they might gain vastly more than at present they do by the Dust Trade; adding, that he should always be ready to use the utmost of his power, which is very considerable in that country, to support them therein.[3]

---

[1] P.R.O., T.70/1447, p. 75.

[2] The incoming correspondence and papers of the Royal African Company for 1709–22 are, as Mr. Geoffrey Beard pointed out to me, to be found among the Chancery Papers in the P.R.O., but I have found no trace of the correspondence for any subsequent year.

[3] *Gentleman's Magazine*, 1736, p. 681.

Job's letter to Sir Hans had, as it was reported, contained only good news, but information reaching his friends in England earlier in the year told of an unfortunate reversal of his affairs. The Duke of Montagu and the Earl of Pembroke replied jointly on 26 April to Job's messages of goodwill sent to them by Francis Moore. They almost matched Job himself in piety of expression. After thanking him for the prayers of both himself and his fellow 'Mussulmans' for their prosperity, they continued, in words chosen carefully to sound as orthodox in the wilds of Africa as in the Strand: 'God Almighty is Great, He is the Common Father of us all, wee all worship Him, tho' in differing Form, and He hears the prayers of all who with a sincere heart call upon Him, and endeavour to follow that Universal law He has given to all mankind.' They condoled with him on the loss of his father, but they were also 'sincerely concerned' at the news they had learnt by 'another hand' of the loss of his goods, through the loss of the French ship to which he had consigned them. All they could do was to pray that God would eventually 'give you all those Blessings and Comforts to which as a good man you are justly entitled'.

They had one comforting item of news, which they tactfully kept to the last. Francis Moore, they were able to inform him, had sailed for Georgia with James Oglethorpe, an appointment that could only have been the result of his connection with Job, and, what was more important, his friend Thomas Bluett had returned to Maryland with their instructions 'to make enquiry for your servant there, and procure his liberty'. And with an assurance that they had presented his duty to their Majesties, these two generous noblemen closed by subscribing themselves Job's 'sincere friends'.[1]

The Duke of Montagu's interest in Job was not transitory. When he learnt that Thomas Hull had kept a diary of his journey to Bondou he borrowed a copy from the Company, though he no doubt found it, as the Company warned him, 'barren of the many usefull observations and Remarks that might undoubtedly have been made by Mr. Thomas Hull during the long time of his residing there'.[2] The Duke was naturally greatly disturbed by the news of Job having lost such a rich cargo so carefully assembled, and he pressed the African Company to make a strict inquiry. The Court of Assistants, who had now heard of the loss from Job himself, promptly wrote to James Fort reprimanding the Governor for his slackness in looking after Job's interest. The

[1] *Hist. MSS. Comm.* xlv. 388.
[2] P.R.O., T.70/55, p. 254.

Company could expect Job to support their trading interests in his own country, but

> we might much more have expected from him had you taken Care to follow our directions and to have sent all his things as farr up the River Gambia as you could with safety and there lodged them till he could have had an Opportunity of taking them away by degrees, and indeed considering the long tedious and dangerous Navigation of the Senegal and the Rival-ship in Trade which you well know subsists between the French and us we are greatly at a loss to guess what could induce you to trust any of them in such hands, or to send them by such a round about way to him, for had Job himself desired to have had them sent this way, you ought, if you had considered the matter rightly, to have opposed it as knowing that if they were they would never be delivered to him, which it seems proves to be the Case, it being now given out, as Job himself informs us that they were lost between Gambia and Senegal, but as Job seems to question the truth of this Report we do therefore earnestly recommend it to you to make the strictest and most particular Enquiry you possibly can into this Affair, and for your own Justification as well as for the Satisfaction of Job's Friends here to acquaint us with the result thereof by the first Opportunity.[1]

Had the Company and his English friends but known it, Job's position was far worse than might ever have been suspected. He had lost his freedom, not to speak of his goods, and stood on the edge of being transported to the French West Indies or Louisiana as a slave again.

The governors of the French India Company at St. Louis had reported back to Paris on 15 June 1736 that the Englishman who had been in Bondou had left on 16 December with an escort of fifty men provided by the people of Bondou. He intended to return immediately, they went on, still exaggerating, with a horse and asses laden with trading goods, but the officers at St. Joseph's were under instructions to chase him out of the country and arrest the Negro Job.[2] The rumours that had reached Hull of French attempts to have him kidnapped were truer than they might have seemed. But the French were finding it hard to put their intentions into effect. They were engaged in a bitter quarrel with Tonca Tuabo, one of the kings of Galam, over the customs due to him, and had been forced to fall back under protection of the guns of the fort, though the fort itself was in

---

[1] P.R.O., T.70/55, pp. 245–6.
[2] '. . . le Conseil de Galam doit faire son possible pour le chasser et faire arrêter le Negre Job.' (Archives Nationales, Colonies C6¹¹.)

bad repair and supplies were low. And then one day, on 6 June, to the astonishment of the French, Job, having just returned from the Gambia, simply walked into the fort to find out whether there was any truth in the alarming rumours that the French sloop in which he had shipped his goods had been wrecked off Portodally.[1] The French promptly clapped him in irons.

The country was at once up in arms at this injustice and the position of the French, already made precarious by their quarrel with Tonca Tuabo, now became grave indeed. On 6 November 1736 Claude St. Adon, the Governor of St. Joseph's, in succession to De Balmauir, wrote despairingly about his position to the Council at St. Louis. The fort was in ruins, the garrison was short of food,[2] the firewood was used up, the laptots had all deserted, and there was no trade to be had at all. In an attempt to redress the situation, the exorbitant customs demanded by Tonca Tuabo had been paid, but the country still refused to be pacified, all on account of Job. Should the Council insist that he should be sent down to them at St. Louis, it was impossible to anticipate what might happen.

When St. Adon wrote again on 2 December the situation had grown even worse. The Marabouts of Bondou and Dramanet (Doramana) and elsewhere, who shared all the trade of the region between them, had been so scandalized by Job's arrest, as St. Adon explained, that they had sworn a solemn vow not to trade with the French during the time of his detention. 'I saw with regret', he continued, 'that their zeal was not at all simulated, that such a scruple was really enjoined by their religion, and that the slave merchants were consequently diverting their trade to the Gambia.'[3] As he dared not set Job free without the consent of his superiors, though this was the course he urged upon them, he had decided to get on as good terms as he could with Job and had been so successful that they had drafted together a circular letter in Arabic, declaring to all the country that Job was living in his friend's house of his own free will and absolved from his vow any merchant who wanted to trade with the French. But they also had to send Job's priestly gown round all the Marabouts, a

---

[1] '. . . ce Négre Job . . . y etoit venu aprés le départ de l'Anglois de Bondou pour répéter quelques éffets que les Anglois avoient embarqués sur un de nos bateaux . . . qui a faire naufrage à la pointe des Cereres auprés de Gorée.' (6 October? 1736, loc. cit.)

[2] '. . . nous etions reduits a vivre entierement avec du lard.' (loc. cit.)

[3] 'Je voyois avec regret que leur zelle n'etoit pas simulé, que c'est reellement un point de leur religion et que les Marchands des Captifs prenoint tout de bon le Chemin de Gambie . . .' (loc. cit.)

formality necessary to absolve them of their oath.[1] As St. Adon cynically observed, all this purported to be for the good of the country and especially of Job, while being in fact vital for the prospects of the trading season.

The governors at St. Louis were exasperated by this ineffectual handling of the problem of Job. As they said, the officers in Galam ought either to have packed Job straight off to St. Louis before the country was aware of what had happened, or to have released him on the first signs of trouble. They wrote immediately to St. Joseph, ordering Job to be set free, and as the direct route up the Senegal was at the moment highly dangerous, they sent a second messenger round by the Gambia and overland, a long and tedious journey. Only the messenger from the Gambia got through, and by that time St. Adon had decided on his own responsibility that Job must be released.

The passage up the Senegal from its mouth to St. Joseph was always difficult from natural hazards; if the natives were hostile, impossible. In 1736 the French had not only to cope with the hostility of Tonca Tuabo and of the Marabouts supporting Job; they suddenly found themselves opposed by the Siratick of Futa Toro, whose realm lay on both banks of the Senegal. On 11 September the vessel carrying the annual tribute to the Siratick was surprised at Guiol by Siratick Conco (Konko Bubu Musa). The Frenchmen on board were slain, the Negro crew either killed or taken prisoner, and the vessel itself was pillaged of all its goods and furnishings, even down to the nails.

The French were exasperated by this insult to their prestige and by the threat to their communications with the interior, and took immediate steps to get Siratick Conco deposed. They put a reward of 3,000 *livres*, in arms, powder, cloth, amber, and other goods, on his head, and they tried to bribe the Brak of Oualo, the ruler of the principality lying between the mouth of the Senegal and Futa Toro, and the commander of the Ormans, the Moroccan troops, who had for several years exercised a great and unsettling influence in the region of Futa Toro, to take the field against the Siratick. But their chief instrument was Job's schoolfellow, Sambo—Sambaguelaye (Samba Clajo)—the deposed Siratick, whom Thomas Hull had met living in exile in Bondou and even then plotting to regain his throne.

---

[1] ' . . . j'ay été obligé de remetre ses hardes entre les mains de Marabous pour les relever de leur serment de fidelité, les casuites ayant decidé que cette formalité suffisoit pour le repos des consciences puisque nous n'avions tous ensemble qu'un seul et même object qui etoit le bien du pais et en particulier du Marabou Yob . . .' (loc. cit.)

The governors at St. Louis sent a messenger express to St. Adon, ordering him to enter into negotiations at once with Sambo.[1]

St. Adon's relations with Job, and consequently with Job's friend Sambo, and Job's fellow Marabouts of Bondou, were now of even greater consequence. When setting him free St. Adon had not been blind to the fact, as he informed his superiors, that Job had been so signally honoured by the king of England in order to secure his help in exploiting the mines of Bambuk, or, at least, in setting up English factories in the country. But in the course of a lengthy and intelligent consideration of the possibilities, St. Adon concluded that if such were the English ambitions, they were bound to be fruitless. The natural hazards, such as distance and terrain and climate, were too great to permit the economic working of the mines, and the Negroes were unlikely to relinquish voluntarily their rights in the land, of which they now very well knew the value. In addition, if the English established factories in Bondou they would overturn the great markets at Caignoux (Médine) and Tamboucany (Tamboucane), a prospect unlikely to enrol the country in their support. Job might be safely released, for the only condition of the country's support of the English was his ill treatment by the French.[2] Upon his release, Job returned quietly home and seemed to forget the English; in fact, St. Adon was able to report on 22 July 1737 that Job had been very useful in supplying him with some fine lustrous black linen and a quantity of excellent cornelians, a very important article of trade.[3] He was certainly behaving himself, and if he did not, St. Adon had the means, he thought, to stop his tricks or even to have him arrested yet again.[4]

Meanwhile, the strict inquiry which the Royal African Company had ordered James Fort to make into the loss of Job's goods showed that the loss was even greater than expected. The French sloop had certainly been wrecked off the coast near Portodally, with the loss of all the goods Job had consigned in her, but the rest, those that he had wisely reserved and stored in the Company's factory at Yamyamacunda, were lost in the fire that destroyed the factory on 9 August 1736.[5] Job could have actually enjoyed only a small part of his English presents,

---

[1] '. . . nous avons de faire attaquer Conco par les Ormans, par le secours desquels nous tenterons de remetre Sambaguelaye sur le thrône des Foules, nous avons envoyé a cet effet un éxprés en Galam . . .' (6 October 1736, loc. cit.).

[2] St. Adon to the Conseil Superieur at St. Louis, 2 December 1736 (loc. cit.).

[3] St. Adon to the Conseil Superieur at St. Louis, 22 July 1737 (loc. cit.).

[4] '. . . en supposant qu'il voulut faire quelque negotiation, j'ay assez d'intrigues dans le pais pour le traverse, et meme pour le faire enlever.' (St. Adon to the Conseil Superieur at St. Louis, 1 March 1737, loc. cit.)

[5] P.R.O., T.70/55, p. 254.

those that he carried with him on his first return to Bondou. When the Court of Assistants in London learnt of his double loss they wrote on 19 May 1737 approving of Richard Hull's 'having ordered Mr. Thomas Hull when he meets him at Bambau [Bambuk] to make him a small present for his encouragement'.[1]

The Court of Assistants had as yet heard nothing at all about Job's arrest by the French and were still counting on him to act as a guide and intermediary to either Thomas Hull or anyone else who might be sent out to develop the inland trade, on which the Company placed its best hopes for its future prosperity. On 19 May 1737, the same day as they were writing to approve of Thomas Hull's giving Job a present when he met him at Bambuk—Hull having been sent again to Bambuk and Nettico—the Court of Assistants were writing a letter to Job himself, which they were sending out to him by a new and remarkable emissary.

A few months earlier, on 13 January, the Court had met to consider two letters from Job dated 19 and 23 July 1736,[2] probably those telling them of the loss of his goods on board ship. Job had written in Arabic and the translations had been made by Melchior De Jaspas, an Armenian. At one point in the meeting the committee called in De Jaspas, who was in attendance, to explain a difficulty in the text: what did 'Cefnil Hull' mean? The Armenian agreed that it could mean 'Captain Hull'. But the Court had met not only to read Job's letters but to consider some proposals put to them by Melchior De Jaspas. He had offered his services as an explorer of the inland parts of Africa.

The Court gladly accepted the Armenian's offer and when writing to James Fort on 19 May 1737 by the *Guinea*, the packet that was taking De Jaspas to the Gambia, they briefly set out the unusual qualifications they believed he possessed for the duties for which he had volunteered, and gave instructions for his employment.

We have received two Letters from Job in which he expresses his good Wishes and Intentions for the Company's Wellfare, and as we think him very sincere and believe he may be of great Service to the Company, we have returned him an Answer by the hands of Mr. Melchior De Jaspas an Armenian—Native of Diarbekir the Capital City of Mesopotamia, who we gott to translate these Letters, and who upon offering his Service to the Company we have thought fit to entertain in the Station of an Assistant to

[1] ibid.

[2] I am unable to reconcile these dates with the date of 6 June given by the French as that of his arrest. These letters must have preceded his arrest and been written on the Gambia before his second return to Bondou. As they were in Arabic—they have not survived—the mistake may have lain in the translation.

be employed by you for carrying on and improving the Company's inland Trade, at the Allowance of Sixty pounds a Year for his own Salary and diet and Twenty pounds a Year for his Servant and we have likewise permitted him to take with him a Young Persian Slave of his own. He is recommended to us as a very honest and able person and as he understands the Arabick spoken in Job's Country, and is capable of learning any Language in a Short time, and is also very desirous of travilling into and making new discoveries in the Inland parts of Africa, we hope he may be of great Service to the Company not only in settling and carrying on a considerable trade between Bunda and our Factorys up the River, but likewise in discovering and settling a trade and Correspondence between the Countries where the Gold Mines lye and our said Factorys: and therefore we do recommend it to you to receive and use him kindly, and to give him all the insight you can into the Nature of the trade of the River while he stays with you, and as soon as the Season will permit to send him up the River with such Orders, Instructions and Assistance as you shall judge most proper and effectual for the purposes he comes for, and for his further Encouragement we have agreed to allow him the same Commissions upon all the Trade which he shall bring to any of our said Factorys as are allowed by our last Establishment to any of our Factors above Joar.[1]

Travelling out to the Gambia with De Jaspas was also a new factor called James Anderson, who hoped to travel inland with De Jaspas before being settled at a factory. Anderson died almost as soon as he arrived.

Melchior De Jaspas brought with him to the Gambia the Company's letter to Job, addressed to him 'at Boonda in Africa', the last of the Company's letters to him. It, too, was dated 19 May 1737.

Sir

1. It was with much satisfaction and pleasure that we received your two Letters to us dated the 19th and 23rd days of July 1736, whereby we were informed of your safe arrival at Boonda after having undergone so many Difficulties and Misfortunes which were however in the latter part of your Absence from your Native Country attended with Blessings and good Success, towards promoting the last of which we have contributed as much as possible, and shall continue to do so.

[1] P.R.O., T.70/55, p. 259. The Commission granted to De Jaspas is the 20 per cent referred to by Francis Moore, see above, p. 160. The Company's initiative in sending out an Arabic speaker came to be entirely forgotten. In 1788, Henry Beaufoy, the Secretary of the newly formed Association for Promoting the Discovery of the Interior Parts of Africa, in drawing up a Plan of the Association, wrote: 'Neither have we profited by the information which we have long possessed, that even on the Western coasts of Africa, the Mahometan faith is received in many extensive districts. . . . That the Arabic, which the Mussulman priests of all countries understand, furnishes an easy access to such knowledge as the Western Africans are able to supply, is perfectly obvious. . . .' (Quoted in Hallet, p. 45.)

2. We are concerned that you lost so many of your things, and wish you had not desired them to be sent in the French Sloop by way of Senegal, but rather left them in the Care of our Chief Merchants at James Fort till they could have found means to send them safe to you up the River Gambia. That French Sloop as we are informed was lost by stress of Weather on the Shore of Portodally, but if she had not been so lost we should have been doubtful of the French conveying and delivering your things safe, by the Way of the River Senegal. Our Chief Merchants at James Fort Gambia inform us that some of your things were destroyed by the fire that burnt down our Factory of Yamyamacunda, and we have ordered them to make a Strict Enquiry into the Truth of the Loss of those which were in the French Sloop.

3. We have delivered the Compliment which you recommended to us in your Letters to the Several persons.

4. We are pleased with the other part of the Contents of your Letters related to the Carrying on a Correspondence, as also a trade in your Country and the better to answer both those purposes have entertained Mr. Melchior De Jaspas the Bearer of this Letter as Assistant to be employed by our Chief Merchants, and we believe you will soon find him to be a very good and a very understanding Man, and therefore we recommend him to your favour and friendship. We have ordered him to make your King a present, and another present to you of which we desire your Acceptance as a token of the Respect and Friendship we bear you. We desire that we may constantly hear from you, we wish you good health, long Life and all other Blessings that it may please God to bestow on you.[1]

And subscribing themselves to this singular epistle as Job's 'Loving Freinds' were Sir Bibye Lake, the Governor of the Company, and fourteen members of the Court of Assistants, great men in the City.

The Company's letter to Job was to be given to him by De Jaspas, but hardly had he set out for the Gambia than a rumour began to circulate in England that Job might be in no position to receive it. The Duke of Montagu was greatly perturbed and immediately sent to the Company to make inquiries. Richard Spence, Secretary to the Company, hurriedly wrote to the Duke from Africa House on 26 August to reassure him.

Mr. Cromwell having called here and acquainted the Gentlemen of this Company that your Grace having heard something of a Report that Job had been secured by the French and sent to Martinico and that your Grace was therefore desirous to know if the Company had any advices that confirmed it. They have ordered me to present their Duty to your Grace and to acquaint you they are in great Hopes that Report is not true, but for your further Satisfaction have directed me to inclose Extracts of all the

[1] P.R.O., T.70/55, p. 257.

advices they have received relating thereto, which I have accordingly done, and with your Grace's Leave shall take the Liberty of informing you of what other advices the Company may hereafter receive concerning him.[1]

The Company's officers in the Gambia, having at last got news of Job's arrest, possibly by means of one of the agents they were now maintaining in Bondou and Bambuk,[2] had already taken steps to secure his release. Richard Hull having died in the previous January, Charles Orfeur, who had succeeded him as Governor, wrote to the French officers at Goree offering to ransom him, declaring that the king of England himself would want him brought back from the French West Indies if he had been sent there. As the Council of Directors at St. Louis remarked when reporting the correspondence back to Paris on 2 August 1737, Job having already been released, the answer to 'Sieur Orpheur's' inquiry was simple.[3] Either because of his uncle's death, or out of pique at De Jaspas's arrival, Thomas Hull, whom the Company had been relying on to initiate De Jaspas into the secrets of inland travel, had asked for his discharge and was returning home.

De Jaspas had arrived at the height of the rains, a sickly season, and he had hardly settled into James Fort with Joseph, his Persian boy slave, and his Scottish secretary, before the secretary, John Buchanan, died, on 11 August. The doctor in the fort, Dr. Gervan, had been unable to save him; and he was unable to save his own wife, Mary, who died at the end of the month, or even himself; the Doctor followed on 4 October. De Jaspas's subsequent career on the Gambia was to be as inauspicious as its beginning.

But good news was about to come, at least for Job. Thomas Bluett had found Job's servant, Loumein Yoai—or Lahamin Joy, as his name appeared in the Company's records—on his return to Maryland and, with the funds so generously supplied by the Duke of Montagu, had redeemed him and put him on a ship bound for London, where he was received and boarded by the Company. He arrived towards the end of 1737 and the Company at once made arrangements for his passage in a man-of-war about to sail for James Fort. Richard Spence

---

[1] P.R.O., T.70/48, p. 17.

[2] '. . . j'ay fait arretter par l'intrigue des Bagueris un espece de Courtier des Anglois qui se tenoit sur la route de Gambie. . .' (St. Adon to the Conseil Superieur at St. Louis, 22 July 1737; Archives Nationales, Colonies C6[11].)

[3] 'Le S[r]. Orpheur Gouverneur du Fort Jacques de Gambie vient d'écrire au Conseil de Gorée pour reclamer le Négre Job qu'il a appris être détenu en Galam offrant de payer son rachat et déclarant que le Roy d'Angleterre le fera revenir des Isles de l'Amerique s'il y a été envoyé, comme ce Négre a été délivre depuis longtems, la réponse est facile.' (loc. cit.)

wrote to Charles Orfeur and the other chief agents at the fort on 2 February 1738 by Loumein Yoai, with instructions on how they were to treat him. He sent a copy of the letter to the Duke of Montagu to reassure him that the African was being properly taken care of.

The bearer, Lahamin Joy, a black Man, is the Person who was taken and sold with Job and carried with him to Maryland; and by the great goodness of His Grace the Duke of Montague, he being redeemed from his Slavery and brought from thence hither; he now takes his passage for your place in the [blank] Man of War, Capt. [blank] in order to return to Job and his own Country, and His Grace having desired that he may be recommended from the Company to you; I am therefore directed particularly to recommend it to you, upon his arrival at James Fort to receive and entertain him at the Company's Expense and treat him kindly, untill you can send him up, either with Mr. De Jaspas, if he be not gone up the Country, or by the first convenient opportunity that may offer, and likewise to give him the best advice and assistance you can for that purpose. I am further to acquaint you that the Company will write to you in favour of this Man by their own ship the Happy Deliverance which will very soon be dispatched from hence for Gambia.[1]

How Loumein Yoai returned home is unknown, but a second providential release from slavery could have been the occasion for Job again galloping a horse in exultation until it dropped under him and summoning his fellow Mussulmans to thank God in the wilds of Africa for such a kind man as the Duke of Montagu, albeit an infidel.

De Jaspas probably did not accompany Loumein Yoai to Bondou. He never seems to have been on sincerely good terms with the officers at James Fort. In fact, he became so discontented that he asked for his discharge in 1738 and withdrew from the Company's service. The Court of Assistants reprimanded the Governor sharply for losing such a useful person. We are 'well satisfied', they wrote to Charles Orfeur, 'that had he but received at James Fort the treatment in general that is required and ought to be expected from persons supposed to be civilised tho' residing in a Barbarous Country,—allowances might have been made for any defects on his part (as we cannot suppose him without them) he would not have desired his discharge but have chosen rather to stay till the proper time and circumstances of Affairs in the Country would have admitted his being sent inland to answer the ends for which we sent him to Gambia.'[2]

As the incoming correspondence from James Fort is missing, it is impossible to tell what prompted this rather splenetic outburst on the

[1] P.R.O., T.70/56, p. 11.
[2] P.R.O., T.70/56, p. 21.

part of London, but De Jaspas, as London expected he would, returned to James Fort, having probably nowhere else to settle if he intended to continue in the Gambia, and re-entered the Company's service. The Court of Assistants at first advised that he should be sent to blaze a trail by travelling overland from the Gambia to Cape Castle, the Company's great fort on the Gold Coast, for which they 'would reward him handsomely for his trouble', but a better scheme presented itself. Almost as soon as Thomas Hull had returned to London in 1738 he petitioned the Company to be taken back into its service. The matter was considered at a meeting on 22 February 1739 when it was decided that Hull should 'be entertained as a Factor, and that Directions be given to the Chief Agents to employ him only for the Discovery and Improvement of the Company's inland trade, and to allow him the necessary Supplies and Assistants for that purpose'.[1] When he returned to the Gambia at the beginning of 1739 he carried instructions that Melchior De Jaspas was to accompany him on his journey inland.[2]

Whether or not Thomas Hull ever travelled again towards Tombo d'Ouro, or the country of the gold mines, is uncertain; his name disappears from the records of the Company after he has been noted as outward bound for James Fort; but De Jaspas was at last able to make one voyage inland, to Bondou, in company with Job. Job came down to James Fort in 1740 on business with the Company, and while he was there he proposed that he should be invited back to London to renew his old and lucrative acquaintance with the Duke of Montagu, Sir Hans Sloane, and all his other friends. Before he returned to Bondou, accompanied by De Jaspas, he put such a strong case for a voyage to England that Charles Orfeur wrote to London forwarding the proposal and asking for advice. The Court of Assistants' advice was prompt and unambiguous; they foresaw endless trouble from having Job once again on their hands. 'You did very well', they replied to Orfeur on 26 March 1741,

in taking the opportunity to send Job up again to his own Country with Mr. Jaspas, and we approve of your treating Job kindly while at the Fort, and of the present of 25 bars you made him on his going away; and if he should apply to you to come to England again, we would have you by all means discourage the same: but as to the 2 slaves and the several other things said to belong to him as mentioned in your 16th paragraph, if you are satisfied those things were applied to the Company's use you may give

---

[1] P.R.O., T.70/105, p. 161.
[2] P.R.O., T.70/56, p. 21.

Job credit for them, and also for the value of the two slaves, in case (as Job asserts) he did deliver them to the Company's Factor Mr. Roots.[1]

De Jaspas returned safely from his expedition on 26 May,[2] and he may have travelled again and even more widely in the region, attended by his Persian slave, but his name appears only once more in the Company's records.

Job's name, too, makes one further appearance in the records. He seems to have pledged his watch, perhaps the same watch that was presented to him by the Queen, against two slaves, and when the watch was lost, claimed its value from the Company. The officials in London were puzzled by the account of what had been going on, but they were at least clear that they were under no obligations to Job on account of his watch for, as they wrote on 11 October 1744, they were 'already sufferers to the amount of those slaves and further he can be no loser, since the two slaves were at least the full of his said watch'.[3]

The last reference to Melchior De Jaspas is of quite another kind. The Court of Assistants wrote to James Fort on 11 December 1746 to express its 'great concern' at the news that Charles Orfeur and De Jaspas had been murdered by the natives of Barrah.[4] The cause that roused the usually friendly natives to such violence is unknown.

De Jaspas's murder ended the Company's schemes of exploring and exploiting the mysterious inland countries with the help of Job, but even if De Jaspas had survived, it is unlikely that any further progress would have been made. The Company itself was on the eve of dissolution. Its only assets were its forts and establishments in the Gambia and on the Guinea Coast and its creditors were becoming as clamorous as its inveterate enemies, the separate traders from Bristol and Liverpool, who resented any attempt by a joint-stock company to control the African trade. The Company's charter was withdrawn by Act of Parliament in 1750. Its forts were to be maintained thereafter at the public expense and the trade itself to be regulated 'by a committee of merchants, representing the chief trading towns in the kingdom, to be superintended by the board of trade and plantations'.[5] James Fort, the symbol of the old Royal African Company's ambitions in the Gambia, was shortly deserted and in ruins. And with the winding up of the Company, Job ben Solomon disappears. He may have kept up some correspondence with his English friends: Thomas Hunt, the Laudian Professor of Arabic, consulted by Joseph Ames

[1] P.R.O., T.70/56, p. 31. [2] P.R.O., T.70/1448, p. 3.
[3] P.R.O., T.70/56, p. 47. [4] ibid. p. 51.
[5] Smollett, *History of England*, 1811, iv. 75.

over an Arabic inscription in 1744, remarked that he had 'not only heard of *Job* the African', but had 'some of his original letters', and thought it might be worth Ames writing to him about his problem.[1] Of Job's closest English friends, the Duke of Montagu died in 1749 and Sir Hans Sloane, at an advanced age, in 1753. Francis Moore seems to have died in Georgia and Thomas Bluett died in Maryland in 1750. The only suggestion that Job might have kept in touch with some well-wisher comes, improbably enough, from the records of the Gentlemen's Society of Spalding. Opposite his name in the list of its members, the date of his death is given as 1773, but there is not a tittle of evidence to show how that distant event could have been known among the flat lands of Lincolnshire.

But his memory, if it survived at all, can have survived only locally in his own country. When travellers at the end of the century crossed the woods and fields of Bondou within a few miles at the most of the village where Job had made his home and possibly died they heard no accounts of him. Mungo Park was not told that many years ago another white man had lived in Bondou, brought there by a native who after the most extraordinary adventures had returned safely home. Job had disappeared so completely into the anonymity of Africa that he was not even a tale to be told.

[1] Hunt to Ames, 31 August 1744; Society of Antiquaries.

CHAPTER SEVEN

Fires by Night

THE efforts of the Royal African Company to divert the trade of Bondou and Bambuk, and the great inland kingdoms lying beyond, towards the Gambia, had ended in failure. Mungo Park's two expeditions of 1795 and 1805, especially the second, which was made in strength, had the same object in view and also failed. Park's disappearance somewhere down the Niger, with the pathetic remains of his company, brought the British efforts to penetrate the region to a halt until 1818, when a large military force, under the command of Major William Gray, was sent into Bondou, largely in response to the renewed efforts of the French to exploit their position on the Senegal.

Major Gray and his troops entered Bondou on 14 May 1818 and left it on 24 September 1821, by descending the Senegal, from Bagnelle, not far from the site of the old fort of St. Joseph, to St. Louis, in a French steamship. By diplomacy and duplicity, by withholding supplies, by endless promises and occasional threats of force, the Almamy and the rapacious chiefs of Bondou effectively contained the expedition for two and a half years, until it was no longer in a position to push farther into the interior. Gray's delight at the arrival of the French trading fleet at Galam and his gratitude to the French officers for their 'most cordial assistance' is indicative of his loss of confidence. He had none of Thomas Hull's coarse but proud truculence.

When Major Gray had arrived in the Gambia in 1818 he had assembled his force at Bathurst, a new settlement (named after Earl Bathurst, Secretary of State for the Colonies), which was designed to replace the old Company's headquarters on James Island. Bathurst had been sited on St. Mary's Island, at the mouth of the river in the former kingdom of Cumbo, across whose burning sands Major Holmes had arduously trudged in the distant past. Gray was astonished on his return to Bathurst from Bondou and St. Louis three years later by the improvements that had taken place. 'Many fine substantial government buildings have been lately erected,' he wrote, 'and the British merchants resident there, have vied with each other in the elegant and convenient arrangement of their dwelling-houses and stores, all of which are built with stone or brick, and roofed with slate or shingles.'[1] The new town was prosperous and looked forward to vast increases in trade as the hinterland was opened up by British initiative.

But Major Gray himself, as he stood admiring the rising streets of Bathurst, was the reason why the colony would be unable to grow, as it seemed it must with such vast and productive territories lying at the head of the river. The failure of his expedition to Bondou, and the consequent resignation of the region to the more pertinacious French, meant that the main British effort in West Africa was finally transferred farther south, to Sierra Leone and beyond, to the Gold Coast and the Slave Coast, where the old Company factories had always outnumbered the French, those countries being far richer in Britain's special and fiercely defended monopoly—slaves; a trade that Britain had now renounced with disgust. The nineteenth-century partition of Africa was being sorted out according to the inescapable logic of the past.

Bathurst grew, but it grew slowly, after the first rush of its foundation. The Albert Market, the principal landmark in the centre, the gay epitome of local life, was opened in 1855. To walk about the town today is to feel arrested in the nineteenth century. The guards, bright in their red and yellow dress uniforms, stand smartly at attention in front of Government House, a private dwelling in appearance rather than an official residence. The Anglican Cathedral is on the same modest scale and suggests that as paternal and unostentatious an authority reigns above as the one who rules locally below. The Joloff women of the town, famous throughout West Africa for their style, who shop for cotton goods in the stores along Wellington Street, fill the duskiness of the arcades with the astonishing brilliance of their *pagnes* and elaborately knotted headtyes; a dress that is sported as naturally as plumage and strangely suits the old-fashioned appearance of the street. Farther down Wellington Street, salt from the saltpans across the river in Barrah, always a famous article of trade, stands stacked in wicker baskets along the road. Beyond the strip of foreshore, where the native craft are built and repaired, stretches the glittering estuary of the great river.

The river is still the principal line of communication; Gambia is

[1] Gray and Dochard, pp. 365–6.

still both banks of the river, from Cape St. Mary to Barracunda, and
little more. A good road, with a hard surface for much of the way, runs
along the south bank, from Bathurst to Basse, but travel on the north
bank is difficult, the tracks meandering crazily along ridges of exposed
laterite or losing themselves in pockets of loose sand. The river may
be a slower means of travel but, in spite of the overcrowding of the
only passenger boat, a more comfortable and far more sociable one.
The *Lady Wright* travels up and down from Bathurst to Basse once a
week, stacked with piles of trading goods and building materials over
which the passengers, representing all the peoples on the river, have
to push and scramble on their way to and from the nooks and niches
where they have managed to camp; good-humoured and accommodat-
ing in spite of every possible inconvenience.

The boat calls at each wharf, or *tenda*, along the river, loading or
unloading goods and passengers, and while it stops the villagers
crowd down to the riverside to trade or just to see and be seen and
chat. The places that Francis Moore and the other early travellers
named and described float into sight round the leisurely bends of the
river, or are glimpsed through openings in the wall of mangroves or
across the marshes lying between the river and the accompanying low
bluffs. Tancrowall, Joar, Brucoe, Yamyamacunda: the spelling has
changed, becoming scientific rather than simply phonetic, but most of
these places still appear on the map. The engines drone away on the
Lady Wright, but the river itself looks exactly as it did when Job ben
Solomon carried his two Negro slaves across; the same empty reaches
which seem to lie stationary under the paralysing weight of the sun; the
same yellowish grey sky of the brief evening, against whose overmaster-
ing emptiness the palms suddenly stand out in angular, black outline;
the same groups of villagers strolling back into isolation once the boat
has passed.

The Gambia is the same and remembers its past; not officially, but
as people remember it, irregularly with lapses and inexactitudes. At
Bintang—or Vintain—where La Courbe had been entertained in 1686
by the Portuguese wife of the notorious Captain Hodges, I was told by
the oldest man in the village, who talked gently, with his eyes half
shut, as if he would lose what he scarce remembered unless he took
care, that the Portuguese village used to stand farther along the bluff,
to the right of the present village, overlooking the lagoon of the Bintang Creek. And over here, he went on, leading the way down a rough
track, was the burial place of a Portuguese lady, a rich lady, once
married to a captain, an Englishman. The grave was among the dry

straw of the field and his hand lightly pointed to a particular but unmarked place. Had this strange memory really come down through so many years, or did a later beachcombing Englishman as brutal as Hodges marry another Portuguese lady? A boy led me across the fields beyond Bwiam to the thick clump of stately baobabs and silk cotton trees which mark the site of Geregia, where the Portuguese had a church; a site that is unmarked on any modern map and is supposed to have been lost. The quietness was complete, like deserted sunlit rooms. At Fattatenda, the highest of the Royal African Company's factories on the river, where Thomas Hull was once factor, the headman of the village unerringly conducted me through the tall dry grass along the river to the site of the post: a flat outcrop of rock, defensible, as well as standing safely above the level of the floods. The hot afternoon was utterly silent, except for the brushing of the grass, and as we stood looking down on the river, glinting as it flowed between its steep rust-coloured banks, without a sign of life in sight, we could feel the weight of Africa—all the miles of wilderness leading up to Bondou and beyond—at our backs.

The Portuguese came first; they are remembered first. The headman at Jufureh—the Gillyfree of Francis Moore's map—pointed out in detail where each of the Portuguese buildings had once stood, few of them marked at all, or only by broken walls. He even indicated the directions in which the roads had crossed, the good roads required by such a busy centre of trade as San Domingo. Only after he and his friends, each complementing the others' information, had disposed of the Portuguese—who were the relations of several of them through ancient marriages, after all—did he lead me down through a dense wilderness of elephant grass towards the river and the burial ground of the English of James Fort. Stones with writing on them, he explained, were to be found when the grass was burnt off annually, but now the thick grass hid all. Here Francis Moore had buried William Rusling, deep enough to prevent his corpse from being dug up by the 'wolves', as he had promised. James Island could be seen lying offshore, hardly more than an accentual mark in the middle of the shimmering estuary, infinitely remote.

The same stories are being told today as in the past. When Francis Moore rode from Cuttejarr to Samy in July 1733 he wanted to ride on across the Samy River to Fendalacunda, but the owners of the horses refused to let them be taken over the river; 'they being more afraid for their Horses', Moore remarked, 'than we were for ourselves, that the Crocodiles should seize them'.[1] Was it really the crocodiles, or were these beasts the excuse? The crocodiles have been almost shot out along the Gambia, but as I stood on the deck of the *Lady Wright* trying to mark the mouth of the Samy River—the Sandugu Bolon on modern maps—my Joloff companion told me that according to legend anyone entering that river never comes out. A short time before when we were passing the point marked as 'Ars Hill' on Moore's map, my companion told me how in order to get a boat to move upstream beyond the hill, it had once been necessary for the crews to dance and bare their arses as they danced.

The grass had not yet been burnt off at San Domingo when I visited it, but it would soon be fired. It was towards the end of December; the dry season, the pleasantest time of the year. The grass and scrub were already being fired across considerable stretches along the river to clear the ground for sowing, and at night the sky was incandescent with the glow of false moons. The fires go back to the oldest report on the Gambia. When Hanno the Carthaginian sailed southwards along the African coast in about 570 B.C. he sailed up a wide estuary and saw fires burning hither and yon in the night. At the moment when night is suddenly about to fall and the sky blazes red, the smoke from these creeping fires could be the smoke from the final conflagration. The air is pungent with the acrid and aromatic smell of burning grasses and woods; the ambiguous light is further confused by the drooping haze; and a country that is strange even by day begins to slip into a metaphysical obscurity. Africa seems as foreign as it must always have been, day in, day out, to the handful of lonely factors along the river in the eighteenth century, men like Job ben Solomon's friend, Francis Moore.

Job ben Solomon himself seems more credible, remembered by the Gambia rather than in Leadenhall Street. As he stood in a drawing-room at Cheshunt chatting with his kindly hosts, as good as any gentleman, by what possible force of the imagination could they place him in his proper relation to these vast spaces of forest and scrub, nearly impassable in the wet season for rain, in the dry season for drought? He was a mystery, but a mystery that they were driven to try and explain in terms of what they already knew, not only of geography and anthropology, but of morality. Job ben Solomon could only be seen where he crossed the narrow intermittent beams of their knowledge; everywhere else he stood in darkness.

The darkness that enclosed him, in so far as it could yield to facts,

[1] Moore, p. 170.

has been greatly reduced, and the customs of Bondou may even be better studied than our own folk ways, but the inner darkness is still impenetrable. Job ben Solomon, 'a great Pholey from Boonda', a forerunner of the emerging millions of his race, is still the challenge that he was, to the understanding and the conscience.

APPENDIX

Thomas Hull's Itinerary of a Voyage to Bondou, 1735

STATIONS & COURSES OF THE INLAND ROAD OF YAMYAMACUNDA

Stations	Miles	Bearings	Remarks
1. From Yamyamacunda to			
2. Cowas	4	N.	a Small Town.
3. Mancadaway	10	E.	Formerly a large Town but was last year destroyed by Fire.
4. Suncobarr	12	N.E.	half-way is a remarkable Hill.
5. Concord	6	N.E.	The Capital Town in Wooley.
6. Cohunt or Count	8	N.E.	A Mahometan Town.
7. Sowro	7	N.	Formerly a large Town but lately destroy'd by ye Warrs.
8. Colingding	5	N.N.E.	a Small Town but ruin'd by the Warrs.
9. Conophy	10	N.N.E.	a large & Strong Town.
10. Condery	8	N.E.	a small Town, 4 Miles East of this town lyes Cassang.
11. Cross'd ye River Samy	10	N.N.E.	This River falls into ye Gambia near Fendalecunda & is said to come out of ye Senegal river.
12. Calore	6	N.E.	a Strong Town, the Master & Inhabitants are Slaves belonging to the King of Wooley.
13. Cambey	9	E.N.E.	a Strong Town & the last in the Kingdom of Wooley.
Carried Forward	95		

Stations	Miles	Bearings	Remarks
Brought forward	95		
14. Cross'd Bajasa or Samy River again	7	E.	
15.	3	E.	
16.	10	E. by S.	
17.	6	E.S.E.	
18.	14	E.S.E.	A large Wilderness which we were four days & 3 Nights going thro'.
19. a River	4	E.	
20.	4	N.E.	
21. Scitadella a large Pond or Spring of good Water & never dry	3	N.E.	
22. River Golore	7	E.	
23. Goodery	7	E. by N.	A Town in a province so call'd belonging to Bundo, its Lat. is 14.33, about one Mile before we came to this Town we cross'd the River Neery or Yarico, which falls into the Gambia at Tinda.
24. Wild	5	E.	a small Town.
25. Bullabuck	15	N.E.	a small Town.
26. Chambey	5	E.	Job's houses or Hutts are in this Town, its Latit. is 14.44. North & from whence I could plainly hear ye Guns at ye French Fort at Gallam.

185

Stations	*Miles*	*Bearings*	*Remarks*
From Chambey to— Phenah	8	S.	A large Town where lives Eleman Maccah King of Bundo.
Conjure	6	E.N.E.	a Town almost close to Fallam River which parts Bundo from the Kingdoms of Gallam & Bombou[c]; Its Inhabitants are Merchants chiefly & is situate not far from the opposite side of the River where the Sanon Colez, or as the French call it, Riviere D'or falls into it, & on which the Gold Mines border; which Mines supplies the Gold Trade to ye French on the Senegall, which is a very considerable one & to all parts Inland and to the River Gambia; The Inhabitants of Goodery, Bundo, Futa & Boumbou[c] & most of the other Inland Countrys are Mahometans.

SELECT BIBLIOGRAPHY

A. MANUSCRIPTS

The Papers of the Royal African Company are among the Treasury Papers in the Public Record Office. Reference T.70/1-1495.

The Papers of the French East India Company bearing on Job ben Solomon's return to Bondou are in the Archives Nationales, Paris. Reference Colonies C6[11].

Thomas Hull's Journal of his voyage to Bondou in 1735 is among the papers belonging to the Duke of Buccleuch at Boughton, Northamptonshire.

Other papers relating to Job are in the British Museum, the Royal Society, the Society of Antiquaries and the Spalding Gentlemen's Society. References to particular locations are given in the footnotes where they are available.

B. PRINTED SOURCES (The place of publication is London unless otherwise stated.)

ADANSON, Michel, *A Voyage to Senegal, the Isle of Goree, and the River Gambia.* 1759

ASTLEY, Thomas, *A New General Collection of Voyages and Travels.* 4 vols. 1745-7

ATKINS, John, *A Voyage to Guinea, Brasil, and the West-Indies.* 1735

BARBOT, John, *A Description of the Coasts of North and South Guinea.* (Churchill's *Collection*, vol. v, 1732)

BARTH, Henry, *Travels and Discoveries in North and Central Africa.* 2nd ed. 5 vols. 1857

BENEZET, Anthony, *A Caution to Great Britain and her Colonies, in a short representation of the calamitous state of the enslaved Negroes in the British dominions.* 1784

——*Some Historical Account of Guinea, Its Situation, Produce and the General Disposition of its Inhabitants. With An Enquiry into the Rise and Progress of the Slave-Trade, its Nature and lamentable Effects.* Philadelphia, 1771

BENNETT, J. Harry, *Bondsmen and Bishops: Slavery and Apprenticeship on the Codrington Plantations of Barbados, 1710–1830.* Berkeley, 1958

BISSELL, Benjamin, *The American Indian in English Literature of the Eighteenth Century.* New Haven, 1925

BLAKE, John William (ed. & trans.), *Europeans in West Africa, 1450–1560.* 2 vols. 1942

BLUETT, Thomas, *Some Memoirs of the Life of Job, the Son of Solomon, the High Priest of Boonda in Africa.* 1734

BOND, Richmond P., *Queen Anne's American Kings.* Oxford, 1952

BOSMAN, William, *A New and Accurate Description of the Coast of Guinea.* 1705 (second edition, 1721)

BOVILL, E. W., *Caravans of the Old Sahara. An Introduction to the History of the Western Sudan.* Oxford, 1933

—— (ed.) *Missions to the Niger*, vol. i. Cambridge, 1964

BRACKETT, Jeffrey R., *The Negro in Maryland. A Study of the Institution of Slavery.* Baltimore, 1889

CHURCH, Leslie F., *Oglethorpe: A Study of Philanthropy in England and Georgia.* 1932

CHURCHILL, A. & J., *A Collection of Voyages and Travels.* 6 vols. 1732

CLARKE, W. K. Lowther, *A History of the S.P.C.K.* 1959

CLARKSON, Thomas, *The History of the Rise, Progress, and Accomplishment of the Abolition of the African Slave-Trade by the British Parliament.* 2 vols. 1808

COLLINS, *Practical Rules for the Management and Medical Treatment of Negro Slaves in the Sugar Colonies.* 1811

COUPLAND, Reginald, *The British Anti-Slavery Movement.* 1933

CULTRU, P., *Histoire du Sénégal du XVe siècle à 1870.* Paris, 1910

—— (ed.), *Premier Voyage du Sieur de la Courbe Fait à la Coste d'Afrique en 1685.* Paris, 1913

CURTIN, P. D. (ed.), *Africa Remembered. Narratives by West Africans from the Era of the Slave Trade.* Madison, 1967

CUSSANS, J. E., *A History of Hertfordshire.* 1876

DAVIES, K. G., *The Royal African Company.* 1957

DE BEER, G. R., *Sir Hans Sloane and the British Museum.* 1954

DELCOURT, André, *La France et les Établissements Français au Sénégal entre 1713 et 1763.* Dakar, 1952

DONNAN, Elizabeth, *Documents Illustrative of the History of the Slave Trade to America.* 4 vols. Washington, 1935

DYKES, Eva Beatrice, *The Negro in English Romantic Thought, or, A Study of Sympathy for the Oppressed.* Washington, 1942

EANNES DE AZURARA, Gomes, *The Chronicle of the Discovery and Conquest of Guinea,* translated by C. R. Beazley and Edgar Prestage. 2 vols. 1896

EDWARDS, Bryan, *The History, Civil and Commercial, of the British Colonies in the West Indies.* 4th ed. 3 vols. 1807

ETTINGER, Amos Aschbach, *James Edward Oglethorpe: Imperial Idealist.* Oxford, 1936

FAIRCHILD, Hoxie Neale, *The Noble Savage: a study in Romantic naturalism.* 1928

FALCONBRIDGE, Alexander, *An Account of the Slave Trade on the Coast of Africa.* 1788

GAILEY, Harry A., *A History of the Gambia.* 1964

GEORGE, Dorothy, *London Life in the Eighteenth Century.* 1930

GOLBERRY (GOLBÉRY), S. M. X. *Travels in Africa, performed during the years 1785, 1786, and 1787 in the Western Countries of this Continent.* 2 vols. 1803

GOUILLY, Alphonse, *L'Islam dans l'Afrique Occidentale Française.* Paris. 1952

GRACE, Edward, *Letters of a West African Trader 1767–70.* 1950

GRAY, J. M., *A History of the Gambia.* 1940

GRAY, William *and* DOCHARD,—, *Travels in Western Africa in the Years 1818, 19, 20, and 21, from the River Gambia.* 1825

HALLETT, Robin, *The Penetration of Africa: European Enterprise and Exploration Principally in Northern and Western Africa up to 1830.* Volume i to 1815. 1965

—— (ed.), *Records of the African Association 1788–1831.* 1964

HASAN IBN MUHAMMAD (LEO AFRICANUS), *The History and Description of Africa.* Trans. John Pory, ed. Robert Brown. 3 vols. 1896

HECHT, J. Jean, *Continental and Colonial Servants in Eighteenth-Century England.* 1954

HODGES, Cornelius, 'The Journey of Cornelius Hodges in Senegambia, 1689–90', *English Historical Review*, 1924, xxxix. 89–95

HOUSTOUN, James, *Some New and Accurate Observations, Geographical, Natural and Historical. Containing a true and impartial Account of the Situation, Product, and Natural History of the Coast of Guinea.* 1725

JOBSON, Richard, *The Golden Trade or A Discovery of the River Gambia, and the Golden Trade of the Aethiopians.* 1623 [1932]

LABAT, J. B., *Voyage du Chevalier des Marchais en Guinée, Isles Voisines et à Cayenne.* 4 vols. Amsterdam, 1731

LASCELLES, E. C. P., *Granville Sharp and the Freedom of Slaves in England.* Oxford, 1928

LAWRENCE, A. W., *Trade Castles and Forts of West Africa.* 1963

LITTLE, K. L., *Negroes in Britain. A Study of Racial Relations in English Society.* 1947

LONG, Edward, *A History of Jamaica.* 2 vols. 1774

MACHAT, J., *Documents sur les Établissements Français de l'Afrique Occidentale au XVIIIe siècle.* Paris, 1906

MACINNES, C. M., *England and Slavery.* 1934

MACKENZIE-GRIEVE, Averil, *The Last Years of the English Slave Trade. Liverpool 1750–1807.* 1941

MATTHEWS, John, *A Voyage to the River Sierra-Leone.* 1788

MOLLIEN, Gaspard, *Travels in the Interior of Africa, to the sources of the Senegal and Gambia.* 1820

MOORE, Francis, *Travels into the Inland Parts of Africa . . . with a particular Account of Job Ben Solomon, who was in England in the Year 1733, and known by the Name of the African.* 1738

NICHOLS, John, *Literary Anecdotes of the Eighteenth Century.* 7 vols. 1813

PARK, Mungo, *Journal of a Mission to the Interior of Africa . . . in the year 1805.* 1815

—— *Travels in the Interior Districts of Africa.* 1799

PHILLIPS, Thomas, *A Journal of a Voyage made . . . along the Coast of Guiney to Whidaw.* (Churchill's *Collection*, vol. vi, 1732)

RAMSAY, James, *An Essay on the Treatment and Conversion of African Slaves in the British Sugar Colonies.* 1784

RANÇON, André, *Le Bondou.* 1894

The Royal African: or, Memoirs of the Young Prince of Annamaboe. n.d. [1749]

'The Life Story of Abou Bekir Sadiki, Alias Edward Doulan.' *Journal of Negro History*, 1936, xxi. 52–5.

SLOANE, Hans, *A Voyage to the Islands Madera, Barbados, Nieves, S. Christophers and Jamaica with the Natural History . . . of the last of those Islands*, vol. i. 1707

SMITH, William, *A New Voyage to Guinea.* 1745

SNELGRAVE, William, *A New Account of some Parts of Guinea and the Slave Trade.* 1734

SOUTHORN, Bella, *The Gambia: the story of the groundnut colony.* 1952

STENNING, Derrick J., *Savannah Nomads: A Study of the Wodaabe Pastoral Fulani of Western Bornu Province, Northern Region, Nigeria.* 1959

SYPHER, Wylie, *Guinea's Captive Kings: British Anti-Slavery Literature of the XVIIIth Century.* Chapel Hill, 1942

THOMPSON, H. P., *Thomas Bray.* 1954

Trade to Africa Consider'd, The, n.d. (1709?)

TRIMINGHAM, J. Spencer, *A History of Islam in West Africa.* Glasgow, 1962

UNIVERSAL HISTORY, FROM THE EARLIEST ACCOUNT OF TIME. *Modern History*, vol. xiv, 1760

VAUX, Robert, *Memoirs of the Life of Anthony Benezet.* York, 1817

WEBER, Henry, *La Compagnie Française des Indes (1604–1875).* Paris, 1904

WILLIAMS, Eric, *Capitalism and Slavery.* Chapel Hill, 1944

The World Displayed: or, a Curious Collection of Voyages and Travels. 3rd ed. vol. xvii. 1778

WYNDHAM, H. A., *The Atlantic and Slavery.* Oxford, 1935

INDEX

Noblemen have been indexed under their titles, and the name most familiar to the reader has also been used—e.g. 'Henry the Navigator', under 'H'. African names have cross-references and are indexed under the initial of the first name. Entries in *italics* indicate titles of books or ships' names; italic numerals refer to footnotes. 'Company' and 'Co.' in the index denote the Royal African Company.

P